GLOBAL TERRORISM

GLOBAL TERRORISM

A HISTORICAL BIBLIOGRAPHY

Suzanne Robitaille Ontiveros
Editor

ABC-CLIO

Santa Barbara, California
Oxford, England

Library of Congress Cataloging-in-Publication Data

Global Terrorism.
  (ABC-CLIO research guides; 16)
  Includes indexes.
  1. Terrorism—History—Bibliography. I. Ontiveros,
Suzanne, R. II. Series.
Z7164.T3G57 1986 016.3036′25′09 86-3339
[HV6431]
ISBN-0-87436-453-1 (alk. paper)

© 1986 by ABC-Clio, Inc.

All rights reserved. No part of this publication may be
reproduced, stored in a retrieval system, or transmitted
in any form, or by any means, electronic, mechanical,
photocopying, recording, or otherwise, without the prior
written permission of ABC-Clio, Inc.

*This book is Smyth sewn and printed on acid-free paper to
meet library standards.*

ABC-Clio, Inc.
2040 Alameda Padre Serra, Box 4397
Santa Barbara, California 93140-4397

Clio Press Ltd.
55 St. Thomas Street
Oxford, OX1 1JG, England

Manufactured in the United States of America.

ABC-CLIO RESEARCH GUIDES

The ABC-CLIO Research Guides are a new generation of annotated bibliographies that provide comprehensive control of the recent journal literature on high-interest topics in history and the related social sciences. These publications are compiled by editor/historians and other subject specialists who examine article entries in ABC-CLIO's vast history data base and select abstracts of all citations that relate to the particular topic of study.

Each entry selected from this data base—the largest history data base in the world—has been reviewed to ensure consistency in treatment and completeness of coverage. The subject profile index (ABC-SPIndex) accompanying each volume has been evaluated and revised in terms of the specific subject presented to allow precise and rapid access to the entries.

The titles in this series are prepared to save researchers, students, and librarians the considerable time and expense usually associated with accessing materials manually or through online searching. ABC-CLIO's Research Guides offer unmatched access to significant scholarly articles on the topics of most current interest to historians and social scientists.

ABC-CLIO RESEARCH GUIDES

Pamela R. Byrne, Executive Editor
Suzanne R. Ontiveros, Managing Editor

1. **World War II from an American Perspective** *(1982)*; ISBN 0-87436-035-8
2. **The Jewish Experience in America** *(1982)*; ISBN 0-87436-034-X
3. **Nuclear America** *(1983)*; ISBN 0-87436-360-8
4. **The Great Depression** *(1983)*; ISBN 0-87436-361-6
5. **Corporate America** *(1983)*; ISBN 0-87436-362-4
6. **Crime and Punishment in America** *(1983)*; ISBN 0-87436-363-2
7. **The Democratic and Republican Parties** *(1983)*; ISBN 0-87436-364-0
8. **The American Electorate** *(1983)*; ISBN 0-87436-372-1
9. **The Weimar Republic** *(1984)*; ISBN 0-87436-378-0
10. **The Third Reich, 1933-1939** *(1984)*; ISBN 0-87436-379-9
11. **The Third Reich at War** *(1984)*; ISBN 0-87436-393-4
12. **American Family History** *(1984)*; ISBN 0-87436-380-2
13. **The Sino-Soviet Conflict** *(1985)*; ISBN 0-87436-382-9
14. **The United States in East Asia** *(1985)*; ISBN 0-87436-452-3
15. **Women in the Third World** *(1986)*; ISBN 0-87436-459-0
16. **Global Terrorism** *(1986)*; ISBN 0-87436-453-1

CONTENTS

USER'S GUIDE TO THE INDEXES viii
LIST OF ABBREVIATIONS ix
INTRODUCTION xi
1. General 1
2. Europe 21
3. Middle East 53
4. Asia and the Pacific Region 80
5. Latin America and the West Indies 94
6. North America 106
7. Africa 111
   SUBJECT INDEX 115
   AUTHOR INDEX 141
   CHRONOLOGY 145

USER'S GUIDE TO THE INDEXES

All titles in this series use ABC-CLIO's unique Subject Profile Index (ABC-SPIndex) and an author index. The following abstract is found in this volume:

Abstract

214. Moss, David. THE KIDNAPPING AND MURDER OF ALDO MORO. *European J. of Sociol. [Great Britain] 1981 22(2): 265-295.* Political terrorism became a feature of Italian politics in the 1970's, culminating in the 1978 murder of Aldo Moro, the leader of the Christian Democrats, by the Red Brigades. The kidnapping is interpreted as a tactic appropriate to the pursuit of political identity. It was a ritual with a solidaristic function for the Red Brigades. It established the continuity of the group and created a frame for subsequent symbolic actions (communiques and show-trials). Biblio.

R. Aldrich

In this Subject Index, each index entry is a complete profile of the abstract and consists of one or more subject, geographic, and biographic descriptors, followed by the dates covered in the article. These descriptors are rotated so that the complete subject profile is cited under each of the terms in alphabetical order. Thus, indexing for the abstract shown above is located in five different places in the index:

Subject Index

Italy. Murder. Politics. Red Brigades. 1970-78. *214*

Murder. Italy. Politics. Red Brigades. 1970-78. *214*

Politics. Italy. Murder. Red Brigades. 1970-78. *214*

Red Brigades. Italy. Murder. Politics. 1970-78. *214*

A dash replaces second and subsequent identical leading terms. Cross-references in the form of *See* and *See-also* references are provided. Refer also to the notes at the head of the Subject Index.

Bogozato *See also* Violencia.

Jews *See also* Anti-Semitism.

The separate Author Index lists the name of the author and abstract number.

Author Index

More, Vishwanath 120
Morell, David 464
Moss, David 214
Mosse, George L. 119
Mottet, George J. 532

LIST OF ABBREVIATIONS

A.	Author-prepared Abstract	*Illus.*	Illustrated, Illustration
Acad.	Academy, Academie, Academia	*Inst.*	Institute, Institut-.
Agric.	Agriculture, Agricultural	*Int.*	International, Internacional, Internationaal, Internationaux, Internazionale
AIA	Abstracts in Anthropology		
Akad.	Akademie		
Am.	America, American		
Ann.	Annals, Annales, Annual, Annali	*J.*	Journal, Journal-prepared Abstract
Anthrop.	Anthropology, Anthropological	*Lib.*	Library, Libraries
Arch.	Archives	*Mag.*	Magazine
Archaeol.	Archaeology, Archaeological	*Mus.*	Museum, Musee, Museo
Art.	Article	*Nac.*	Nacional
Assoc.	Association, Associate	*Natl.*	National, Nationale
Biblio.	Bibliography, Bibliographical	*Naz.*	Nazionale
Biog.	Biography, Biographical	*Phil.*	Philosophy, Philosophical
Bol.	Boletim, Boletin	*Photo.*	Photograph
Bull.	Bulletin	*Pol.*	Politics, Political, Politique, Politico
c.	century (in index)	*Pr.*	Press
ca.	circa	*Pres.*	President
Can.	Canada, Canadian, Canadien	*Pro.*	Proceedings
Cent.	Century	*Publ.*	Publishing, Publication
Coll.	College	*Q.*	Quarterly
Com.	Committee	*Rev.*	Review, Revue, Revista, Revised
Comm.	Commission	*Riv.*	Rivista
Comp.	Compiler	*Res.*	Research
DAI	Dissertation Abstracts International	*RSA*	Romanian Scientific Abstracts
		S.	Staff-prepared Abstract
		Sci.	Science, Scientific
Dept.	Department	*Secy.*	Secretary
Dir.	Director, Direktor	*Soc.*	Society, Societe, Sociedad, Societa
Econ.	Economy, Econom-.		
Ed.	Editor, Edition	*Sociol.*	Sociology, Sociological
Educ.	Education, Educational	*Tr.*	Transactions
Geneal.	Genealogy, Genealogical, Genealogique	*Transl.*	Translator, Translation
		U.	University, Universi-.
Grad.	Graduate	*US*	United States
Hist.	History, Hist-.	*Vol.*	Volume
IHE	Indice Historico Espanol	*Y.*	Yearbook

INTRODUCTION

The increasing frequency of bombings, hijackings, assassinations, and sabotage suggests that terrorist activities during the past 10 years are the prologue to a disturbing future. According to a State Department spokesperson, acts of violence attributed to terrorist groups are increasing at the rate of about 15 percent per year, and there are now as many as 60 target nations. The abstracts included in this volume typify and summarize the published literature dealing with terrorism. The accompanying chronology lists the acts of terrorism, and related events, reported in the media from January 1975 through December 1985.

This bibliography is not a comprehensive or definitive treatment of terrorism; rather, it outlines a religious and political phenomenon that is not widely understood or readily controlled. The term itself evades definition. According to *Webster's* it is both "a mode of governing" and a means "of opposing government." In ordinary parlance terrorism is "wrong" when used to intimidate a righteous regime and "right" when applied to correct injustice. Terrorism has no doctrinal, ethnic, political, or legal boundaries. It has been employed by ethnic and religious groups—Catholics and Protestants; Jews and Muslims; Shi'ites and Ba'hais; Blacks and Whites—and by ideological and political factions in tribal societies, developing nations, and in the industrial states. It is an essential tool of revolutionary governments both left and right. In 1901 Lenin declared that "we have never rejected terror on principle, nor can we do so," and Hitler's July 1944 *Terror and Sabotage Decree* stated that "terror can be countered only by terror." The historical record suggests that international terrorism has become tacitly legitimized. Some nations openly support terrorists; attempts to define the term in the United Nations stir more controversy than agreement; and international law has no effective sanctions to control its frequent occurrence.

Terrorism is supported, directly and indirectly, by nations that provide money, weapons, and training for dissident groups engaged in terrorist activities. Some nations provide asylum to individuals accused of terrorist acts. Other nations silently disapprove but are reluctant to publicly condemn threats or specific acts of terrorism. Direct action against terrorists taken in another nation's territory or airspace (e.g., the Israeli raid on Entebbe, the abortive U.S. attempt to free hostages in Iran, and the interception of an Egyptian airliner carrying the Achille Lauro hijackers) may be regarded as an act of war by the offended nation.

Terrorism is sometimes effective in gaining specific concessions from target nations. It is used to attract worldwide publicity, support revolutions, create anarchy, and provoke reprisal. It is capable of demoralizing whole societies; repressive regimes employ it to enforce public obedience and cooperation. If the following record is a prologue, global terrorism promises to alter world politics in the future. Terrorist groups that share similar ideologies will ally themselves in the international struggle; new weapons and new technologies will increase the vulnerability of their targets; radical governments will employ terrorists and their techniques to wage surrogate warfare—and they may yet achieve the ultimate terror by gaining access to weapons of mass destruction. In any event, terrorism threatens to irreversably alter traditional theories of national security, military strategy, and perhaps the very concept of government itself.

The techniques employed by ethnic/religious and ideological/political zealots to terrorize their enemies and achieve their particular goals include all of the following: agitation, assassination, attack, bombing, break-in, conspiracy, coup, demand, guerrilla war, hijack, hostage, massacre, murder, raid, random killing, ransom, rape, sabotage, sniper fire, strike, violence, and war. The appearance of those words in news reports identified the events listed in the following chronology as terrorist activities.

Terrorism, and the potentially destructive events subsumed under that rubric, must be studied, explained, understood, and eventually controlled. This abbreviated bibliography is an initial step toward summarizing the journal scholarship in history on the subject to date.

Global Terrorism contains 598 abstracts and citations of journal articles drawn from ABC-CLIO's vast history database, which covers over 2,000 periodicals published in some 90 countries. In creating this annotated bibliography, editors reviewed thousands of article abstracts and selected only those relevant to terrorism as traditionally defined, that is, the activities of state or nonstate actors who use techniques of violence in their efforts to attain political objectives. Entries are arranged alphabetically by author within geographic chapters. Chapter 1 includes overviews treating one or more countries or entries that are not country-specific. Chapters 2-7 cover Europe, the Middle East, Asia and the Pacific Region, Latin America and the West Indies, North America, and Africa, respectively. Differences in the size of chapters do not represent editorial predisposition; rather, they reflect the relative volume of journal coverage. Consequently, this bibliography says as much about what has not been written or published as it does about what has appeared in the journal literature of history.

Additional access to the abstracts and citations in *Global Terrorism* is provided through ABC-SPIndex (Subject Profile Index), a highly specific subject index. Key subject terms are linked with the historical dates to form a complete profile of the article. Each set of index terms is rotated alphabetically so that the complete profile appears under each of the subject terms. Thus, the accuracy and specificity of subject access is enhanced as compared to conventional, hierarchical indexes. Care has been taken to eliminate inconsistencies that might have appeared in the subject index as a result of merging many years of database material. The explanatory note at the beginning of the subject index provides further information for using ABC-SPIndex.

This volume represents the collaboration of a skilled and diverse group. Managing Editor of *Historical Abstracts* Roger W. Davis reviewed the subject index. Production Supervisor Deborah Looker, Computer Operator Glen Kaltunbrun, and Applications Programmer Tracy Kaltenbrun ably manipulated the database to fit the editorial specifications of this bibliography. David R. Blanke provided critical support in assuring high-quality photocomposition. Tanya Cullen was responsible for essential paste-up corrections and book design.

Sincere appreciation is extended to the worldwide community of scholars who wrote the abstracts and citations that comprise this volume. Their efforts mark an early contribution to the growing scholarly interest in terrorism. If the human community fails to rid itself of this currently incomprehensible and apparently uncontrollable phenomenon, civilization as we know it will be radically altered, perhaps terminated.

We can no longer afford to believe that "the only thing we have to fear is fear itself."

Lloyd W. Garrison
Santa Barbara, California

1

GENERAL

1. Abramovsky, Abraham. MULTILATERAL CONVENTIONS FOR THE SUPPRESSION OF UNLAWFUL SEIZURE AND INTERFERENCE WITH AIRCRAFT.
THE HAGUE CONVENTION. *Columbia J. of Transnational Law 1974 13(3): 381-405.* Describes how nations have used international law from 1930 to the Hague Convention of 1970 to combat aircraft hijacking.
THE MONTREAL CONVENTION. *Columbia J. of Transnational Law 1975 14(2): 268-300.* Discusses issues raised at the 1972 conference of the International Civil Aviation Organization (in Montreal).
THE LEGALITY AND POLITICAL FEASIBILITY OF A MULTILATERAL AIR SECURITY ENFORCEMENT CONVENTION. *Columbia J. of Transnational Law 1975 14(3): 451-484.* Discusses proposals made in 1973.

2. Aggarwala, Narinder. POLITICAL ASPECTS OF HIJACKING. *Internat. Conciliation 1971 (585): 7-27.* A general discussion of international aerial hijacking and conventions pertaining to it. The goal should be to declare hijacking a universal crime so hijackers become the enemy of every state. The main problem is enforcement of International Civil Aviation Organization (ICAO) Conventions, especially where extradition conflicts with rights of political asylum and involves a threatened interference with national sovereignty. Based on secondary sources and UN documents; table, 43 notes.
C. A. Gallacci

3. Akinsanya, Adeoye A. THE ENTEBBE RESCUE MISSION: A CASE OF AGGRESSION? *J. of African Studies 1982 9(2): 46-57.* An analysis of aircraft hijackings and national and international measures taken against them between 1961 and 1976, from which the June-July 1976 hijacking of Air France Flight 139 at Athens and subsequent events at Entebbe, Uganda, are examined. Both the Arab hijackers and the Ugandan regime violated international law. Idi Amin's government ignored provisions of the 1970 Hague Convention for the Suppression of Unlawful Seizure of Aircraft. The Israeli response, however, is depicted as an illegal overreaction, disproportionate to the threat posed to the Israeli hostages detained at Entebbe. Concludes that the United Nations should have condemned Israel's action as aggression against Uganda and "a clear breach of international peace." Based on published documents, international law texts, and secondary sources and accounts; 3 tables, 44 notes.
L. W. Truschel

4. Akinsanya, Adeoye A. THE ENTEBBE RESCUE MISSION: A CASE OF AGGRESSION? *Pakistan Horizon [Pakistan] 1981 34(3): 12-35.* Considers whether the Israeli raid on Entebbe, Uganda to rescue civilian hostages taken by the Popular Front for the Liberation of Palestine (PFLP) in the aircraft hijacking of an Air France Jumbo Jet was an act of aggression under international law and concludes that, while Israel defended the 4 July 1976 raid as a humanitarian act in defense of innocent civilians, such actions are probably illegal by international standards of law.

5. Alexander, Yonah. TERRORISM, THE MEDIA AND THE POLICE. *J. of Int. Affairs 1978 32(1): 101-113.* The communications purposes which revolutionary terror groups seek through the media are attention, recognition, and legitimacy; the law enforcement agencies, which now lack the legal authority and practical ability to control coverage of terrorist activities, in general look upon the media as a powerful force which should somehow be restrained, so that these aims of the terror groups could not be achieved. 43 notes. V. Samaraweera

6. Aquarone, Alberto. VIOLENZA E CONSENSO NEL FASCISMO ITALIANO [Violence and consensus in Italian Fascism]. *Storia Contemporanea [Italy] 1979 10(1): 145-155.* The Fascist regime in Italy based itself on the Fascist Party and beyond that on a shifting consensus embracing different groups at different times. The Great Depression caused people to give more support to regime and party as the only institutions capable of helping them through this "natural catastrophe." The war of conquest against Ethiopia also won support for the regime, but Italian intervention in the Spanish Civil War alienated many. So did the alliance with Nazi Germany. But consensus in Fascist Italy was a passive thing. The people tolerated the regime, they did not participate in it. Post-Fascist Italy was very similar to pre-Fascist Italy; the social institutions had not been fundamentally altered. J. C. Billigmeier

7. Aston, Clive C. THE UNITED NATIONS CONVENTION AGAINST THE TAKING OF HOSTAGES: REALISTIC OR RHETORIC? *Terrorism 1981 5(1-2): 139-160.* Reviews the central political issues that have pervaded the debates on a convention proposed by West Germany to the UN to ban the taking of hostages and suggests that the resulting compromise is flawed with an inherent tautology which will impede successful implementation.

8. Bailey, Sydney D. THE UNITED NATIONS AND THE TERMINATION OF ARMED CONFLICT, 1946-64. *Int. Affairs [Great Britain] 1982 58(3): 465-475.* The reasons for armed conflicts are not easy to determine; the UN is not well equipped to deal with participants not representing government, such as the Turkish-Cypriot community in Cyprus, the Palestine Liberation Organization, and others.

9. Bassiouni, M. Cherif. MEDIA COVERAGE OF TERRORISM: THE LAW AND THE PUBLIC. *J. of Communication 1982 32(2): 128-143.* Because media coverage of events often interrupts or impedes law enforcement-terrorist negotiations, and because media can exacerbate problems with crowd control, conflicts between the two groups arise; suggests measures that might

control media coverage of terrorist activities in spite of government protection of free speech; 1968-78.

10. Becker, Jillian. THE MOST IMPORTANT QUESTION. *Terrorism 1980 4(1-4): 311-322.* Review article of terrorism and liberal democracy through Paul Wilkinson's *Terrorism and the Liberal State* (New York: New York U. Pr., 1979) and Christopher Dobson and Ronald Payne's *The Weapons of Terror* (London: Macmillan, 1979).

11. Bell, Daniel. FIRST LOVE AND EARLY SORROWS. *Partisan Rev. 1981 48(4): 532-551.* In this autobiographical article, the author weaves his varied personal and intellectual experiences with the Left and Max Weber's injunction about the ethic of responsibility in dealing with the prosaic world. The Left, particularly the Bolsheviks, are eschatologists or chiliasts; therefore, for them, the end is so important, so cosmic, that any (including systematic repression) means to that end is justifiable. Cites two examples of men who believed that philosophy and how they paid for their beliefs. Communism drawing on gnostic sources of political religion thereby uses terrorism and violence to "save" or "redeem" the world. Bell's biography and writings are one man's testament against fearful fascination that the Left offers the alienated intellectual in this century. D. K. Pickens

12. Bell, J. Bowyer. TRANSNATIONAL TERROR AND WORLD ORDER. *South Atlantic Q. 1975 74(4): 404-417.* Increasing acts of international terrorism have not really disturbed world order, which has been remarkably stable for over 20 years. The tactics of terrorists may have limited success, but terrorism really frightens no one except persons directly involved. The use of terrorism implies weakness, and terrorists may be safely ignored as disturbers of world order. Terrorist tactics will no doubt change in the future and technological advances will have to supply new weapons to oppose them. 11 notes. V. L. Human

13. Beres, Louis René. GUERRILLAS, TERRORISTS, AND POLARITY: NEW STRUCTURAL MODELS OF WORLD POLITICS. *Western Pol. Q. 1974 27(4): 624-636.* Shows how "private" acts of terrorism fit into new structural models of world politics.

14. Blair, Bruce G. and Brewer, Garry D. THE TERRORIST THREAT TO WORLD NUCLEAR PROGRAMS. *J. of Conflict Resolution 1977 21(3): 379-403.* Terrorism in the global setting has become the predominant form of confrontation between differing subcategories of societies that seek to overcome each other, regardless of size. In the case of nuclear terrorism, the consequences of failure are potentially catastrophic. While the logic of our strategic nuclear policy is clear, the same clarity does not hold for policies directed at nuclear terrorism. In the former case, a prevailing view is that the risk of nuclear war is low because the United States responds vigilantly to nuclear threats posed by other nations. In the latter case, there is no terrorist prevention doctrine, nor is there an institutional focus for preventing terrorism that is even remotely commensurate with that which exists for deterring nuclear war. We here consider the dimensions of the nuclear terrorism

problem, discuss these with respect to the Minuteman Intercontinental Ballastic Missile system, consider the capabilities and objectives of potential terrorist groups, and formulate some basic recommendations for improving the current state of affairs. J

15. Blaufarb, Douglas S. TERRORIST TRENDS AND TIES. *Problems of Communism* 1982 31(3): 73-77. A review of Robert H. Kupperman and Darrell M. Trent's *Terrorism: Threat, Reality, Response* (1979), Claire Sterling's *The Terror Network* (1981), Yonah Alexander, David Carlton, and Paul Wilkinson, ed., *Terrorism: Theory and Practice* (1979), and Herbert Romerstein's *Soviet Support for International Terrorism* (1981). Even though urban terrorists in the industrialized democracies are viewed by their contemporaries as dangerously disturbed minds rather than the vanguard of the future, Moscow continues to encourage them in order to achieve maximum disruption of other societies at minimal cost and political risk to itself. 6 notes.
J. M. Lauber

16. Blishchenko, I. P. and Zhdanov, N. V. SOTRUDNICHESTVO GOSUDARSTV V BOR'BE PROTIV TERRORISTICHESKIKH AKTOV MEZHDUNARODNOGO KHARAKTERA [The cooperation of states in the struggle against international acts of terrorism]. *Sovetskoe Gosudarstvo i Pravo [USSR]* 1981 (8): 110-119. Attempts to define the optimal response of the world's nations to the problem of international terrorism, stressing the difficulty of definition and cooperation in such an emotion-laden issue, and criticizes US efforts to portray the USSR as the chief supporter of terrorist activities.

17. Bonante, Luigi. DIMENSIONI DEL TERRORISMO POLITICO [Dimensions of political terrorism]. *Comunità [Italy]* 1977 31(177): 76-122. Provides thorough analysis of the phenomenon of terrorism in all of its manifestations, whether perpetrated by the state or against the state, and stemming from political movements of the far left to the far right.

18. Booth, John A. RURAL VIOLENCE IN COLOMBIA, 1948-1963. *Western Political Q.* 1974 27(4): 657-679. An application of factor analysis to certain social, economic, and political variables and the intensity and persistence of violence in rural Colombia, 1948-63. S

19. Brandt, Niels. DIE TÄTIGKEIT DER ORGANISATION DER AMERIKANISCHEN STAATEN (OAS) IN DEN JAHREN 1970 UND 1971 [The activity of the Organization of American States (OAS), 1970-71]. *Jahrbuch für Int. Recht [West Germany]* 1973 16: 475-494. Covers the first two years of the Organization of American States under its reformed Charter of 27 February 1970; includes its resolutions and actions concerning terrorism, the El Salvador-Honduras war of 1969, and the problem of tariffs instituted by developed countries against imports from less developed countries.

20. Braungart, Richard G. and Braungart, Margaret M. INTERNATIONAL TERRORISM: BACKGROUND AND RESPONSE. *J. of Pol. and Military Sociol.* 1981 9(2): 263-288. Reviews 14 books on international terrorism. In the

section on background characteristics of terrorism, summarizes material on the definition, history, causes, organization, membership, and strategy of terrorism. In the second section—responses to terrorist threats—crisis management and negotiations, victim response, the role of the media, legal response, and the future of terrorism are examined. Ref. — J. V. Coutinho

21. Capurso, Armando. NATURA E TENDENZA DEI CONFLITTI NEL PERIODO 1945-1974 [Nature and tendencies of conflicts in the period 1945-74]. *Riv. Militare [Italy] 1977 100(2): 2-10.* Examines limited warfare in various parts of the world, 1945-74, including guerrilla warfare and terrorism.

22. Carrère, René and Valat-Morio, Pierre. LA VIOLENCE MONDIALE EN 1970-1971 (COMPARAISON AVEC 1968-1969) [World violence in 1970-71 (a comparison with 1968-69)]. *Études Polémologiques [France] 1972 (6): 16-70.* Interprets and analyzes 882 instances of collective international violence, 1970-71, noting the end of three wars and the outbreak of a fourth, a general overall stability, the easing of tension in China, the evolution of political morality, and a concentration of violence in the capitals.

23. Carrère, René and Valat-Morio, Pierre. LA VIOLENCE MONDIALE EN 1972 (COMPARAISON AVEC 1968-1971) (RECHERCHE AVEC ORDINATEUR) [World violence in 1972 compared with 1968-71: computer research]. *Études Polémologiques [France] 1973 (10): 65-91.* An analysis of 541 instances of collective violence during 1972, which is compared with previous studies, noting the tendency toward diminution in wars in Vietnam, the Middle East, and other areas, an increase in internal microconflicts in Europe and elsewhere, and an increase in terrorism. Also offer conclusions on the evolution and thresholds of collective aggression.

24. Carrère, René. LA VIOLENCE POLITIQUE MONDIALE EN 1981 (COMPARAISON AVEC LA PERIODE 1968/1980) [World political violence in 1981 compared to 1968-80]. *Etudes Polémologiques [France] 1982 (25-26): 131-195.* Since 1968 the Institut Français de Polémologie has given annual accounts of the quantitative evolution and the qualitative transformations in manifestations of collective political violence in the world. The present study, ending with the beginning of this year, gives the characteristics for 1981. J

25. Carrère, René and Valat-Morio, Pierre. LA VIOLENCE POLITIQUE MONDIALE EN 1978-1979-1980 (COMPARAISON AVEC 1968-1977) [Political violence in the world in the years 1978-79-80: a comparison with the years 1968-77]. *Etudes Polémologiques [France] 1981 (24): 120-166.* Compares armed conflicts in the world occurring in the years 1968-77 with those of 1978-80, aiming at establishing trends in the quality of recent disturbances. It seems, on statistical evidence, that foreign interventions have become more frequent, and that the religious factor—the "holy war"—has been gaining ground. The sea has become the recent zone of conflict, and terrorism, rooted in the 1960's, has gained ground among threatened political and ethnic minorities. 7 tables. — M. Hernas

26. Carrère, René and Valat-Morio, Pierre. MESURE DU TERRORISME DE 1968 À 1972 [A measure of terrorism, 1968-72]. *Études Polémologiques [France] 1973 (8): 47-57.* Describes principle trends in increasing world terrorism, and outlines its battlegrounds, noting the decline of racial and student violence and the increase in ethnic difficulties, especially in the Middle East and Latin America.

27. Chapman, Robert D. STATE TERRORISM. *Conflict 1982 3(4): 283-298.* Discusses state terrorism in Libya, Iran, Liberia, Nicaragua and the United States.

28. Dasnabedian, Hratch. THE A.R.F. RECORD: THE BALANCE SHEET OF NINETY YEARS. *Armenian Rev. 1981 34(2): 115-126.* Examines the political, social, and economic factors in Armenia from 1830 to 1889 and the Armenian cultural renaissance of the 1840's, which led to the formation in 1890 of the Armenian Revolutionary Federation. Discusses the federation's military activity from 1890 to 1921 and mounting terrorism from 1890 to 1895.

29. Derriennic, Jean Pierre. THE NATURE OF TERRORISM AND THE EFFECTIVE RESPONSE. *Int. Perspectives [Canada] 1975 (3): 7-10.* Analyzes the psychological gains and effectiveness of terrorism, its relation to the development of democracy, and the ability of a society to resist terrorism.

30. Duculescu, V. PROTECTION ET INVIOLABILITÉ DIPLOMATIQUE. QUELQUES QUESTIONS D'INTÉRÊT ACTUEL [Protection and diplomatic inviolability: some questions of present interest]. *Rev. Roumaine d'Études Int. [Rumania] 1975 9(3): 247-264.* Examines the Vienna diplomatic and consular Conventions of 1961 and 1963 which precisely define the special protection accorded the diplomatic corps, and provides examples of international approaches to the problem of special protection and several UN decisions on the problem. Discusses as well the historic roots of diplomatic immunity and the impact of contemporary terrorism on diplomatic life. 42 notes. G. F. Jewsbury

31. Dugard, John. INTERNATIONAL TERRORISM: PROBLEMS OF DEFINITION. *Internat. Affairs [Great Britain] 1974 50(1): 67-81.* It is difficult to define international terrorism, although this must be done in order to facilitate its suppression. Analyzes the obstacles confronting any convention to combat international terrorism, and examines the US Draft Convention submitted in 1972. Based on a paper delivered in 1973 to the American Society of International Law, and other primary and secondary sources; 54 notes.
P. J. Beck

32. Duperier, B. LES PIRATES DE L'AIR [The skyjackers]. *Rev. des Deux Mondes [France] 1970 (5): 331-344.* Recalls the first air piracy, March 1950, when a group of Czechoslovakians diverted three transport planes toward the American occupied zone in Germany. Gives statistics on all hijackings since, the people involved, the problems of the pilots' responsibility

for passengers, and the role of the advisory committee of the Aéro-Club of France. 3 tables. R. K. Adams

33. Durán Ros, Manuel M. EL TERRORISMO EN LA GUERRA MODERNA [Terrorism in modern war]. *Rev. General de Marina [Spain] 1975 188(6): 613-618.* Analyzes terrorism as a psychological weapon in guerrilla warfare. Terrorism comes in two basic forms (assassination and sabotage), two classes (selective and indiscriminate), and two operational levels (strategic and tactical). Examples of the theory of terrorism in the Algerian and Cuban revolutions are included. A people attacked by terrorism may lose its cohesion and surrender to the terrorists or rebel against the established government for not providing effective protection. But should there be an escalation of terrorism, the same people may become sufficiently indignant as to unite around the established government or form a force of its own to combat terrorism. The results of terrorism are so unpredictable that it is a dangerous weapon to utilize to further a specific political objective. W. C. Frank

34. Efremov, V. "MEZHDUNARODNYI TERRORIZM"—ORUDIE IMPERIALIZMA I REAKTSII ["International terrorism" is the weapon of imperialism and reaction]. *Aziia i Afrika Segodnia [USSR] 1981 (7): 24-26.* Shows the Soviet concepts of international terrorism and the US role in it at the beginning of 1981.

35. Eshov, V. D. PROISKHOZHDENIE I KLASSOVAIA SUSHCHNOST' FASHIZMA [The origin and class nature of fascism]. *Novaia i Noveishaia Istoriia [USSR] 1976 (5): 28-52.* Discusses the causes of the rise of fascism and the conditions of state power used by fascists, and examines fascism as a system of terror, violence, and demagogy. J

36. Evans, Alona E. AIRCRAFT HIJACKING: WHAT IS BEING DONE. *Am. J. of Internat. Law 1973 67(4): 641-671.*

37. Finger, Seymour Maxwell. SECURITY OF INTERNATIONAL CIVIL AVIATION: THE ROLE OF ICAO. *Terrorism 1983 6(4): 519-527.* The International Civil Aviation Organization has, since 1963, sponsored international agreements which accompany a reduction of aircraft hijackings from 245 in 1969-71 to 147 in 1978-80.

38. Fitzgerald, Gerald F. TOWARD LEGAL SUPPRESSION OF ACTS AGAINST CIVIL AVIATION. *Internat. Conciliation 1971 (585): 42-82.* A discussion of the legal rules passed by the International Civil Aviation Organization during three conventions: Tokyo (1963), Hague (1970), and Montreal (1971). The problems considered were: offenses committed on board aircraft, the unlawful seizure of aircraft, and the suppression of unlawful acts against the safety of civil aviation. Attempts have also been made to determine sanctions against offending states, but because of a lack of unanimity among states on the issue of concerted action, discussion was abandoned. Based on ICAO documents; 32 notes, appendix. C. A. Gallacci

39. Fitzhugh, David. TERRORISM AND DIPLOMACY. *Foreign Service J. 1977 54(2): 14-17.* Discusses incidents of international terrorism, 1968-76, and the effect which it has on traditional diplomacy.

40. Fox, K. O. REVOLUTIONARY WAR: A REAPPRAISAL. *Army Q. and Defence J. [Great Britain] 1974 104(2): 160-167.* Defines and analyzes contemporary and historical examples of revolutionary war. Revolutionary war can succeed only if a base area, or a state within a state, is established which is diametrically opposed "to the established government whose authority its inhabitants refuse to recognize." Pure ideology, Communist or otherwise, does not in itself produce a successful movement. Describes tactics of urban revolutionaries, such as the IRA in Londonderry, and considers governments' reactions. They should avoid identifying themselves with totalitarianism which revolutionaries can exploit to obtain a nationwide cause on which to base their claim to power. 11 notes. R. G. Neville

41. Fox, K. O. THE ROLE OF FORCE IN THE INTERNATIONAL WORLD. *Army Q. and Defence J. [Great Britain] 1974 104(5): 538-546.* Discusses the utility of force for industrialized countries in the 20th century and the increased use of force and terrorism by developing nations and terrorist groups.

42. Franck, Thomas M. and Lockwood, Bert B., Jr. PRELIMINARY THOUGHTS TOWARDS AN INTERNATIONAL CONVENTION ON TERRORISM. *Am. J. of Int. Law 1974 68(1): 69-90.*

43. Friedlander, Robert A. TERRORISM AND VIOLENCE: SOME PRELIMINARY OBSERVATIONS. *Int. Studies Notes 1976 3(1): 1-3.* Defines terrorism and deplores the lack of agreement in the world community and the UN on the cause or cure of the terrorist phenomenon in the 1970's.

44. Fromkin, David. THE STRATEGY OF TERRORISM. *Foreign Affairs 1975 53(4): 683-698.* Discusses the modern use of terrorism since its first use in the context of organized politics during the Reign of Terror (1793-94) and subsequent use to destroy governments, as in the cases of the Russian Socialist Revolutionaries, Irish republicans, the Irgun, and the Algerian National Liberation Front. In the 1960's and 1970's terrorism struck randomly, killing the innocent deliberately. Too much attention is devoted to preventing terrorist actions and too little to foiling terrorist purposes. "The overriding questions are not legal or technological, they are philosophical and political. Terrorism is the indirect strategy that wins or loses only in terms of how you respond to it." C. W. Olson

45. Glaser, Stefan. LE TERRORISME INTERNATIONAL ET SES DIVERS ASPECTS [International terrorism and its various aspects]. *R. Internat. de Droit Comparé [France] 1973 25(4): 825-850.* Although international terrorism and the efforts to suppress it have a long history, international cooperation against it in effect dates only from the beginning of the 20th century. The problem has been studied by the UN and other international organizations. Several states have included provisions in their criminal codes.

However, effective international action has been hampered by the difficulty of defining international terrorism and by the barrier of the principle of granting asylum to political fugitives. Moreover, no action has been taken against the terrorism perpetrated by states against individuals, despite the worldwide prevalence of this type of terrorism. The problem of international terrorism will not be solved simply by repressive police measures, but will require a global amelioration both at the social-political level and in cultural and psychological conditions. Based on official documents and published works; 66 notes. J. S. Gassner

46. Goldblatt, Murray. THE UN'S 27TH SESSION IN REVIEW. *Int. Perspectives [Canada] 1973 (2): 20-31.* Summarizes actions of the UN during its 27th session on issues such as terrorism, the UN budget, the situation in the Middle East, the status of Bangladesh, and the progress of arms control measures. L. S. Frey

47. Gravel, Mike. PLUTONIUM RECYCLE: THE CIVIL LIBERTIES VIEW. *Civil Liberties Rev. 1976 3(1): 38-42.* The important point is not that we must watch for infringements of civil liberties under the guise of plutonium security. Rather, it is that the horrific consequences of plutonium terrorism could indeed justify the curtailment of such liberties. J

48. Green, L. C. ASPECTS OF TERRORISM. *Terrorism 1982 5(4): 373-400.* Examines attempts by both the League of Nations and the UN to define and outlaw terrorism, largely unsuccessful because of the continued insistence of some member nations that terrorism in the cause of national liberation is justified.

49. Green, L. C. DOUBLE STANDARDS IN THE UNITED NATIONS: THE LEGALIZATION OF TERRORISM. *Archiv des Völkerrechts [West Germany] 1979 18(2): 129-148.* Since the adoption of the Universal Declaration of Human Rights in 1948 the UN has not carried through a clear policy regarding terrorism, decisions having been strongly influenced by political sympathies of the member states.

50. Gutman, David. KILLERS AND CONSUMERS: THE TERORIST AND HIS AUDIENCE. *Social Res. 1979 46(3): 517-526.* Describes the political and psychological effects of terrorism upon those who view it from a distance.

51. Hacker, Susan. VIOLENT AND NON-VIOLENT APPROACHES IN REVOLUTION. *Mawazo [Uganda] 1972 3(3): 1-10.* Examines the theories of revolutionary action of Mahatma Gandhi (nonviolence) and Franz Fanon (violence), discussing movements in India, South Africa, Portuguese Africa, and the United States, 1918-70.

52. Häggman, Bertil. THE VULNERABLE MODERN INDUSTRIAL SOCIETY. *Jerusalem J. of Int. Relations [Israel] 1978 3(4): 1-18.* Because of increased technological development in the United States, Western Europe,

particularly Sweden, and Japan, modern industrial society is seen as being vulnerable to threats of political terrorism.

53. Henry, Ernst. TERRORIZM I NEOFASHIZM [Terrorism and neofascism]. *Mirovaia Ekonomika i Mezhdunarodnye Otnosheniia [USSR] 1981 (11): 107-116.* Examines the activities of various terrorist and fascist groups in Europe and the United States during 1977-81.

54. Hopple, Gerald W. TRANSNATIONAL TERRORISM: PROSPECTS FOR A CAUSAL MODELING APPROACH. *Terrorism 1982 6(1): 73-100.* Bibliographical essay on the literature on terrorism, 1960-81.

55. Horowitz, Irving Louis. POLITICAL TERRORISM AND THE STATE. *J. of Pol. and Military Sociol. 1973 1(1): 147-158.* "Attempts to locate the problem of political terrorism within the larger context of the current blending and fusion of radical political practice and social deviance generally. Beyond that, it attempts to develop a profile of the terrorist that distinguishes the terrorist from the guerrilla or the national revolutionary. It also seeks to show how the problem of terrorism manifests particular concern within the Marxist tradition, where this issue of the use of terror remains a viable theoretical and pragmatic consideration—unlike the older western democratic political traditions. Finally, the paper offers some brief remarks on the control of terror and the limits of such control within a democratic society." J

56. Hutchinson, Martha Crenshaw. THE CONCEPT OF REVOLUTIONARY TERRORISM. *J. of Conflict Resolution 1972 16(3): 383-396.* "This paper deals with the definition and explanation of the concept of revolutionary terrorism, considered a part of insurgent strategy in internal war. It contends that such terrorism is a rational method of action, employing acts of extraordinary violence against selected physical victims, deliberately creating a psychological effect and thereby influencing political behavior and attitudes. This definition is tested against the activity of the FLN during the Algerian War and used as a basis to explain the theoretical and empirical significance of terrorism. The paper compares the relative costs and benefits of a terrorist strategy from the revolutionary point of view and concludes that the attractiveness of terrorism derives from the combination of economy and facility of means with high psychological and political effectiveness. The risks of the strategy are controllable, and the results are predictable. Revolutionary terrorism combines low cost with potentially high yield." J

57. Ingram, Timothy H. NUCLEAR HIJACKING: NOW WITHIN THE GRASP OF ANY BRIGHT LUNATIC. *Washington Monthly 1973 4(11): 20-28.*

58. Jacomy-Millette, Annemarie. LA VIOLENCE, LE DROIT ET LA POLITIQUE: RÉFLEXION SUR LE PROBLÈME DE LA PROTECTION INTERNATIONALE DES DIPLOMATES [Violence, law and politics: Thoughts on the problem of international protection of diplomats]. *Études Int. [Canada] 1975 6(1): 103-109.* The dramatic increases in juvenile delinquency,

airplane hijacking, and assaults on diplomats are indicators of the rising incidence rate for acts of violence and terrorism in the United States and Western Europe. Curtailment of such behavior depends on international agreement on such issues as defining an act of violence and accepting a common course of action. However, acts of violence can be viewed as destructive or beneficial and there is considerable divergence of opinion concerning the rights of the individual in relation to the collective. The issue of violence and terror should be addressed regionally rather than internationally, and partial resolutions are better than no agreements. Primary and secondary sources; 17 notes. J. F. Harrington, Jr.

59. Jenkins, Brian M. INTERNATIONAL COOPERATION IN LOCATING AND RECOVERING STOLEN NUCLEAR MATERIALS. *Terrorism* 1983 6(4): 561-575. Several thefts of nuclear material beginning in 1966, which preceded a wave of terrorism, inspired the 1981 UN Convention on the Physical Protection of Nuclear Materials and similar US measures.

60. Jenkins, Brian Michael. NEW MODES OF CONFLICT. *Orbis* 1984 28(1): 5-16. Examines armed conflict during 1964-84, dividing it into three categories—conventional war, guerrilla war, and international terrorism. International terrorism is a reflection of the postindustrial age and will increase due to the means at its disposal. Note. J. W. Thacker, Jr.

61. Johnson, Chalmers. TERROR. *Society* 1977 15(1): 48-52. Maintains that growing terrorist activities, 1944-77, can be curtailed, but such curtailment entails agreement among nonterrorist nations to suspend certain civil liberties in order to suppress terrorism.

62. Joyner, Christopher C. OFFSHORE MARITIME TERRORISM: INTERNATIONAL IMPLICATIONS AND THE LEGAL RESPONSE. *Naval War Coll. Rev.* 1983 36(4): 16-31. The dependency of the West on oil assures the construction of more offshore installations, which may become the target of terrorist attacks. A review of international law reveals that the coastal states will generally have jurisdiction over such incidents and must prepare a defense policy to protect themselves. 45 notes. D. Powell

63. Kanin, David B. THE OLYMPIC GAMES. *Midstream* 1979 25(8): 14-18. Traces Jews' interests in the Olympic Games focusing on the issues of terrorism and boycotts, 1930's-70's.

64. Karber, Phillip A. URBAN TERRORISM: BASELINE DATA AND A CONCEPTUAL FRAMEWORK. *Social Sci. Q.* 1971 52(3): 521-533. "Presents and evaluates data on bombing incidents and discusses such terrorism as symbolic violence employed to maximize significance and minimize the actor's vulnerability. Karber notes that viewing terrorism as an attempt to communicate rather than as a form of revolution provides theoretical insight into its components, functions and pathologies." J

65. Kimche, Jon. CARRINGTON'S "CAVIARE." *Midstream* 1981 27(6): 3-7. Discusses the role of British Foreign Secretary Lord Carrington during

1980 in fashioning the "European initiative" as a plan to bring peace to the Middle East. Examines the general background and the reaction of the Palestine Liberation Organization.

66. Kogan, Eugen. STAATSTERROR ALS ORDNUNGSFAKTOR [State terror as a factor in keeping order]. *Frankfurter Hefte [Germany] 1976 31(6): 9-16.* A reflection on the history of terrorism, both by governments and revolutionaries, in the Western world.

67. Korey, William. MORAL BANKRUPTCY AT THE UN. *Midstream 1973 19(2): 34-42.* The 1972 UN decision to make no statements regarding international terrorism was a travesty.   S

68. Krieger, David M. TERRORISTS AND NUCLEAR TECHNOLOGY. *Bull. of the Atomic Scientists 1975 31(6): 28-34.* Warns that terrorist groups will achieve nuclear weapon capability unless steps are taken "almost immediately to halt both nuclear weapon and nuclear power plant proliferation." Explores ways in which terrorist groups "may gain possession of nuclear materials, including weapons; the way in which they may use nuclear weapons and other nuclear technologies to their benefit; and various courses of action designed to minimize the possibilities of terrorists utilizing nuclear technology to their benefit and society's detriment." Based on primary and secondary sources; map, 21 notes.   D. J. Trickey

69. Laqueur, Walter. FEHLGEDEUTETER TERRORISMUS [Misinterpreted terrorism]. *Schweizer Monatshefte [Switzerland] 1976 56(7): 567-574.* Discusses changes in 20th-century terrorism, an analysis of which requires attention to the special political, economic, social, and historical situation of the countries involved.

70. Laqueur, Walter. GUERRILLAS AND TERRORISTS. *Commentary 1974 58(4): 40-48.*

71. Laqueur, Walter. INTERPRETATIONS OF TERRORISM—FACT, FICTION AND POLITICAL SCIENCE. *J. of Contemporary Hist. [Great Britain] 1977 12(1): 1-42.* A long excursion into the facts of modern terrorism and modern European and Asian literature treating the subject reaches the conclusion that the origin, the character, the participants, and the motivation of political or social violence follow no discernible pattern. 83 notes.
M. P. Trauth

72. Leber, Jeffrey R. INTERNATIONAL TERRORISM: CRIMINAL OR POLITICAL? *Towson State J. of Internat. Affairs 1973 7(2): 129-142.* Analyzes legal and political aspects of terrorism on land, sea, and air, and describes the difficulty eradicating it.   S

73. Lee, Edward G. and April, Serge. BEHIND-THE-SCENES NEGOTIATION OF TREATY TO PROTECT DIPLOMATS. *Int. Perspectives [Canada] 1976 (3): 3-7.* General discussion of the background to and adoption of the Convention on the Prevention and Punishment of Crimes Against Internation-

ally Protected Persons by the UN General Assembly, 14 December 1973, in order to better protect the lives of diplomatic agents and to combat international terrorism.

74. Leites, Nathan. UNDERSTANDING THE NEXT ACT. *Terrorism 1979 3(1-2): 1-46.* Discusses the ideological and tactical motives which inspired terrorist groups in the 1970's, such as the Weathermen, the Japanese United Red Army, the Italian Brigate Rosse, the West German Rote Armee Fraktion, and others, to commit acts of "microviolence."

75. Livingstone, N. C. WEAPONS FOR THE FEW. *Conflict 1979 1(4): 303-325.* Discusses the kinds of weapons that are or could become available to terrorists.

76. Livingstone, N. C. THE WOLVES AMONG US: REFLECTIONS ON THE PAST EIGHTEEN MONTHS AND THOUGHTS ON THE FUTURE. *World Affairs 1983 146(1): 7-22.* Since 1982, the Palestine Liberation Organization (PLO) has been defeated, France has become the battleground for terrorists, Armenian violence against Turkey and its diplomats has escalated, in Northern Ireland the Irish Republican Army has continued its terrorist campaign against the British, and in general the modern face of terrorism appears to be undergoing a transformation.

77. Mallin, Jay. TERRORISM AS A POLITICAL WEAPON. *Air U. R. 1971 22(5): 45-52.* Discusses 20th-century terrorism, especially Communist terror in the Vietnam War. S

78. May, William F. TERRORISM AS STRATEGY AND ECSTASY. *Social Res. 1974 41(2): 277-298.* Concentrates on instances and definition of revolutionary terrorism. S

79. McDonald, John W., Jr. THE UNITED NATIONS CONVENTION AGAINST THE TAKING OF HOSTAGES: THE INSIDE STORY. *Terrorism 1983 6(4): 545-560.* After negotiating from 1976 to 1979 and despite last-minute obstructionism by the USSR, the UN General Assembly adopted a treaty criminalizing hostage-taking.

80. Miller, David. THE USE AND ABUSE OF POLITICAL VIOLENCE. *Pol. Studies [Great Britain] 1984 32(3): 401-419.* Examines the ethics of using violence for achieving political ends within a liberal democracy. Secondary sources; 28 notes. G. L. Neville

81. Monroe, Charles P. ADDRESSING TERRORISM IN THE UNITED STATES. *Ann. of the Am. Acad. of Pol. and Social Sci. 1982 (463): 141-148.* Terrorism presents a serious threat to democratic governments that must protect themselves without trampling individual rights. Federal Bureau of Investigation successes have shown that the US government can effectively deal with this threat while protecting the constitutional rights of citizens. J

82. Nemes, Dezső. A FASIZMUS KÉRDÉSÉHEZ [On the question of fascism]. *Párttörténeti Közlemények [Hungary] 1974 20(4): 3-64.* Scolds Marxist historians who have accepted some parts of Western redefinitions of fascism. The East Germans and the Soviets have maintained a leading role in the international ideological struggle while Miklós Lackó, Mihály Vajda, and even Party historians Mária Ormos and Ince Miklós have deviated from Georgi Dimitrov's definition of fascism: An openly terrorist dictatorship of the most reactionary, most chauvinistic, and most imperialistic elements of finance capital. 35 notes. P. I. Hidas

83. Paletz, David L.; Fozzard, Peter A.; and Ayanian, John Z. THE I.R.A., THE RED BRIGADES, AND THE F.A.L.N. IN THE *NEW YORK TIMES.* *J. of Communication 1982 32(2): 162-171.* A study of the *New York Times*'s coverage of the activities of the Irish Republican Army (IRA), the Red Brigades, and the Fuerzas Armadas de Liberacion (FALN), shows that the media do not always cover incidents of terrorism sympathetically, thereby encouraging the terrorists; instead, the newspaper "generally ignores the motivations, objectives, and long-term goals of violent organizations, thereby preventing their causes from gaining legitimacy with the public."

84. Palm, Thede. AMERIKANSK UTRIKESPOLITIK [American foreign policy]. *Svensk Tidskrift [Sweden] 1981 68(5-6): 247-252.* The Reagan administration aims to fight terrorism—in the shape of Soviet-supported "liberation movements"—and to supply her allies with arms to redress the international balance of power. The apparent success of Soviet imperialism during the Carter administration forces the present administration to support even authoritarian regimes to prevent Communist takeovers. The redressed balance of power following rearmament in the Western world will make SALT meaningful. Ref.
H. C. Andersen

85. Parry, Albert. WHEREFROM THIS ERROR OF TERROR? *Georgia R. 1972 26(2): 169-182.* Though today's terrorists maintain that they are Marxist-Leninists, they are often ignorant of the ideas of the great writers on revolution. They tend to acquire ideas about revolution second hand, often lacking an intelligent, comprehensive program with which to replace the society they intend to destroy. M. B. Lucas

86. Patkó, Imre. AZ EGYESÜLT ÁLLAMOK KÉT TAKTIKÁJA AZ "EMBERI JOGOKTÓL" A "NEMZETKÖZI TERRORIZMUSIG" [The two tactics of United States: from "human rights" to "international terrorism"]. *Társadalmi Szemle [Hungary] 1981 36(3): 61-72.* The abnormal stress on human rights, introduced as a political red herring by the Carter government did not pay the dividend expected. Consequently it was replaced in the Reagan administration by the more impressive sounding "fight against international terrorists." T. Kuner

87. Pierre, Andrew J. THE POLITICS OF INTERNATIONAL TERRORISM. *Orbis 1976 19(4): 1251-1269.* There has been a tremendous growth of international terrorism since 1969, but there is nothing new about terrorism. International terrorism is usually political in intent and carried out by

nongovernment groups across national boundaries, sometimes with financial and moral support from nation states. International terrorism is not a transitory phenomenon. Its suppression will require both "measures of prevention and measures of deterrence"; terrorism could become a new form of warfare. 13 notes. A. N. Garland

88. Poulantzas, Nicholas M. SOME PROBLEMS OF INTERNATIONAL LAW CONNECTED WITH URBAN GUERRILLA WARFARE: THE KIDNAPPING OF MEMBERS OF DIPLOMATIC MISSIONS, CONSULAR OFFICES AND OTHER FOREIGN PERSONNEL. *Ann. d'Études Int.* [Switzerland] 1972 (3): 137-167. Studies the theory and practice of urban guerrilla warfare in the various countries of Europe, Latin America, and Asia, discussing the legal problems arising from the abduction of persons, ca. 1960-72, especially in the prevention and punishment of terrorism.

89. Pozefsky, Abby L. AIR LAW—WARSAW CONVENTION AND MONTREAL AGREEMENT— HIJACKING VICTIMS MAY RECOVER DAMAGES FROM AIRLINE. *New York U. J. of Internat. Law and Politics* 1973 6(3): 555-568. A stated purpose of the Warsaw Convention, as modified by the Montreal Agreement, was to maximize and expedite recovery by those who need it most. Stresses that victims of hijacking fit into this category and that both emotional and physical damage are compensable. Based on primary and secondary sources; 66 notes. M. L. Frey

90. Price, H. Edward, Jr. THE STRATEGY AND TACTICS OF REVOLUTIONARY TERRORISM. *Comparative Studies in Soc. and Hist.* [Great Britain] 1977 19(1): 52-66. Discusses political theory regarding the tactics and aims of terrorism by revolutionaries in the 1960's and 1970's; considers recent cases in Uruguay, Northern Ireland and Palestine.

91. Raab, Earl. ANTI-SEMITISM IN THE 1980'S. *Midstream* 1983 29(2): 11-18. Examines current trends and reports concerning public opinion and Jews; notes the rise in acts of terrorism directed toward Jews worldwide.

92. Raditsa, Leo. THE SOURCE OF WORLD TERRORISM. *Midstream* 1981 27(10): 42-48. Reviews Claire Sterling's *The Terror Network,* which explores the organization of world terrorist activities and accuses the USSR of being its chief supporter.

93. Russell, Charles A. and Bowman, H. Miller. PROFILE OF A TERRORIST. *Military Rev.* 1977 57(8): 21-34. Studies terrorists from different organizations and countries active since 1966 in terms of age, sex, marital status, rural-urban origins, socioeconomic background, education, occupation, the method and place of recruitment, and political philosophy. 5 illus., 24 notes. D. J. Kommer

94. Russell, Charles A. TRANSNATIONAL TERRORISM. *Air U. Rev.* 1976 27(2): 26-35. Since 1970 two significant changes have taken place in many of those insurgent movements active in the non-Communist world: 1) the focus of the movement has shifted from the rural to the urban areas, and 2)

terrorist activity has become transnational. Middle Eastern and South American guerrilla movements are discussed in detail. Also the organization, tactics, and growing ties among terrorist groups are analyzed as well as some of the counterinsurgency measures of the Western countries. Based on newspapers and government reports; 5 illus., 14 notes. J. W. Thacker, Jr.

95. Saddy, Fehmy. INTERNATIONAL TERRORISM, HUMAN RIGHTS, AND WORLD ORDER. *Terrorism 1982 5(4): 325-352.* Examines the efforts made in the 1970's to define international terrorism, its causes, and measures to combat it, and evaluates these efforts in the context of the simultaneous interest in the promotion of human rights.

96. St. John, Peter. ANALYSIS AND RESPONSE OF A DECADE OF TERRORISM. *Int. Perspectives [Canada] 1981 (Sept-Oct): 2-5.* The international terrorist threat that emerged in the late 1960's is likely to escalate in intensity in the 1980's, a decade that may see widespread assassination attempts and the use of advanced weaponry. Control of this phenomenon will require good intelligence networks, well-trained police, a cooperative press, and removal of the causes of terrorism. Terrorism, perceived as a legitimate response to an affluent and uncaring West, may also become a continuing feature of North-South conflict. E. Palais

97. Sanakoyev, Sh. THE UN AND THE SECURITY OF NATIONS. *Int. Affairs [USSR] 1972 (12): 16-21.* Discusses the USSR's positions in issues involving disarmament, terrorism and the Middle East in the 1972 meeting of the UN General Assembly; accuses the United States and other Western nations of imperialism.

98. Schleimer, Joseph D. THE DAY THEY BLEW UP SAN ONOFRE. *Bull. of the Atomic Scientists 1974 30(8): 24-27.* A scenario for sabotaging atomic power plants, including possible sources of nuclear materials, entrance to plant facilities, and results of destruction of the plant for surrounding urban areas; examines the threat of nuclear power in the hands of terrorist groups.

99. Segre, D. V. and Adler, J. H. THE ECOLOGY OF TERRORISM. *Encounter [Great Britain] 1973 40(2): 17-24.* The combination of violence and modern technology has transformed the nature of terrorism. "Extremist attitudes to legitimate power are becoming self-fulfilling" and require coordinated international reaction. "They are no longer a political phenomenon linked with particular historical or economic situations; they are becoming a retrograde socio-ecological feature." 8 notes. D. H. Murdoch

100. Segre, D. V. and Adler, J. H. THE ECOLOGY OF TERRORISM. *Survival [Great Britain] 1973 15(4): 178-183.* Discusses sociopathic and behavioral aspects of international terrorism and air hijacking in the 1970's.

101. Shamwell, Horace F., Jr. IMPLEMENTING THE CONVENTION ON THE PREVENTION AND PUNISHMENT OF CRIMES AGAINST INTERNATIONALLY PROTECTED PERSONS, INCLUDING DIPLOMATIC AGENTS. *Terrorism 1983 6(4): 529-543.* The prevention program

has not been authorized to curb terrorism against diplomats although all administrative steps have been taken in the UN and in the United States.

102. Sloan, Stephen. SIMULATING TERRORISM: FROM OPERATIONAL TECHNIQUES TO QUESTIONS OF POLICY. *Int. Studies Notes 1978 5(4): 3-8.* Discusses a training technique developed at the University of Oklahoma, with cooperation of police and military organizations, to handle terrorism; 1970's.

103. Smart, I. M. H. THE POWER OF TERROR. *Int. J. [Canada] 1975 30(2): 225-237.* Discusses the effect of terrorism in international politics, cities and the mass media in the 1970's.

104. Snitch, Thomas H. TERRORISM AND POLITICAL ASSASSINATIONS: A TRANSNATIONAL ASSESSMENT, 1968-80. *Ann. of the Am. Acad. of Pol. and Social Sci. 1982 (463): 54-68.* Presents the results of a seven-year, cross-national survey of 721 political assassinations in 123 nations. Certain nations, targets, and terrorist actors account for a large portion of all assassination activity. Statistical analysis could not link terrorist-inspired assassinations to the developing world, nor was any international network of assassins discovered. The findings point to growing levels of separatist-inspired violence and a distinct shift in target selection toward the international business community and the diplomatic corps. Terrorists appear to be increasingly successful because they are targeting relatively unprotected public individuals. J/S

105. Tapia Salinas, Luis. LA POLÍTICA AÉREA INTERNACIONAL Y LA "PIRATERÍA AÉREA" [International air policy and air piracy]. *Rev. de Politica Int. [Spain] 1977 (150): 97-110.* Studies judicial attempts to prevent aircraft hijacking and recommends the implementation of greater precautionary measures by political and security agencies.

106. Taylor, Edmond. THE TERRORISTS. *Horizon 1973 15(3): 58-65.* Terrorism began with The Terror during the French Revolution. Terrorists are seldom loyal to a state or a group; often they are easily converted, providing that they can continue to practice terrorism for their new group. They need not be revolutionaries; many have been safely ensconced in government offices. Terrorism may be an individual or a group activity. Terrorism is becoming increasingly prevalent. It will not disappear until injustice disappears, but measures must be taken to lessen its prevalence and impact in the modern world. Based on secondary sources; 6 photos. V. L. Human

107. Unger, Leopold. WIDZIANE Z BRUKSELI [The view from Brussels]. *Kultura [France] 1983 (3): 70-81.* Examines links between the secret services of the East European countries, notably the USSR and Bulgaria, and political assassinations in the West, such as Leon Trotsky's and his son's and the attempt on the life of Pope John Paul II in 1981.

108. Vitiuk, V. V. O PONIATII "MEZHDUNARODNYI TERRORIZM" [Understanding international terrorism]. *Sotsiologicheskie Issledovaniia*

[USSR] 1982 (2): 59-68. International terrorism is the work of a band of brothers, quarrelsome but still only one band, of whose activities the Western nations take too superficial a view.

109. Warren, G. I. ASSESSING PROGRESS IN DEVELOPING SYSTEMS TO CURB AERIAL HIJACKINGS. *Internat. Perspectives [Canada] 1974 (1): 37-39.* Efforts 1970-73 in international law to stop aircraft hijackings.
S

110. Wilkinson, Paul. INTRODUCTION. *Terrorism 1981 5(1-2): 1-12.* Points out that while Great Britain has been free from major internal strife for the past 150 years, its colonies have been the scene of constant terrorist activities, which finally convinced the British to withdraw rather than pay the high price in lives and material necessary for a colonial presence. Introduction to a special section on Northern Ireland.

111. Wilkinson, Paul. TERRORISM: THE INTERNATIONAL RESPONSE. *World Today [Great Britain] 1978 34(1): 5-13.* Experience since 1967 shows that as long as pro-terrorist states exist, there is little hope for universal conventions and treaties against terrorism; meantime, stringent antiterrorist measures and sophisticated intelligence gathering networks are necessary.

112. Wilkinson, Paul. TERRORISM, THE MASS MEDIA AND DEMOCRACY. *Contemporary Rev. [Great Britain] 1981 239(1386): 35-44.* Discusses the role and responsibilities of the mass media in reporting terrorist activities in liberal democracies.

113. Wilkinson, Paul. THREE QUESTIONS ON TERRORISM. *Government and Opposition [Great Britain] 1973 8(3): 290-312.* Discusses three forms of terrorism: wartime terror, repressive terror, and revolutionary terror. Refers particularly to the cases of the USSR, Cuba, Malaya, and the Middle East.

114. Wurth-Hough, Sandra. NETWORK NEWS COVERAGE OF TERRORISM: THE EARLY YEARS. *Terrorism 1983 6(3): 403-421.* Discusses news coverage of terrorist activities from 1968-71 by the three major television networks, and examines each network's treatment of terrorism stories as reflected by story emphasis and depiction, frequency, length of coverage, and location in newscasts.

115. Yoder, Amos. THE EFFECTIVENESS OF U.N. ACTION AGAINST INTERNATIONAL TERRORISM: CONCLUSIONS AND COMMENTS. *Terrorism 1983 6(4): 587-592.* Since the 1963 Tokyo Convention on aviation security, some antiterrorist measures have been taken, but important gaps remain, especially those pertaining to nuclear terrorism.

116. Yoder, Amos. UNITED NATIONS RESOLUTIONS AGAINST INTERNATIONAL TERRORISM. *Terrorism 1983 6(4): 503-517.* Although the 1981 UN resolution against terrorism lacks effectiveness for political reasons, it has promoted individual, specific, bilateral antiterrorist pacts.

117. —. INTERNATIONAL CONVENTION AGAINST THE TAKING OF HOSTAGES. *Terrorism* 1981 5(3): 293-300. Reproduces the 20-article International Convention against the Taking of Hostages adopted 17 December 1979 by the UN General Assembly in an effort to improve the instruments of international law directed against terrorism.

118. —. THE KGB ABROAD: "MURDER INTERNATIONAL, INC." *Survey [Great Britain]* 1983 27: 80-87. This collection of documents, charts and interviews on Committee of State Security (KGB) "wet affairs" abroad is selected from *Hearings before the Subcommittee to Investigate the Administration of the International Security Act and Other Internal Security Laws of the Committee on the Judiciary,* United States Senate, 89th Congress, First Session, 26 March 1965. It includes testimony by former Soviet state security officer Petr S. Deryabin, an interview with Isaac Don Levine on Soviet acceptance of the murderer of Trotsky, a chart listing some of the terrorist actions between 1926 and 1960, an extract from Flora Lewis's *The Red Pawn* on Ignace Reiss [Ludwig], and an article from the *New York Times* of 9 June 1960 on the kidnapping and murder of Dr. Walter Linse from West Germany in 1953. Chart. L. J. Klass

119. —. LEFT-WING FASCISM. *Society* 1981 18(4): 19-40.
Horowitz, Irving Louis. LEFT-WING FASCISM: AN INFANTILE DISORDER, *pp. 19-24.*
Pells, Richard. HUNTING EMBRYONIC FASCISTS, *pp. 25-27.*
Nisbet, Robert. MYTHS AND MIRRORS, *pp. 27-28.*
Woolf, S. J. PROTOTYPES AND TERRORISTS, *pp. 28-29.*
Fischer-Galati, Stephen. FASCIST-COMMUNIST CONVERGENCE, *pp. 30-31.*
Joes, Anthony James. BLACK SHIRT, RED HEART, *p. 32.*
Robbins, Thomas. A PERIPHERAL DISORDER, *pp. 33-36.*
Gregor, A. James. THE SOCIALISM OF FOOLS, *pp. 36-39.*
Mosse, George L. RETREAT TO THE STATUS QUO, *pp. 39-40.*
Horowitz sees the existence of left-wing fascism (or, as he also calls it, "right-wing communism") internationally and in the United States—a blend of socialism, nationalism, criticism of mass culture, anti-Semitism, ideological fanaticism, and authoritarianism—and the other authors comment on his thesis about renewed totalitarianism.

120. —. NEW DEVELOPMENTS IN THE LAW OF INTERNATIONAL AVIATION: THE CONTROL OF AERIAL HIJACKING. *Am. J. of Internat. Law* 1971 65(4): 71-96.
McWhinney, Edward. ADDRESS, *pp. 71-75.*
Malmborg, K. E., Jr. ADDRESS, *pp. 75-80.*
Lissitzyn, Oliver J. INTERNATIONAL CONTROL OF AERIAL HIJACKING: THE ROLE OF VALUES AND INTERESTS, *pp. 80-86.*
Lowenfeld, Andreas F. COMMENTS, *pp. 86-89.*
Evans, Alona E. COMMENTS, *pp. 89-91.*
More, Vishwanath, et al. DISCUSSION, *pp. 92-96.* Discussion at the 1971 meeting of the American Society of International Law on changes in

international law from 1944-70 which were designed to control aircraft hijacking. S

121. —. [THE SPREAD OF INTERNATIONAL TERRORISM]. *Int. Studies Q. 1980 24(2): 262-310.*
Midlarsky, Manus I.; Crenshaw, Martha; and Yoshida, Fumihiko. WHY VIOLENCE SPREADS: THE CONTAGION OF INTERNATIONAL TERRORISM, *pp. 262-298.* A statistical study of over 500 incidents of terrorism in Latin America and Western Europe demonstrates that violence spread between countries and regions by means of either diffusion (1968-71) or contagion (1973-74). Differences between regions also exist in the contagion effects of various forms of terrorism. 9 tables, 40 notes.
Heyman, Edward and Mickolus, Edward. OBSERVATIONS ON "WHY VIOLENCE SPREADS," *pp. 299-305.* Rejects conclusions of Midlarsky et al. due to the unreliability of the data base and other grounds. 12 notes.
Midlarsky, Manus I.; Crenshaw, Martha; and Yoshida, Fumihiko. REJOINDER TO "OBSERVATIONS ON 'WHY VIOLENCE SPREADS,' " pp. 306-310. E. Palais

122. —. TERRORISM AND POLITICAL CRIMES IN INTERNATIONAL LAW. *Am. J. of Internat. Law 1973 67(5): 87-110.*
Evans, Alona E., Chairman.
Moore, John Norton. TOWARD LEGAL RESTRAINTS ON INTERNATIONAL TERRORISM, pp. 88-94.
Dugard, John. TOWARDS THE DEFINITION OF INTERNATIONAL TERRORISM, pp. 94-100.
AbuLughod, Ibrahim. UNCONVENTIONAL VIOLENCE AND INTERNATIONAL POLITICS, pp. 100-104.
Kittrie, Nicholas. COMMENTS, pp. 104-107.
Sewell, Alan F. COMMENTS, pp. 107-110. Panel discussion at 67th Annual Meeting, American Society of International Law, 12-14 April 1973. S

123. —. [TERRORISM IN THE 20TH CENTURY]. *Dissent 1975 22(3): 227-237.*
Howe, Irving. THE RETURN OF TERROR, *pp. 227-237.*
O'Brien, Conor Cruise. AN IRISH VOICE AGAINST TERRORISM, *pp. 330-331.*

124. —. A U.S. OFFENSIVE AT THE U.N. (STATEMENTS BY THE U.S. DELEGATION BEFORE THE GENERAL ASSEMBLY). *World Affairs 1981-82 144(3): 196-295.* Presents documents and statements presented by the US representatives to the UN on human rights, Soviet policies, the prospects for peace in the Middle East and Asia, disarmament, the international economic situation, and the extradition of Ziad Abu Eain to Israel in 1979 for alleged terrorism.

2

EUROPE

125. Alder, Douglas D. ASSASSINATION AS POLITICAL EFFICACY: TWO CASE STUDIES FROM WORLD WAR I. *East European Q. 1978 12(2): 209-231.* Describes the assassinations of Archduke Francis Ferdinand in 1914 and Austrian Minister President Karl Stürgkh in 1916 by Gavrilo Princip and Friedrich Adler, respectively. Contrasts and compares the victims, the assassins, and the consequences. Both assassins killed for political ideologies, and neither foresaw the results of his actions. 44 notes. C. R. Lovin

126. Alder, Douglas D. FRIEDRICH ADLER: EVOLUTION OF A REVOLUTIONARY. *German Studies Rev. 1978 1(3): 260-284.* Friedrich Adler, Austrian Social Democratic Party official, led a small but sophisticated antiwar movement during World War I. The son of moderate party leader Victor Adler, he pursued a scientific career in Switzerland until 1911. After completing his doctorate, he abandoned his career in physics and turned to Austrian socialist politics. When the war broke out in 1914, Friedrich rejected his father's wait-out-the-war policy, demanding open opposition. Because this policy failed to win party support, he decided to assassinate the Austrian prime minister in order to get his message before the citizens. The assassination (October 1916), his interrogations, and his trial (May 1917) became a cause célèbre, contributing to the transformation of Austrian socialism from a moderate to a more radical or "orthodox" mold. Based on records in Viennese archives. A

127. Alexiev, Alex. THE KREMLIN AND THE POPE. *Ukrainian Q. 1983 39(4): 378-388.* Recounts the history of Pope John Paul II's impact on the Catholics of Eastern Europe, especially Poland, and implies that this influence is of sufficient concern to the USSR that the Soviets might have instigated, supported, or at least condoned the allegedly Bulgarian-led attempted assassination of the pope in 1981.

128. Amort, Čestmír. SPOLEČNÝ BOJ ČESKOSLOVENSKÝCH A BULHARSKÝCH KOMUNISTŮ PROTI FAŠISMU V ROCE 1925 [Joint struggle of Czechoslovak and Bulgarian Communists against fascism in 1925]. *Slovanský Přehled [Czechoslovakia] 1979 65(1): 90-96.* In 1925 the Communist press in Czechoslovakia exposed the terrorist anti-Communist campaign of the fascist regime of Alexander Canek in Bulgaria. Czech Communists gave asylum to Communist exiles and staged a number of demonstrations against the Bulgarian regime. Georgi Dimitrov was sheltered from the police by

members of the Czech Communist Party. The Czech Communist observer in Bulgaria, Karel Kreibich, called a mass meeting in Prague in September of 1925 which the Czech police broke up. In spite of such obstacles the Czech Communists continued to help Bulgarian emigrants in their antifascist struggles. 46 notes. B. Reinfeld

129. Andreadēs, Chrēstos G. ANEKDOTA ENGRAPHA TŌN KATOIKŌN MEGAROVOU KAI TYRNOVOU [Unpublished documents from Megarovo and Veliko Turnovo]. *Makedonika [Greece] 1981 21: 309-318.* In 1870 the Ottoman Empire, hoping to provoke clashes between the Bulgarians and Greeks in Macedonia, created the Bulgarian Exarchate which freed the Bulgarian church from the ecumenical patriarchate. In 1893 the Turks permitted the Bulgarians to create a Macedonian committee—an organ that used propaganda and ultimately violence to drive the Greeks out of Macedonia or to bring them into the Bulgarian Exarchate. The author publishes two letters from 1904 illustrating the resistance of Greeks living in Megarovo and Veliko Túrnovo to the terrorist tactics of the Macedonian committee. 12 notes, 2 letters, English summary. A. J. Papalas

130. Andreoli, Marcella. LINEA ROMA-MILANO-CATANZARO [The Rome-Milan-Catanzaro line]. *Ponte [Italy] 1977 33(8-9): 906-915.* Reviews the judicial processes and the press revelations of the past eight years in connection with the bombing in Piazza Fontana in Milan in 1969; substantiates the crucial role played by top-level government officials and neo-Fascists who, however, will most likely not be prosecuted.

131. Andreoli, Marcella and Obici, Giulio. PER UN'ANALISI (FINALMENTE) POLITICA DEL TERRORISMO [Finally, a political analysis of terrorism]. *Ponte [Italy] 1979 35(6): 688-698.* Political analysis of the growth of terrorism in Italy in the 1970's and the responses to it, particularly from the left.

132. Andreoli, Marcella. PROCESSO PER LA STRAGE DI BRESCIA. 1974, UN ALTRO ANNO-CHIAVE [Trial for the Brescia massacre, 1974: another key year]. *Ponte [Italy] 1978 34(3-4): 265-270.* Recounts the trial in 1978 of a group of fascists accused of a 1974 outrage in Brescia that cost eight lives; 1974 was a key year in the development of right-wing terrorism in Italy.

133. Arbatova, N. K. TERRORIZM V SOVREMENNOI ITALII [Terrorism in modern Italy]. *Voprosy Istorii [USSR] 1981 (12): 176-181.* Both ultraleft-wing and right-wing terrorism have recently been endemic in Italy, united in their fear of Communist Party electoral success. Leftist terrorism has been based on a class of intellectuals, rejecting the organized working class, proclaiming instead that the future belongs to the new working class. Reviews prominent terrorist murders in Italy and the international ramifications of terrorism. Based on Italian newspapers and reports of Italian authorities; 19 notes. A. J. Evans

134. Audoin, Stephanie. LE PARTI COMMUNISTE FRANÇAIS ET LA VIOLENCE: 1929-1931 [The French Communist Party and violence:

1929-31]. *Rev. Hist. [France] 1983 269(2): 365-384.* Prodded by the Comintern, the French Communist Party set class struggle in the streets as its policy. The Party newspaper *Humanité* raised expectation of massive violence to begin 1 August 1929, but the Party's fighting groups were in fact weak and the outcome was unimpressive. After a year of failures, the Communists moderated their policy of violence but were then unable to prevent several elements of the Party from random outbreaks of violence. Despite neglect by historians, the period of agitation to street violence was an important era in the history of French Communism. Based on Archives Nationales, police dossiers, and files of *Humanité*; 33 notes. G. H. Davis

135. Avrus, A. I. MOPROVSKIE KAMPANII PROTIV TERRORA V POL'SHE [The MOPR campaigns against terror in Poland]. *Sovetskoe Slavianovedenie [USSR] 1979 (3): 29-41.* The International Red Aid (known also by its Russian initials, MOPR) was formed in 1922 with the active participation of Polish Communists and played a great role in giving aid to political prisoners and their families in Poland. The author describes the first MOPR campaign for aid to victims of terrorism in Poland of March 1923 and discusses the various subsequent campaigns, which received support in many countries.
S. R. Gudgin

136. Ayçoberry, Pierre. LA GUERRE DE RUES DANS L'ALLEMAGNE DE WEIMAR [The street war under the Weimar Republic]. *Histoire [France] 1979 (10): 86-88.* Street fighting by political paramilitary forces ranging from the Far Right to the Communists helped bring down the republic in Germany, 1920-32.

137. Banfi, Arialdo. TERRORISMO FUORI E DENTRO LO STATO [Terrorism without and within the state]. *Ponte [Italy] 1978 34(3-4): 311-328.* Surveys terrorist violence in the 20th century with emphasis on Italy, discussing that perpetrated by government opponents and that by the government itself.

138. Bell, J. Bowyer. THE ESCALATION OF INSURGENCY: THE PROVISIONAL IRISH REPUBLICAN ARMY'S EXPERIENCE, 1969-1971. *R. of Pol. 1973 35(3): 398-411.*

139. Bertoldi, Silvio. IL "RITORNO ALLE ORIGINI" DEL FASCISMO REPUBBLICANO [The "return to the origins" of republican Fascism]. *Problemi di Ulisse [Italy] 1976 13(82): 112-118.* The Italian Social Republic proclaimed at Salò in 1943 shows the two faces of Fascism: the one terrorist and violent, the other standing for order, law, and consensus.

140. Bibes, Geneviève. LE TERRORISME ITALIEN: ESSAI D'EXPLICATION [Italian terrorism: attempt at an explanation]. *Etudes [France] 1982 357(4): 293-306.* Discusses Italian terrorist activity since the 1960's as an outgrowth of this nation's own sociocultural factors and its political life rather than as the result of the worldwide terrorist crisis or foreign complicity.

141. Billig, Michael and Cochrane, Raymond. THE NATIONAL FRONT AND YOUTH. *Patterns of Prejudice [Great Britain] 1981 15(4): 3-15.* During the 1970's in Great Britain, the National Front, whose fascist and racist political platform attracted urban, working-class white youth, particularly males who left school early, shifted from "respectable" to a blatant display of anti-Semitism, including resort to violence against ethnic groups much like that of the SA and SS in Germany.

142. Bishop, Joseph W., Jr. CAN DEMOCRACY DEFEND ITSELF AGAINST TERRORISM? *Commentary 1978 65(5): 55-62.* Discusses the problem of defense against terrorism, citing the example of Great Britain's handling of the Irish Republican Army. Britain has had some success with internment, arrest and search, interrogation in depth, and other measures. The United States could conceivably use some of these measures, although many would be subject to review by the Supreme Court. J. Tull

143. Blatt, Joel. RELATIVES AND RIVALS: THE RESPONSES OF THE ACTION FRANÇAISE TO ITALIAN FASCISM, 1919-26. *European Studies Rev. [Great Britain] 1981 11(3): 263-292.* The Action Française was a conduit for Italian Fascist influences on French politics, 1919-26. The two movements were hostile toward liberalism and the political left. They endorsed authoritarianism, nationalism, violence, and the political tradition of the right. Action Française was more than a reactionary movement, but it fell short of fascism. It was monarchist, elitist, and doctrinaire. Its leaders were unwilling to seek mass support or to pursue revolutionary action. Action Française made fascism a political issue and helped polarize French politics after 1923. Based on a paper presented to the Southern Historical Association, St. Louis, Missouri, November 1978. Sources include newspapers, the papers of the Minister of the Interior, and the writings of Charles Maurras, Jacques Bainville, Léon Daudet, and Georges Valois; 148 notes.

H. M. Narducci, Jr.

144. Bowden, Tom. THE IRISH UNDERGROUND AND THE WAR OF INDEPENDENCE 1919-21. *J. of Contemporary Hist. [Great Britain] 1973 8(2): 3-23.* From the 1880's, militant nationalism inspired the Irish revolutionary movement against British domination which culminated in the 1916 Easter Rising and the War of Independence, 1919-21. This guerrilla warfare between British security forces and the Irish Volunteers led by Michael Collins (1890-1922), was characterized by systematic assassinations and terrorism by both sides. The tactically and organizationally sound Irish Republican Army prevailed due to the British forces' weak strategy and command structure and lack of popular support. Primary and secondary sources; 46 notes.

B. A. Block

145. Boyce, D. George. NORMAL POLICING: PUBLIC ORDER IN NORTHERN IRELAND SINCE PARTITION. *Éire-Ireland 1979 14(4): 35-52.* The new government in Northern Ireland passed the controversial Special Powers Act (1922), which gave wide powers for preservation of order to the home minister, his undersecretary, and the new Royal Ulster Constabulary (RUC). The northern government reorganized its 50,000 Protestant police

into the RUC and the Ulster Special Constabulary, which were supported by the British army. The police authority was directed against Catholics, and only rarely against Protestant militants. This approach worked until the civil rights movement of 1968 but has backfired since. Reasons for the change include the willingness of Catholics to support the Provisional Irish Republican Army, the discrediting of the northern regime, resumption of British direct rule in 1972, Protestant backlash caused by political stalemate, and the existence of a civil liberties-oriented segment of British public opinion. The IRA remains durable and flexible; the current combination of British Army, RUC, and the Ulster Defense Regiment (UDR), the Specials' replacement, faces an indeterminate period of hostilities. 40 notes. D. J. Engler

146. Cappadocia, Ezio. TERRORISM IN ITALY: A COMMENTARY. *Queen's Q. [Canada] 1982 89(4): 770-782.* Terrorism in Italy can be seen as a reaction to the extreme Right, a reaction to the politics of the Italian Communist Party, a consequence of the history of Fascism in Italy, a result of uneven economic factors that historically left out the Catholic Church and the mass of the working class, or a combination of the preceding. In a country that has never had a civil war or a revolution, the fabric of society seems infinitely stronger and more resilient than the agencies of the state, and so the mass of Italians have not reacted to terrorism by moving to either the Right or the Left. L. V. Eid

147. Carr, Raymond. THE REGIONAL PROBLEM IN SPAIN. *Bijdragen en Mededelingen Betreffende de Geschiedenis der Nederlanden [Netherlands] 1979 94(3): 639-659.* Liberals not monarchists imposed centralization on Spain in the 19th century. The revival of Catalan nationalism occurred in the 19th century and was inspired by literary figures and based on historic memories and language. In 1932 Catalonia received autonomous status but the statute was revoked by Franco. Basque nationalism is based more on blood and race than Catalan consciousness. It also lacked widespread middle-class support. The Basques received autonomy in 1936 but lost it during the Spanish Civil War. Catalonia received autonomy in 1977, a status that might not satisfy the radical Basque Euzkadi Ta Azkatasuna (ETA) which demands complete independence and a union of all Basques in Spain and France. Basque terrorism constitutes the most serious threat to Spanish democracy today. Biblio. G. D. Homan

148. Ceausescu, Ilie and Talpeş, Ioan. INDEPENDENȚA NAȚIONALĂ ȘI INTEGRITEA TERITORIALĂ A PATRIEI ÎN OPERA ȘI ACTIVITATEA LUI NICOLAE IORGA [National independence and the territorial integrity of the country in the work and activity of Nicolae Iorga]. *Magazin Istoric [Romania] 1980 14(11): 26-29.* A tribute to Nicolae Iorga (1871-1940), President of the Romanian Council, on the 40th anniversary of his assassination by the Iron Guard. Historian, patriot, and politician, he championed the freedom of Romania and the smaller powers. 3 illus.

149. Chamberlin, Brewster S. DER ATTENTATSPLAN GEGEN SEECKT 1924 [The assassination plot against Seeckt, 1924]. *Vierteljahrshefte für Zeitgeschichte [West Germany] 1977 25(4): 425-440.* An analysis of the conception

and political exploitation of the January 1924 assassination attempt against Colonel General Hans von Seeckt (1866-1936), Chief of Army Command, 1920-26, in the post-World War I German Republic. The affair revealed the scheming and bitter conflicts among rightist groups, primarily Heinrich Class's Pan-Germans and Volkish groups close to Hitler, and the disastrous intriguing of the rightist-dominated RKO (Reich Commissioner for Public Order). Based on records in East German (Potsdam) and West German (Bavarian State Archive, Research Center of National Socialism, Hamburg) archives, the contemporary press, and secondary works; 69 notes. D. Prowe

150. Chiesa, G. POKUSHENIE NA ITAL'IANSKUIU DEMOKRATIIU (DELO OB UBIISTVE AL'DO MORO) [The attack on Italian democracy: the murder of Aldo Moro]. *Sovetskoe Gosudarstvo i Pravo [USSR] 1983 (8): 104-110.* Analyzes the events connected with the kidnapping and murder of the leader of the Italian Christian Democratic Party, Aldo Moro, in 1978 and shows that it was the reactionary wing of the CDP and not the Red Brigades that made political capital out of the affair. Secondary sources; 2 notes.

151. Clutterbuck, Richard. INTIMIDATION OF WITNESSES AND JURIES. *Army Q. and Defence J. [Great Britain] 1974 104(3): 285-289.* The intimidation of witnesses as a technique used by political terrorists is primarily designed to force authorities to abandon liberal legal processes and adopt repressive measures, thus playing into the enemy's hands. Examines the internment measures introduced in Northern Ireland from August 1971 as an example of this problem and notes the success of the recommendations of the Diplock Report. D. H. Murdoch

152. Clutterbuck, Richard. TERRORISM AND THE SECURITY FORCES IN EUROPE. *Army Q. and Defence J. [Great Britain] 1981 111(1): 12-29.* Compares the antiterrorist capabilities and doctrines of various Western European countries, primarily Great Britain, West Germany, and Italy, and analyzes the differing situations faced by these nations in combating terrorism.

153. Clutterbuck, Richard. TERRORIST INTERNATIONAL. *Army Q. and Defence J. [Great Britain] 1974 104(2): 154-159.* Discusses urban guerrilla operations in 1972-73, with particular reference to the IRA, and concludes that there is increasing international collaboration between underground terrorist groups. Particularly dangerous are the small number of free lance anarchists not firmly attached to any terrorist organization. Governments are desperately striving to discover an answer to the terrorist problem. Three optimistic developments relating to the IRA can be discerned; 1) the IRA suffered enormous losses during 1973, 2) the formation of the Protestant-Catholic Executive at Stormont is encouraging, and 3) in general, British public opinion is vehemently opposed to all forms of terrorism. 2 notes. R. G. Neville

154. Cooke, A. B. and Vincent, J. R. LORD SPENCER ON THE PHOENIX PARK MURDERS. *Irish Hist. Studies [Ireland] 1973 18(72): 583-591.* Reprints a statement by John Poyntz Spencer, fifth earl Spencer (1835-1910), relating to the murder of the chief secretary for Ireland, Lord Frederick Charles Cavendish, and the under secretary by Irish terrorists in Dublin

(1882). The statement, recorded in 1889, sheds additional light on the event and on the character of Spencer, who was lord lieutenant of Ireland at the time. 29 notes. P. H. Hardacre

155. Demi, Ahmet. NGJARJË TË JETUARA NË VITIN 1924 [Events of 1924]. *Studime Hist. [Albania] 1984 38(2): 207-213.* An account of a failed plot to kill Zog I organized by Avni Rustem, who was later assassinated. The 1924 democratic revolution followed and Ahmet Demi joined it, fighting to keep Zog I from returning from Yugoslavia where he had previously fled. Ahmet Demi was wounded and then escaped abroad. G-D. L. Naçi

156. Denitch, Bogdan. VIOLENCE AND SOCIAL CHANGE IN THE YUGOSLAV REVOLUTION: LESSONS FOR THE THIRD WORLD? *Comparative Pol. 1976 8(3): 465-478.* Analyzes three stages of the post-World War II Yugoslav revolution: consolidation of power, struggle for national independence, and the creation of a social and political system based on the workers. Indicates the similarities of the Chinese and Yugoslav revolutions. Traces the phases in Yugoslavia from 1942, covering the partisan forces, the rationale for the Communist purges, the relationship of peasants to the partisans, and the Chetnik movement (recruited from the peasants). The revolution proves that social structures, types, and attitudes can be changed. The guerrilla-nature of the struggle provided for a less repressive society because unlike most new nations, the elite established a bond with the people. 13 notes. R. I. Vexler

157. Dodd, Norman L. THE CORPORALS' WAR: INTERNAL SECURITY OPERATIONS IN NORTHERN IRELAND. *Military Rev. 1976 56(7): 58-68.* Discusses the British Army's military training in specialized internal security duties against potential Irish Republican Army terrorism in Northern Ireland, 1969-70's.

158. Dowling, Kathryn. CIVIL RIGHTS, HUMAN RIGHTS, AND TERRORISM IN NORTHERN IRELAND. *J. of Intergroup Relations 1979-80 7(4): 3-23.* Political background to the civil strife in Northern Ireland.

159. Dragne, Florea. LOCUL BLOCULUI MUNCITORESC-ȚĂRĂNESC ÎN ACTIVITATEA PENTRU FĂURIREA DE ALIANȚE POLITICE A FORȚELOR DEMOCRATICE ȘI PROGRESISTE [The place of the Workers and Peasants Bloc in creating the political alliance of progressive and democratic forces]. *Anale de Istorie [Romania] 1976 22(4): 61-71.* Elaborates on Romanian Communist Party tactics of alliance with other left-wing parties and even petit-bourgeois groups, 1922-33, aimed at concentrating democratic forces against the bourgeois-monarchical regime. The Comintern was mistaken in condemning the PCR for rightist tendencies and lack of discipline. The PCR never lost sight of the class struggle and the long-range goal of installing working-class order. The forces of oligarchy remained strong, making Party activity nearly impossible without political collaboration, especially with the Socialist and Peasant Parties. The principal work of the bloc was in electoral campaigns for communal and district councils and for parliament. Despite many successes, including the election of five members to parliament in 1931,

the government through terrorism dissolved the bloc two years later. 21 notes.
G. J. Bobango

160. Duhamel, Luc. LÉNINE, LA VIOLENCE ET L'EUROCOMMUNISME [Lenin, violence, and Eurocommunism]. *Can. J. of Pol. Sci. [Canada] 1980 13(1): 97-120.* Examines the attitudes of the Communist parties of France, Italy, and Spain toward violence and its role in the revolutionary movements in Western Europe in order to learn if these positions are consistent with the theories of V. I. Lenin. Emphasizes the evolution of Lenin's views on violence as they related to the real condition of the working-class movement and the revolutions in Russia. Outlines agreement and disagreement between the theories of Lenin and those of Marchais, Berlinguer, and Carillo. 53 notes.
S

161. Dülffer, Jost. BONAPARTISM, FASCISM, AND NATIONAL SOCIALISM. *J. of Contemporary Hist. [Great Britain] 1976 11(4): 109-128.* It is imprecise and anachronistic to apply the term Bonapartism to 20th-century phenomena like Fascism and Nazism. One of the earliest models of Bonapartism was set up in Karl Marx's *The Eighteenth Brumaire of Louis Bonaparte*, in which he saw a dictator supported by Lumpenproletariat and peasantry—a useful pointer to Hitler. Engels redefined Bonapartism as the form of government in a country in which an advanced working class is outnumbered by small peasantry and defeated by the capitalists and the army. So defined, Bonapartism became a necessary stage in the revolution. The German Communist, August Thalheimer, saw a comparison between the France of Louis Bonaparte and contemporary Italy under Mussolini, though he dealt only briefly with Germany. He sought to prove that the political situation was, in principle, open to various possibilities of Communist Party action. Leon Trotsky inflated the Bonapartist model by seeing it in purest form in General Kurt von Schleicher. Franz Borkenau, official of the Comintern, saw an analogy between Mussolini and Napoleon. The comparison between Napoleon's strategy and that of Hitler in World War II was obvious. On the other hand, "the theory of Bonapartism can do little to explain the paralysis of the old power centres during the course of the Third Reich in favor of bureaucratic and terrorist National Socialist elites, which were in turn opposed to each other." Printed primary and secondary sources; 47 notes.
M. P. Trauth

162. Dunin-Wąsowicz, Krzysztof. DZIAŁACZE I GRUPY POLSKIEGO RUCHU ROBOTNICZEGO W HITLEROWSKICH OBOZACH KONCENTRACYJNYCH [The activists and groups of the Polish workers' movement in Nazi concentration camps]. *Z Pola Walki [Poland] 1979 22(1): 53-79.* Describes various kinds of resistance movements in concentration camps. Beyond the struggle for biological survival and the mutual aid activities of various types, there was a struggle for the preservation of human dignity, the organization of cultural, religious, and political life. Finally, there was activity directly destructive for the Third Reich, sabotage, escapes, assassinations, intelligence activities, documentation of Nazi crimes, and military organizations in camps. Describes the contribution of Polish worker activists to all forms of resistance.
J/S

163. Eytan, Walter. THE CHERBOURG BOATS. *Midstream 1981 27(10): 34-38.* Discusses the decline in Israeli-French relations following the 1967 Six-Day War, and the subsequent hijacking of seven embargoed Israeli motor boats from Cherbourg in 1969.

164. Fields, Rona M. PSYCHOLOGICAL GENOCIDE: THE CHILDREN OF NORTHERN IRELAND. *Hist. of Childhood Q. 1975 3(2): 201-224.* Evaluates longitudinal personality testing of children in Northern Ireland during the height of sectarian upheaval, military occupation, terrorist actions, and a series of political responses, 1971-74. The experience of dislocation and terror during civil strife combined with extreme prejudice during their formative years seriously disrupted the normal psychological maturity of Irish children. They came to accept fear as the normal condition of life, became fatalistic, denied the possibility of any independent justice, and sought to right wrongs individually by violent acts. The result will be genocide (as defined by the UN) since the psychological damage inflicted on the children "has seriously decreased the probable survival of the group." Based on the results of the author's personality testing and primary and secondary sources; 35 notes.
R. E. Butchart

165. Fortier, David H. BRITTANY: "BREIZ ATAO." Foster, Charles R., ed. *Nations Without a State: Ethnic Minorities in Western Europe* (New York: Praeger, 1980): 136-152. Discusses the origin and development of ethnic nationalism in Brittany from 1880, when an agrarian syndicalist movement gave a sense of unity to farmers and landowners in Brittany, to 1978. Discusses the appearance of the so-called "new ethnicity" and terrorism after World War II, and the history of *Breiz Atao* [Brittany forever], a Breton nationalist journal.

166. Francis, Samuel T. TERRORIST RENAISSANCE: FRANCE, 1980-1983. *World Affairs 1983 146(1): 54-68.* In the 1970's France escaped most of the dramatic terrorist acts that disrupted other Western European countries, but since 1980 international terrorism, driven out elsewhere, has taken refuge in France. The most notable terrorist actions in France are not perpetrated by Frenchmen and are often not directed at the French state or society, but derive principally from immigrant or internationally active elements that seek revenge, "liberation," or media attention by targeting their traditionally identified enemies, who happen to be located in a country that is providing inadequate security against such terrorist attacks.

167. Fraser, John. THE INNER CONTRADICTIONS OF MARXISM AND POLITICAL VIOLENCE: THE CASE OF THE ITALIAN LEFT. *Social Res. 1981 48(1): 21-44.* Discusses the forms of political and economic intervention through the state advocated in Italy by the Communist Party and political scientist Antonio Negri's call to violence against the state.

168. Glandon, Virginia E. THE IRISH PRESS AND REVOLUTIONARY IRISH NATIONALISM. *Éire-Ireland 1981 16(1): 21-33.* From 1896 to 1922, Irish nationalist newspapers, which outnumbered labor, independent, and unionist newspapers, informed the Irish people at home and abroad, and

enkindled the national spirit, despite censorship and suppression by the British. The survival of the nationalist press demonstrates the people's faith in it. Describes newspapers from the *Shan Van Vocht* (Poor Old Woman) of 1896-99, two newspapers of the Irish War of Independence in 1919-21, the Irish Republican Army organ *An tÓglach* (The Volunteer) and the shadow Irish government's *The Irish Bulletin*. 21 notes. D. J. Engler

169. Glees, Anthony. ALBERT C. GRZESINSKI AND THE POLITICS OF PRUSSIA, 1926-1930. *English Hist. Rev. [Great Britain] 1974 89(353): 814-834.* Examines the career of Albert C. Grzesinski as Prussian Minister of Interior, 1926-30, to demonstrate that the Social Democratic Party (SPD) was not responsible for failing to stop the rise of Hitler and other antirepublican organizations. Denies that the SPD was not energetic enough in pursuit of the enemies of the Weimar Republic, and defends the use of authoritarian methods by Grzesinski to build a pro-republic civil service. In addition to reconstituting the civil service, Grzesinski dissolved paramilitary extremist organizations of both the right and left and battled with courts and the Reich president to keep the ban on groups that used terror, violence, and intimidation to prevent others from freely exercising their democratic rights. Based mainly on published works and unpublished papers in the *Nachlasz Grzesinski*, Amsterdam; 128 notes. R. J. Gromen

170. Grahn, Gerlinde, ed. DIE IRH GEGEN DEN JUSTIZTERROR IN BULGARIEN 1927 [International Red Aid versus administrative terrorism in Bulgaria, 1927]. *Beiträge zur Gesch. der Arbeiterbewegung [East Germany] 1984 26(1): 45-55.* Introduces and prints documents relating to Communist foreign aid to revolutionary movements in Bulgaria. Most are circular letters from the central European office of the International Red Aid headquartered in Potsdam. 9 notes. R. Grove

171. Greer, Herb. ULSTER: IN THE EMPTY HOUSE OF THE STARE. *Commentary 1982 73(1): 55-64.* Whatever the dreams of Irish terrorists and their friends in the United States, the logic of 800 years of Irish history is against them, and Ireland's political wounds must now be healed.

172. Gregory, F. E. C. THE BRITISH POLICE AND TERRORISM. *Terrorism 1981 5(1-2): 107-123.* Evaluates the function of the police in Great Britain and stresses the complexity of countering terrorism in a democracy, which depends on good relations between police and public.

173. Hennig, Eike. REGIONALE UNTERSCHIEDE BEI DER ENSTE-HUNG DES DEUTSCHEN FASCHISMUS: EIN PLÄDOYER FÜR MI-KROANALYTISCHE STUDIEN ZUR ERFORSCHUNG DER NSDAP (NATIONALSOZIALISTISCHE DEUTSCHE ARBEITER PARTEI) [Regional differences and the origin of German fascism: a model for a microanalytical study of the NSDAP]. *Politische Vierteljahresschrift [West Germany] 1980 21(2): 152-173.* Examines the origins of the German National Socialist Workers' Party (NSDAP) and the factors affecting its growth and development, particularly at the regional level, and reception by various sectors of the population, grouped according to profession, trade, age, and sex. Considers

socioeconomic conditions in Germany for their effect on the formation of the NSDAP, and in uniting otherwise incompatible elements of society. Political activism, a climate of violence, world economic depression, and the weakness of the Weimar government also played a part. Contrary to a common view, the NSDAP is seen as appealing to both rural and urban populations. The propaganda was provincial but not geographically localized. 2 tables, 36 notes, biblio. S. Bonnycastle

174. Henze, Paul B. ORIGINS OF THE PLOT TO KILL THE POPE. *Washington Q. 1983 6(4): 3-20.* Speculates on the probable course of planning and events that led to Soviet intentions to assassinate Pope John Paul II with the aid of Bulgarian agents and Mehmet Ali Agca, a hired Turkish assassin, whose trail led all over Europe and the Middle East until the assassination attempt was made in Rome in May 1981.

175. Henze, Paul B. THE PLOT TO KILL THE POPE. *Survey [Great Britain] 1983 27: 2-21.* "The attempt to kill the Polish Pope, John Paul II, on 13 May 1981 was not a casual intrigue undertaken for the amusement of the plotters." Nor were its origins to be found in the Middle East, Turkey, or even Bulgaria. Instead, there is conclusive evidence that the attempted assassination of Pope John Paul II by a Turk was a scheme created in the Kremlin to "exacerbate strains between Turkey and its NATO allies and reinforce doubts about Turkey's reliability," but most of all to deal a significant blow to Poland and thus tip the scales in Polish-Soviet relations in favor of the USSR. Adapted from Paul B. Henze's *The Plot to Kill the Pope,* the first scholarly study of the episode and its background; 33 notes. L. J. Klass

176. Herman, Valentine and Bouma, Rob van der Laan. NATIONALISTS WITHOUT A NATION: SOUTH MOLUCCAN TERRORISM IN THE NETHERLANDS. *Terrorism 1980 4(1-4): 223-257.* Examines the socioeconomic conditions of the South Moluccans in the Netherlands, the incidents of terrorism, and the reaction of the Dutch government and public opinion, 1950's-70's.

177. Hermet, Guy. LE DÉSENCHANTEMENT: L'ESPAGNE RETROUVE-T-ELIE SES DÉMONS? [Disillusionment: has Spain rediscovered her devils?]. *Défense Natl. [France] 1979 35(10): 25-33.* Assesses the performance of the government of Adolfo Suárez in Spain, 1977-79, and the influence of the rise of the Left and of Basque terrorism.

178. Hoffman, Bruce. RIGHT-WING TERRORISM IN EUROPE. *Orbis 1984 28(1): 16-27.* Analyzes the incidence of right-wing terrorism in Italy, Germany, and France between 1980 and 1984. Although right-wing terrorist activities have not been publicized much since the bombings in Bologna, Munich, and Paris in 1980, there have been some disturbing developments. The right-wing terrorists have established connections with the PLO, been more willing to cooperate with the left and started terrorist activities against US personnel stationed in Germany. Based on published works; 19 notes.
J. W. Thacker, Jr.

179. Horchem, Hans Josef. EUROPEAN TERRORISM: A GERMAN PERSPECTIVE. *Terrorism 1982 6(1): 27-51.* Describes the membership, philosophy, activities, and outlook for terrorist groups in West Germany, Spain, and Italy, with special reference to international, especially Soviet, connections.

180. Horchem, Hans Josef. TERRORISM AND GOVERNMENT RESPONSE: THE GERMAN EXPERIENCE. *Jerusalem J. of Int. Relations [Israel] 1980 4(3): 43-55.* Describes the structure of the Baader-Meinhof Gang and other terrorist organizations, their tactics, and West Germany's effort to deal with them using security forces and new laws.

181. Husbands, Christopher T. THE DECLINE OF THE NATIONAL FRONT: THE ELECTIONS OF 3RD MAY 1979. *Wiener Lib. Bull. [Great Britain] 1979 32(49-50): 60-66.* The National Front won only 1.3% of the votes in the 1979 British general election, a decline from 3.1% in 1974. One factor in the decline is the Conservative Party's appropriation of the National Front's themes of race and immigration. There is a possibility of the National Front turning, like frustrated continental extremist groups, to terrorist activities, likely to be relatively unorganized and take such forms as random attacks on immigrants. 11 notes. R. V. Layton

182. Iliescu, Crişan. 1923—BULGARIA [1923—Bulgaria]. *Anale de Istorie [Romania] 1979 25(1): 169-186.* Summarizes events in Bulgaria from the overthrow of Alexander Stamboliski's government in June, 1923 by the rightist Democratic Entente coalition, to the successful liberation movement of September, 1944. Describes the terrorism and suppression of democratic liberties during the interwar period and the Bulgarian Communist Party's struggle against the reactionary bourgeois-military regime of Boris III. 114 notes.
G. J. Bobango

183. Johnston, A. BRITAIN, IRELAND AND ULSTER. *Rev. of Int. Studies [Great Britain] 1981 7(3): 187-198.* Reviews six books, published from 1975 to 1978, on the unrest in Northern Ireland and the events, which since 1918, have led to violence.

184. Jones, Mervyn. VERDICT IN LONDON: TERRORISTS ON TRIAL. *Present Tense 1983 10(4): 25-28.* Describes the trial of a group of Arabs for the 1982 shooting of Israel's ambassador to Great Britain.

185. Jorgensen, Birthe. DEFENDING THE TERRORISTS: QUEEN'S COUNSEL BEFORE THE COURTS OF NORTHERN IRELAND. *J. of Law and Soc. [Great Britain] 1982 9(1): 115-126.* Studies the motivations, work, and careers of counsel in criminal courts in Northern Ireland, 1973-81.

186. Katris, John. POLITICAL ASSASSINATIONS. *J. of the Hellenic Diaspora 1976 3(3): 17-23.* Discusses political assassinations in Greece in the 20th century, emphasizing the 1956-76 era and the dictatorship of George Papadopoulos.

187. Kearney, Richard. TERRORISME ET SACRIFICE, LE CAS DE L'IRLANDE DU NORD [Terrorism and sacrifice: the case of Northern Ireland]. *Esprit [France] 1979 (4): 29-44.* The terrorists of Northern Ireland, whether of the Catholic Irish Republican Army (IRA) or of the Protestant and Loyalist Ulster Volunteer Force (UVF), are united by a spirit of sacrifice as well as by their violence. The true Christians, ready to sacrifice in purity, are the pacifists of both faiths. Discusses the views of René Girard.

188. Keller, Elke. "ES GEHT NICHT UM IHRE GUTEN VORSÄTZE". (W. I. LENIN) VOM REVOLUTIONÄREN SOZIAL-DEMOKRATEN ZUM ZENTRISTEN. HUGO HAASE ["It's not a question of their good intentions" (V. I. Lenin): from revolutionary Social Democrat to centrist—Hugo Haase]. *Beiträge zur Gesch. der Arbeiterbewegung [East Germany] 1981 23(4): 583-596.* Traces the life and political career of the German Social Democrat Hugo Haase (1863-1919), paying particular attention to his activities and influence within the Social Democratic Party, 1894-1919, his opposition to World War I, and his work as a lawyer to defend many German revolutionaries, including Ernst Toller in 1919. Haase was assassinated in 1919. Based on documents of the German Social Democratic Party in Berlin and secondary sources; 75 notes. G. L. Neville

189. Kirby, D. G. REVOLUTIONARY FERMENT IN FINLAND AND THE ORIGINS OF THE CIVIL WAR 1917-1918. *Scandinavian Econ. Hist. Rev. [Denmark] 1978 26(1): 15-35.* The development of revolutionary sentiment in Finland was partly due to economic conditions—a developing economy in which industrialization's effects were negative, inadequate control by the unions and political institutions, and a consequent tendency to violence. World War I caused the Finns to turn from political controls which had caused economic chaos and labor violence. The formation of paramilitary organizations (Security Corps) led to civil war. In addition, the Social Democratic Party followed an opportunistic policy and presented no authority either to its members or to the masses. R. E. Lindgren

190. Kirkaldy, John. ENGLISH CARTOONISTS: ULSTER REALITIES. *Éire-Ireland 1981 16(3): 27-42.* Political cartoons in English newspapers since the Northern Ireland civil rights campaign in 1968 and through the subsequent hostilities "have fulfilled their traditional function—expressing anti-Irish prejudice that in any other form would be unacceptable, even in England." They have blamed only the Irish for events since 1968, and have simplified and distorted reality. The ignorance, racism, stereotypes, and hostility of the cartoons have played and continue to "play an essential part in preventing English comprehension of the realities of Northern Ireland," such as "English responsibility for the violence." The author discusses specific events since 1968 and misrepresentation of them by cartoonists. Secondary sources and newspapers; 31 notes. D. J. Engler

191. Kline, Rayna. PARTISANS, GODMOTHERS, BICYCLISTS, AND OTHER TERRORISTS: WOMEN IN THE FRENCH RESISTANCE AND UNDER VICHY. *Pro. of the Ann. Meeting of the Western Soc. for French Hist. 1977 5: 375-383.* The women of France played a significant role in the

Resistance movement during the occupation, 1940-44. They were an extremely diverse group that cut across social classes, political alignments, and religious persuasions. The range of their activities and the flexibility in their roles challenge pervasive French notions about women's nature and separate spheres. The World War II crisis had placed French women in responsible roles. Ironically, under the Vichy government, the domestic policy of France moved in a direction that reinforced the most conservative tendencies regarding women's roles. Women in the Resistance anticipated that the part they played in the crisis would result in significant change, but they carried over prewar attitudes and political structures. Based on interviews and secondary work; 38 notes. A/J

192. Komolova, N. P. GIBEL' AL'DO MORO [Death of Aldo Moro]. *Novaia i Noveishaia Istoriia [USSR] 1981 (3): 140-160.* A detailed appraisal of the last two decades of the political career of Aldo Moro, sometime prime minister and leader of the Italian Christian Democrats, abducted and murdered by ultra-left-wing terrorists in 1978. He had appeared to be on the edge of reconstituting a political understanding with the Communist Party, such as had existed briefly at the end of the war. 112 notes. J. P. H. Myers

193. Korzec, Pawel. THE STEIGER AFFAIR. *Soviet Jewish Affairs [Great Britain] 1973 3(2): 38-57.* Discusses the arrest and trial of Jewish student Stanislaw Steiger for the alleged assassination attempt on President Stanislaw Wojciechowski of Poland, 1924-25, including its relation to political crises and subsequent anti-Semitism.

194. Kujala, Antti. SUOMALAISET VALLANKUMOUSJÄRJESTÖT JA POLIITTINEN RIKOLLISUUS 1906-1908 [Finnish revolutionary organizations and political criminality, 1906-08]. *Hist. Aikakauskirja [Finland] 1981 79(2): 106-124.* Examines persons and organizations among Finnish socialists responsible for politically-inspired armed robberies, murders, and other terrorist acts in Finland from August 1906 to January 1908. Many of the leaders were former members of the workers' Red Guard who attempted to support the revolutionary movements in Russia and to prepare for armed class struggle in Finland. The leaders of the official Finnish Social Democratic Party were ambivalent, but they gradually withdrew their support as they shifted toward tactics of parliamentary gradualism. Based on archives of Finnish judicial and executive agencies and of the Finnish labor movement; 87 notes.
R. G. Selleck

195. Kukushkin, U. M. NEKOTORYE OSOBENNOSTI PORTUGAL'SKOGO FASHIZMA [Certain peculiarities of the ideology and the political regime in Portugal]. *Voprosy Istorii [USSR] 1973 (2): 54-70.* Examines the basic principles of the Salazar doctrine which forms the ideological foundation of Portuguese fascism, its concept of the nation, state, and family, and its attitude to democracy, bringing out the sum and substance of the corporative system, its attitude to the colonial question, and the structure of the fascist party in Portugal. Analyzes the social basis of Salazarism, its policy of unbridled terrorism, repression, and colonial oppression thinly camouflaged

by unrestrained social demagogy, and reveals a number of specific features and peculiarities which distinguish this policy from other forms of fascism. J

196. Kyle, Keith. SUNNINGDALE AND AFTER: BRITAIN, IRELAND, AND ULSTER. *World Today [Great Britain] 1975 31(11): 439-450.* Evaluates the outcome of the Sunningdale Conference (1973) attended by Great Britain and Ireland. The formation of a Council of Ireland linking Northern Ireland and the Republic was discussed, as well as the sharing of political power and the extradition of Irish Republican Army terrorists.

197. Lasky, Melvin J. ULRIKE MEINHOF AND THE BAADER-MEINHOF GANG. *Encounter [Great Britain] 1975 44(6): 9-23.* Discusses the imprisonment and pending trial of political radicals Ulrike Meinhof and the Baader-Meinhof Gang in West Germany, 1975.

198. Lawlor, S. M. IRELAND FROM TRUCE TO TREATY: WAR OR PEACE? JULY TO OCTOBER 1921. *Irish Hist. Studies [Ireland] 1980 22(85): 49-64.* Examines the attitudes toward Anglo-Irish relations after the truce of July 1921 between the British army and the Irish Republican Army (IRA). Lloyd George used the threat of war to force the Irish to negotiate the treaty conferring dominion status on the Irish Free State. Conflicting interests divided the Irish leaders, many of whom were IRA officers. Among these, the politicians mainly supported the treaty, although officers and men in the field assumed that war was inevitable. De Valera, President of the Dail, was privately hesitant to go to war, but publicly encouraged IRA preparations. Based on manuscripts in the Public Record Office, the House of Lords Record Office (London), and State Paper Office and University College, Dublin. 61 notes. P. H. Hardacre

199. Lebow, Richard Ned. THE ORIGINS OF SECTARIAN ASSASSINATION: THE CASE OF BELFAST. *J. of Int. Affairs 1978 32(1): 43-61.* Sectarian assassination in Belfast, which is both a cause and result of social disintegration, has revealed two distinct patterns; the year of the imposition of direct British rule over Northern Ireland, 1972, marks the dividing line. While the pre-1972 pattern conforms to the social group control vigilantism typology, the post-1972 pattern has been more determined by the new political context of direct rule, especially the sense of rage and frustration felt by the Protestants. Based on interviews, other primary, and secondary sources; table, 25 notes.
V. Samaraweera

200. Lee, Alfred McClung. THE DYNAMICS OF TERRORISM IN NORTHERN IRELAND, 1968-1980. *Social Res. 1981 48(1): 100-134.* Reviews the history of the conflict in Northern Ireland, provides a definition of "terrorism," and shows that so-called "terrorist" activities have much in common with officially sanctioned actions such as "legal force," and "security measures."

201. Legault, Albert. LA DYNAMIQUE DU TERRORISME: LE CAS DES BRIGADES ROUGES [The dynamic of terrorism: the case of the Red Brigades]. *Etudes Int. [Canada] 1983 14(4): 639-682.* The dynamics of terror-

ism seem to follow a double track evolution. On the one hand, terrorism presents at the beginning a strong ideological component. As events unfold, the ideology gradually changes to one of violence for its own sake. On the other hand, the state ideological commitment to the preservation of the state creates a process whereby terrorist movements are increasingly viewed as criminal. Uses the Red Brigades in Italy as an example of this dual evolution. 2 tables, chart, 140 notes. J. F. Harrington, Jr.

202. Leshukov, A. S. NEKOTORYE VOPROSY BOR'BY MARKSISTOV-LENINTSEV PROTIV ANARKHISTSKOI PSEVDOREVOLIUTSION-NOSTI [Aspects of the Marxist-Leninist struggle against pseudorevolutionary anarchism]. *Voprosy Istorii KPSS [USSR] 1979 (12): 52-62.* Examines the development of anarchist movements, anti-Marxist and pseudorevolutionary in character, attacks anarchist concepts, and demonstrates the basic directions of Communist opposition to anarchism. Particular reference is made to Italy and West Germany's extreme-left and terrorist groups, and to the efforts of Communists to prevent the spread of anarchist influence among the young. 48 notes. J. S. S. Charles

203. Lévy, Claude. L'AFFICHE ROUGE [The Red Poster]. *Histoire [France] 1979 (18): 22-30.* The *L'Affiche Rouge* affair was a striking aspect of the psychological campaign launched in 1944 by German and Vichy regime propagandists, on the occasion of the trial and execution of 24 foreign Resistance "terrorists," most of them Jews, in an attempt to discredit the French Resistance by playing on feelings of xenophobia. J/S

204. Loney, Martin. DIRTY TRICKS (UK) LTD. *Can. Dimension 1974 10(3): 21-22.* Examines the activities of the Special Branch, a British police agency which collects information on militants and possible disrupters of security, in the context of the murder of Kenneth Joseph Lennon, a Special Branch informer, by the IRA. S

205. Lubau, Robert. HAUTE-SILÉSIE: 1921 L'ASSASSINAT DU COMMANDANT MONTALÈGRE [Upper Silesia: 1921, the assassination of Commandant Montalègre]. *Écrits de Paris [France] 1978 382: 67-78.* The author, who was assistant to the controller of a district in Beuthen (Bytom), Upper Silesia, during the plebiscite after World War I, describes the political and military situations at that time and narrates the facts and circumstances surrounding the assassination of garrison commander Montalègre (1921).

206. Lumley, Bob and Schlesinger, Philip. THE PRESS, THE STATE AND ITS ENEMIES: THE ITALIAN CASE. *Sociol. Rev. [Great Britain] 1982 30(4): 603-626.* Discusses representations of the state and terrorists in the Italian press from the Moro case in 1978 to 1982.

207. Lyttelton, Adrian. FASCISMO E VIOLENZA: CONFLITTO SOCIALE E AZIONE POLITICA IN ITALIA NEL PRIMO DOPOGUERRA [Fascism and violence: social conflict and political action in Italy after World War I]. *Storia Contemporanea [Italy] 1982 13(6): 965-983.* Three types of motivation account for Fascist violence: violence bred by frustration, social

disorganization and anomie; violence in reaction to a perceived threat to fundamental values; and violence deliberately employed as part of a strategy designed to achieve particular ends. Fascism was a movement based on an irrational ideology pursuing a calculated, programmed, and unusually effective policy of violence. 46 notes. J. V. Coutinho

208. Machefer, Philippe. L'UNION DES DROITES, LE P.S.F. ET LE FRONT DE LA LIBERTÉ, 1936-1937 [The Union of the Right, the Parti Social Français and the Freedom Front, 1936-37]. *R. d'Hist. Moderne et Contemporaine [France] 1970 17(1): 112-126.* Studies internecine battles of right-wing parties that sprang up in reaction to the electoral success of the Popular Front in 1936. Rightist groups hesitated to tip their hand in the choice between traditional political activity and violence as they vied for dominance in the anti-Communist fight. The Freedom Front was Jacques Doriot's ploy to neutralize the Parti Social Français and its leader, Colonel de la Rocque, in favor of his Parti Populaire Français. Based on newspapers and party records; 27 notes. C. Bates

209. Mack Smith, Denis. L'AFFAIRE MATTEOTTI [The Matteotti affair]. *Histoire [France] 1983 (52): 10-18.* Describes the abduction and murder of opposition leader Giacomo Matteotti in 1924 by Mussolini henchmen as part of the violent terrorist activities conducted during the early years of Italian fascism.

210. Mack Smith, Denis. THE MURDER OF MATTEOTTI. *Italian Q. 1983 24(93): 11-20.* Describes the assassination of Giacomo Matteotti, Italian socialist, in 1924, and the consequent investigation. The author suggests that there is little doubt that Benito Mussolini was responsible for his political opponent's murder.

211. Marrus, Michael R. FRENCH ANTISEMITISM IN THE 1980'S. *Patterns of Prejudice [Great Britain] 1983 17(2): 3-20.* Patterns of violence against Jews and Jewish institutions seem to be part of the overall drift toward terrorism since surveys show a general reduction in anti-Semitism; makes comparisons with the 1930's.

212. McAllister, Ian. THE LEGITIMACY OF OPPOSITION: THE COLLAPSE OF THE 1974 NORTHERN IRELAND EXECUTIVE. *Éire-Ireland 1977 12(4): 25-42.* After the failure of the Unionist, Protestant Stormont provincial government in 1972, and then of direct British rule, the British government set up a Northern Ireland Executive, which ruled 1 January-28 May 1974 until the (Protestant) Ulster Workers' Council's general strike toppled it. In the Executive, for the first time since Ireland was partitioned in 1921, Catholics were allowed to participate in government in Northern Ireland. (Catholic) Social Democratic Labour Party (SDLP) participation, however, was undermined by the issues of British internment and the continuation of the mistrusted Royal Irish Constabulary. Protestants objected to the Executive because the southern Irish government could not satisfy them concerning extradition of fugitive IRA members and implementation of the 1973 Sunningdale Agreement. Protestants refused to recognize the legitimacy of the SDLP:

that it accepted the system—retention of Northern Ireland in the United Kingdom—as the (Catholic) Nationalist Party never had. 66 notes.

D. J. Engler

213. Mitchell, James K. SOCIAL VIOLENCE IN NORTHERN IRELAND. *Geographical Rev. 1979 69(2): 179-201.* Contemporary social violence in Northern Ireland has been viewed as an outgrowth of colonialism, sectarianism, and class politics. A heavy toll of deaths and injuries has been compounded by major property damage, intimidation, high levels of emigration, and decade-long disruptions in social life. Punitive social controls, physical design constraints, and governmental reforms have been used with limited success to curb violence. Complex spatial patterns of death tend to substantiate colonial and sectarian theories of violence and to refute a class politics explanation. Regions with differing propensities are enumerated, and appropriate public policies are proposed for each region. Based on police reports, personal correspondence, and secondary sources; 5 photos, maps, 7 tables, graph, 32 notes.

J

214. Moss, David. THE KIDNAPPING AND MURDER OF ALDO MORO. *European J. of Sociol. [Great Britain] 1981 22(2): 265-295.* Political terrorism became a feature of Italian politics in the 1970's, culminating in the 1978 murder of Aldo Moro, the leader of the Christian Democrats, by the Red Brigades. The kidnapping is interpreted as a tactic appropriate to the pursuit of political identity. It was a ritual with a solidaristic function for the Red Brigades. It established the continuity of the group and created a frame for subsequent symbolic actions (communiqués and show-trials). Biblio.

R. Aldrich

215. Moxon-Browne, E. THE WATER AND THE FISH: PUBLIC OPINION AND THE PROVISIONAL IRA IN NORTHERN IRELAND. *Terrorism 1981 5(1-2): 41-72.* The Irish Republican Army (Provisionals) is not a terrorist movement in the accepted sense of the term because its longevity, history, and goals suggest that it has popular support in Irish society and will be eliminated only when the state gains the support of those sections of the Catholic community which until now have had reason to mistrust it.

216. Natoli, Claudio. FASCISMO E CRISI DEL CAPITALISMO NELL'ANALISI DELL'INTERNAZIONALE COMUNISTA 1921-1939. [The Comintern's analysis of fascism and the crisis of capitalism, 1921-39]. *Italia Contemporanea [Italy] 1980 32(139): 19-50.* In 1923 and 1924, the Comintern considered fascism as found in Italy to be essentially the same as social democracy. Further analysis clarified the difference between the two systems: fascism was the expression of both the most aggressive nationalist tendencies and of the crisis of democracy and classic parliamentarianism. By 1935, the Communist view of fascism was that it involved open terrorist dictatorship. Primary sources; 95 notes.

E. E. Ryan

217. Neeler, V. E. FALSIFIKATORY ISTORII "ISHCHUT" KORNI TERRORIZMA [The falsifiers of history "in search" of the roots of terrorism]. *Novaia i Noveishaia Istoriia [USSR] 1981 (6): 158-160.* Having suffered

a fiasco in trying to associate terrorism with the USSR, certain bourgeois historians started to dig even deeper. In Italy, searching for the roots of the Red Brigade's outrage, they arrived at an absurd conclusion that even such revered figures of Italian history as Mazzini and Garibaldi were also terrorists. Enraged by this impudence, the progressive public of Italy gave a worthy rebuff to the falsifiers. V. Bender

218. Nello, Paolo. LA VIOLENZA FASCISTA OVVERO DELLO SQUADRISMO NAZIONALRIVOLUZIONARIO [Fascist violence or the problem of national revolutionary *squadristi*]. *Storia Contemporanea [Italy]* 1982 13(6): 1009-1025. Fascist political violence must be understood in the context of Italian society and its fundamental questions. The Fascist *squadristi* must be studied in their ideological motivations, political backgrounds and social origins. The success of the Fascist national revolutionary ideology throws light on the failure of the national culture, of liberal democratic institutions, and of the maximalist socialist ideology, with its myth of violent revolution. 42 notes.
J. V. Coutinho

219. Newsinger, John. REVOLUTION AND CATHOLICISM IN IRELAND, 1848-1923. *European Studies Rev. [Great Britain]* 1979 9(4): 457-480. The decision to excommunicate members of the irregular Irish Republican Army and the fact that revolutionary activity had existed in Ireland since 1848, did not diminish the strength of Catholicism there. Rather, the revolutionary movement was infused with Catholic sentiment. This was partly due to British rule, whether military or civilian, being regarded as a Protestant phenomenon, and partly because the Catholic Church identified itself with Irish nationalism. When the Church condemned revolutionary activity, a strong bond of sympathy and identity remained, the fight being for the Father and the Fatherland. Mainly secondary sources; 60 notes. E. J. Adams

220. Nowak, Jan. ZAMACH NA PAPIEŻA [The attempt on the Pope's life]. *Kultura [France]* 1983 (5): 53-66. Surveys facts and speculations on the attempted assassination of Pope John Paul II in 1981 by M. A. Agca, retracing the latter's itinerary throughout 1979-81 and his connections with the Bulgarian secret service.

221. O'Ballance, Edgar. IRA LEADERSHIP PROBLEMS. *Terrorism* 1981 5(1-2): 73-82. Traces the development of the present leadership of the Irish Republican Army (IRA), explores its doubts and uncertainties, and analyzes the split between the Officials and the Provisionals and the appearance of the Irish National Liberation Army.

222. O'Beirne-Ranelagh, John. THE I.R.B. FROM THE TREATY TO 1924. *Irish Hist. Studies* 1976 20(77): 26-39. Discusses the Irish Republican Brotherhood during the struggle for independence (1916-21) and the civil war over acceptance of the treaty of 1921 with Britain. Describes its organization and its relations with Sinn Fein, the Dail Eireann, and the Irish Republican Army. Estimates the importance of the IRB leaders at various stages, summarizes their attitude toward the issues, and traces their loss of authority

to the IRA. Based on printed and manuscript sources, including statements by survivors; 54 notes. P. H. Hardacre

223. Oestereicher, Emil. FASCISM AND THE INTELLECTUALS: THE CASE OF ITALIAN FUTURISM. *Social Res. 1974 41(3): 515-533.* "The elitist ideology of the Futurist movement, its admiration for technological progress, its obsession with violence and extreme nationalism, prepared many intellectuals to see in Fascism the concrete political resolution of a contradiction." S

224. O'Leary, Cornelius. NORTHERN IRELAND, 1945-72. Lee, J. J., ed. *Ireland 1945-70* (Dublin: Gill and Macmillan; New York: Barnes & Noble, 1979): 152-165. Recounts the politics of Northern Ireland under the government of Sir Basil Brooke (1945-63), the resurgence of the Irish Republican Army in 1954, the economic moves of Terence O'Neill's government, and civil strife in Northern Ireland after 1968.

225. O'Riordan, M. and Sinclair, B. IRISH COMMUNISTS AND TERRORISM. *World Marxist Rev. [Canada] 1976 19(10): 87-96.* Examines the political activities, 1950-76, of both Northern and Southern Irish; examines terrorism and maintains that the Communist Party has little faith in it as a means of national liberation.

226. Pastorelli, Pietro. I RAPPORTI ITALO-AUSTRIACI DALL'ACCORDO DE GASPERI-GRUBER ALLE INTESE PIÙ RECENTI (1946-1969) [Italo-Austrian relations from the De Gasperi-Gruber Accord to more recent agreements (1946-69)]. *Storia e Politica [Italy] 1974 13(1-2): 283-307.* In 1945, the revived Austrian Republic laid claim to the German-speaking areas of the South Tyrol taken from it in 1919. The Allied Foreign Ministers, after much disagreement, rejected this, but the Gruber-De Gasperi Accord (1946) between Austria and Italy provided for some autonomy for the South Tyrol. After 1956, Austria began to revive its claim, pointing out that the promised autonomy was not being fully granted. During this period, terrorism by South Tyrol extremists against the Italians was frequent. From 1965 on, with help from the UN, the two nations moved toward a settlement, culminating in agreements signed in 1969, granting the South Tyrol wide autonomy in matters of culture and language. The agreements were helped by the victory within the Südtiroler Volkspartei (SVP) of the moderate wing. 64 notes. J. C. Billigmeier

227. Patsavos, Christos C. ARCHBISHOP MAKARIOS III: A BIOGRAPHICAL SKETCH. *Int. Rev. of Hist. and Pol. Sci. [India] 1976 12(2): 89-92.* Archbishop Makarios, appointed ethnarch of the Cypriot Greek Orthodox community in 1950, headed a peaceful political movement to unite Cyprus with Greece, 1950-55, and when this failed was associated with the violent EOKA campaign against British rule, 1955-56. Deported by the British to the Seychelles, he returned from exile to negotiate Cyprus's independence 1957-59, and then became first president of the Cypriot republic. From 1968 until his overthrow by Greek Cypriot rebels in 1974, Makarios resisted the terrorist

activities of former EOKA members, directed after 1971 by their ex-leader, Gen. George Grivas. D. M. Cregier

228. Pavlov, E. A. VDOKHNOVLENNYI OKTIABREM: (K 90-LETIIU SO DNIA ROZHDENIIA MAKSA GEL'TSA) [Inspired by October: the 90th birthday of Max Holz]. *Voprosy Istorii KPSS [USSR] 1979 (10): 128-131.* Max Holz was born in 1889 to a working-class family. During World War I he came into contact with Spartacists and on his return to Germany took up political activity, headed a local council of the unemployed and organized military detachments. Even though the Social Democratic government of Saxony sought his arrest he did not receive the support of the local Communist leaders, many of who subsequently joined the right opportunist wing of the party. After the events of March 1921, he fled to Czechoslovakia and then Austria, continuing his revolutionary activities, including the bombing of courthouses. He was caught later that year and remained in prison until 1928. Secondary sources; 18 notes. L. Waters

229. Payne, Stanley G. TERRORISM AND DEMOCRATIC STABILITY IN SPAIN. *Current Hist. 1979 77(451): 167-171, 182-183.* Discusses political and economic developments in Spain, including the role of the energy crisis and Basque nationalism, since the death of Franco in 1975.

230. Perillo, Gaetano. I COMUNISTI E LA LOTTA DI CLASSE IN LIGURIA: NOVEMBRE 1922-NOVEMBRE 1926 [Communists and class struggle in Liguria, November 1922-November 1926]. *Movimento Operaio e Socialista [Italy] 1971 17(1): 57-104, (2): 159-198.* Part I: L'ANNO 1923 (CON DOCUMENTI) [The Year 1923, with documentation]. Describes the failure of Communist and Socialist groups in Liguria to combat Fascism. Points up lack of agreement between Communists and Socialists. Shows how Fascist police violence and press censorship broke down the Communist Party of Liguria. Describes underground activities of Communists and trade unionists during the Fascist regime. Based on newspapers, Communist Party and Fascist documents; 90 notes, appendix. Part II. DALLE ELEZIONI POLITICHE ALLA RIFORMA DELLA CGL (1924) [From the elections to the reform of the CGL (1924)]. Recounts the elections of 6 April 1924, which strengthened Fascist power in the Chamber of Deputies. Analyzes the failure of leftist parties to agree on common policy. Notes workers' congress of Como and the Matteotti case, Communist activity among maritime workers, and results of the third regional Communist congress of 1924. Based on newspapers and secondary works; 58 notes. C. Bates

231. Petersen, Jens. IL PROBLEMA DELLA VIOLENZA NEL FASCISMO ITALIANO [The problem of violence in Italian Fascism]. *Storia Contemporanea [Italy] 1982 13(6): 985-1008.* Recent events in Italy have heightened awareness of the problem of violence and the need is felt to acquire a more precise understanding of political violence in the aftermath of World War I. Perception of those events seems to be totally different according to the political position, personal experience, generation, and moral and political beliefs of the observer. A survey of available literature confirms this impression. 85 notes. J. V. Coutinho

232. Pollo, Stefanaq. LUIGJ GURAKUQI: DEMOCRAT REVOLUCIONAR I SHQUAR [Luigj Gurakuqi: a distinguished revolutionary democrat]. *Studime Hist. [Albania] 1979 33(2): 17-32.* Describes the life and character of the militant Albanian nationalist Luigj Gurakuqi (1878-1925). He was the director of the first secondary school at Elbasan, one of the leaders of the anti-Ottoman liberation movements of 1911-12, minister in the first independent government of Albania, and Director of Public Instruction 1916-18. He served as a democratic deputy in the first Albanian parliament, staunchly defended Albania's international interests, firmly opposed the reactionary politics of Ahmet Zogu and was a minister in the democratic government after the June 1924 revolution. After its collapse in December he fled to Bari, Italy where he was assassinated by the agents of Zogu. 34 notes. French summary.

R. O. Khan

233. Power, Paul F. VIOLENCE AND CONSENT IN THE NORTHERN IRELAND PROBLEM. *J. of Commonwealth and Comparative Pol. [Great Britain] 1976 14(2): 119-140.* Examines Northern Ireland and the consequences of the notions of political violence and political consent. Traces the development of violence theory in the Irish Republican Army (IRA) and the Ulster Loyalists and examines the role of violence as envisaged by both groups. Northern Ireland has been experiencing a war of national liberation, not a civil or sectarian war. Based on secondary material; 57 notes. C. Anstey

234. Preston, Paul. THE STABILITY OF DEMOCRATIC SPAIN: CURRENT ANXIETIES AND DISTURBING PRECEDENTS. *Contemporary Rev. [Great Britain] 1979 234(1356): 8-15.* Discusses factors in terrorist attempts to destabilize the democratic process in Spain since the accession of Juan Carlos and changes made in Spain's administration and social structure to allow participation in international relations, 1974-79.

235. Preston, Paul. WALKING THE TERRORIST TIGHTROPE. *Contemporary Rev. [Great Britain] 1979 234(1358): 119-123.* Considers the problems of social and political change in Spain in particular the growing movement in favor of democratic change and the threat of terrorism not only from the socialists and communists but from the Basque organizations Euzkadi Ta Azkatasuna (ETA) and GRAPO.

236. Puaux, François. IL Y A CINQ ANS, ALDO MORO... [Five years ago Aldo Moro...]. *Rev. des Deux Mondes [France] 1983 (6): 646-657.* Describes Italy's politics and terrorist activities, 1978-81.

237. Quagliariello, Ernesto. LA TESTIMONIANZA DI GIOVANNI AMENDOLA [The witness of Giovanni Amendola]. *Studium [Italy] 1982 78(5): 545-554.* Recalls the memory of a politician who during the critical period of the decline of the liberal state and the rise of Fascism was conspicuous by his high moral standards and sense of public responsibility and was assassinated by a Fascist squad in 1925.

238. Rammelstedt, Otthein. DIE INSTRUMENTALISIERUNG DER BAADER-MEINHOF-GRUPPE [The instrumentalization of the Baader-Me-

inhof Group]. *Frankfurter Hefte [West Germany] 1975 30(3): 27-38.* The Baader-Meinhof gang did not become a political factor by its own efforts, but by those of politicians who have made the existence of the terrorist group a political issue.

239. Randolph, Virgil P., III. THE WHYS OF VIOLENCE IN NORTHERN IRELAND. *Foreign Service J. 1972 49(4): 22-24, 28.*

240. Reiche, Eric G. FROM SPONTANEOUS TO LEGAL TERROR: SA, POLICE, AND THE JUDICIARY IN NÜRNBERG, 1933-34. *European Studies Rev. [Great Britain] 1979 9(2): 237-264.* The SA (Sturmabteilung) established a rule of terrorism against individuals and groups by working through the existing police and judicial system in Nuremberg, 1933-34. The use of terrorism was justified by the Nazis in the interest of the state. Based on the author's dissertation and research in the Nuremberg Municipal Archives and the Berlin Document Center; 87 notes. J. G. Smoot

241. Ronchery, Robert. ITALIEN ZWISCHEN SCHWARZEN BANDEN UND ROTEN BRIGADEN [Italy between black gangs and red brigades]. *Schweizer Monatshefte [Switzerland] 1978 58(4): 275-284.* Analyzes the development and interaction of right- and left-wing terrorism in Italy between the late 1960's and 1977. R. Wagnleitner

242. Ronchey, Alberto. GUNS AND GRAY MATTER: TERRORISM IN ITALY. *Foreign Affairs 1979 57(4): 921-940.* Traces Italian terrorism during the past decade and attempts to place it in sociological, psychological, and ideological perspective. Despite a constantly rising incidence of political violence, the antiterrorist forces have scored some important successes. 16 notes. M. R. Yerburgh

243. Russell, Charles A. EUROPE: A REGIONAL VIEW, 1970-1978. *Terrorism 1979 3(1-2): 157-171.* A statistical analysis of terrorism in Europe between 1970 and 1978.

244. Scelsi, Filippo. BURGOS. IL FASCISMO CONTINUA [Burgos: fascism is still there]. *Ponte [Italy] 1970 26(12): 1630-1633.* Studies the Basque autonomy movement in the light of the Burgos court martial 28 December 1970 and heavy sentences for 16 members of the Basque liberation group Euzkadi Ta Askatatuna (ETA). Reviews recent Spanish economic events, analyzing the activities of the Spanish "technocrats" of the Opus Dei and the financial scandal of the Matesa company. Touches on the Franco regime's dealings with the United States, the USSR, and other socialist countries.
C. Bates

245. Schlesinger, Philip. "TERRORISM," THE MEDIA, AND THE LIBERAL-DEMOCRATIC STATE: A CRITIQUE OF THE ORTHODOXY. *Social Res. 1981 48(1): 74-99.* Discusses how the concept of terrorism is related to the question of legitimate political activity and the role of the media in reporting on terrorism, with special reference to reporting in Great Britain, and emphasizes the need for an analysis of the causes of political violence.

246. Scott, R. D. NORTHERN IRELAND: THE POLITICS OF DISINTEGRATION. *Australian Outlook [Australia] 1973 27(1): 40-49.* Protestant and Catholic sectors in Northern Ireland seemed to be in a process of social integration. Prime Minister Terence O'Neill's unsuccessful attempt to give Catholic aspirations a political role led to violence, intervention by the British Army, and, eventually, direct rule. By 1972 Northern Ireland was a wholly compartmentalized society where the threat of armed force was likely to remain. Based on secondary sources. E. Plumridge

247. Serfaty, Meir. SPANISH DEMOCRACY: THE END OF THE TRANSITION. *Current Hist. 1981 80(466): 213-217, 227-228.* Discusses Spain's transition from the regime of Francisco Franco since 1976 and examines the impact of Basque terrorism and a floundering economy.

248. Serfőző, Lajos. A TITKOS TÁRSASÁGOK ÉS A KONSZOLIDÁCIO 1922-1926-BAN [The secret societies and the consolidation in 1922-26]. *Acta Hist. [Hungary] 1976 57: 3-60.* In spite of the victory of the right-wing Party of National Unity in the 1922 election, numerous Social Democrats became members of the Second National Assembly. From 1923, secret societies were founded and committed acts of terrorism against the left-wing opposition. The article follows the history of the strongest secret society, the Awakening Hungarians. 234 notes. G. Hetzron

249. Settembrini, Domenico. LENINISMO E ANARCHISMO IERI E OGGI [Leninism and anarchism yesterday and today]. *Storia e Politica [Italy] 1972 11(4): 583-622.* Marxism and anarchism took separate directions when Karl Marx and Friedrich Engels broke with Mikhail Bakunin in 1872. Anarchism emphasized immediate action; Marxism stressed organization and planning. When Lenin brought a Marxist regime to power in Russia, he became a leader and a model for most Marxists around the world. Despite the antagonism of official Marxism-Leninism to anarchism, there have been a number of recent attempts to reconcile the two, as with Cohn-Bendit in France and the Baader-Meinhof gang in West Germany. 117 notes.
J. C. Billigmeier

250. Shamir, Haim. "ANKLAGE GEGEN DEN VOLKSVERDERBER HITLER": EIN BEITRAG ZUR GESCHICHTE DER OPPOSITION IM DRITTEN REICH (MIT DOKUMENTENANHANG) ["Accusations against the destroyer of the nation": a contribution to the history of the opposition in the Third Reich]. *Jahrbuch des Inst. für Deutsche Geschichte [Israel] 1976 5: 449-466.* Reprints a 1943 handbill attacking Adolf Hitler and his regime and demanding his downfall. The author concludes that it is a remaining sample of brochures sent out to prepare for the Beck-Goerdeler attempt to assassinate Hitler in 1943. Describes in some detail the last stages of preparation of the plot and its failure. Based on government document preserved in Würzburg; 36 notes. M. Faissler

251. Siltala, Juha. LAPUAN LIIKE JA KYYDITYKSET 1930 [The Lapua movement and the kidnappings of 1930]. *Hist. Aikakauskirja [Finland] 1982 80(2): 105-123.* Examines the political kidnappings by right-wing activists in

the Lapua movement in Finland from May through December 1930. Of 213 known cases, some 110 can be directly associated with the informal but tightly-knit network of extremists centered around Vihtori Kosola (1884-1936). The kidnappings were timed to put pressure on the Finnish government to adopt anti-Communist legislation and bring conservative politicians into office. Though not a highly disciplined conspiracy, the acts of violence were by no means random or spontaneous local events. Based on police records and other government archives, newspapers, interviews and memoirs; map, 3 tables, 83 notes. R. G. Selleck

252. Spălățelu, Ion. THE MILITANT POSITION OF THE DEMOCRATIC PROGRESSIVE FORCES WITH THE ROMANIAN COMMUNIST PARTY AT THEIR HEAD AGAINST THE SOCIAL-POLITICAL CONCEPTS OF LEGIONARISM. *Romania [Romania] 1981 6(1): 64-85.* The Romanian Communist Party headed the offensive against the Iron Guard, a fascist, antinational organization used by the Nazis as their agency in Romania. This legionary movement used terrorism to curb resistance and annihilate the hostility of Romanian democratic public opinion.

253. Sterling, Claire. ITALIAN TERRORISTS: LIFE AND DEATH IN A VIOLENT GENERATION. *Encounter [Great Britain] 1981 57(1): 18-31.* Traces the development of the terrorist underground known as The Organization in Italy from 1971, when the group was formed in Padua as an umbrella group for terrorists throughout Italy, to 1978-81, when Carlo Fioroni and other terrorists were arrested. Discusses such branch groups as the Red Brigades and the reasons for the lenient attitude of the general public and of judicial leaders toward terrorism.

254. Sundberg, Jacob. OPERATION LEO: DESCRIPTION AND ANALYSIS OF A EUROPEAN TERRORIST OPERATION. *Terrorism 1981 5(3): 197-232.* Discusses Operation Leo, an aborted terrorist action that was to take place in Stockholm in 1977, and the background of Norbert Kroecher, the instigator of Operation Leo, and his group, as obtained from court records.

255. Tamburino, Giovanni. QUANDO LA LUNA NON HA OMBRE [When the moon has no shadows]. *Ponte [Italy] 1979 35(9): 953-966.* Discusses the upsurge of political violence of the Left and Right in Italy during the past decade; focuses on the Padua magistrate who 7 April 1979 implicated members of Autonomia Operaia (organizzata) as conspirators with the Red Brigades in political crimes including the Moro assassination.

256. Terchek, Ronald J. CONFLICT AND CLEAVAGE IN NORTHERN IRELAND. *Ann. of the Am. Acad. of Pol. and Social Sci. 1977 433: 47-59.* The ethnic conflict in Northern Ireland is more than a repetition of ancient native-Catholic/Protestant-settler conflicts. One of the major contemporary issues, partition, dates back to 1921 and is the basis of the declaration of war by the Irish Republican Army on Great Britain. The other conflict is of more recent origin and involves the inclusion of the Catholic third of the population in the government and an end to institutionalized discrimination against the minority. Protestants have uniformly opposed any unification with the Irish

republic, but intense internal disagreements characterize the Protestant reaction to the other conflict. Moderate Protestant elites have been unable to bind their loyalist constituents to a compromise with the Catholic politicians, but neither Protestant nor Catholic paramilitary groups have been able to impose a military solution on the province. Traces the roots of the first conflict to the historical ethnic cleavage separating the two communities, while explaining the second conflict by the volatile mixture of ethnicity and the strains of modernization. Any solution to the current troubles must address the nature and causes of each conflict. J

257. Titley, Alan. ROUGH RUG-HEADED KERNS: THE IRISH GUNMAN IN THE POPULAR NOVEL. Éire-Ireland 1980 15(4): 15-38. Since the mid-1970's, socially and politically influential British and some Irish popular novels set in Northern Ireland have displayed literary worthlessness, and England's age-old anti-Irish bigotry, in their use of every imaginable form of invective against, and vicious characterization of, the Irish Republican Army and the Irish people. Novelists have used stereotyped characters and dialects, reflected colonial disdain for the natives, replaced German and Communist villains with Irish ones, called Ireland insane, incomprehensible, and innately bloodthirsty, and deliberately made no distinction between IRA men and Irishman. Strangely, some Irish readers may have come to accept this external view of themselves. Based on the novels and on secondary sources; 151 notes. D. J. Engler

258. Townsend, Charles. THE IRISH RAILWAY STRIKE OF 1920: INDUSTRIAL ACTION AND CIVIL RESISTANCE IN THE STRUGGLE FOR INDEPENDENCE. Irish Hist. Studies [Ireland] 1979 21(83): 265-282. Illustrates the degree of civil resistance in the Anglo-Irish conflict of 1916-21 by tracing the embargo by Irish railway workers on the transportation of government troops and munitions. Ship cargoes were immobilized and train schedules were disrupted. The government response was to close down railways which failed to discharge strikers, but at the same time the railway workers who defied the embargo were subject to intimidation by the Irish Republican Army. In December 1920 the strikers gave way, however, and resumed carrying troops. Notwithstanding their surrender, the strike contributed to the Irish attack on the legitimacy of British rule. Based on Cabinet papers in Public Record Office, London, manuscripts in the national Library of Ireland, and on contemporary printed materials; 71 notes. P. H. Hardacre

259. Townsend, Charles. THE IRISH REPUBLICAN ARMY AND THE DEVELOPMENT OF GUERRILLA WARFARE, 1916-1921. English Hist. Rev. [Great Britain] 1979 94(371): 318-345. Examines the organization, armaments, tactics, and achievements of the Irish Republican Army and its development from a volunteer movement or brotherhood into an "organized" army. For the period 1919-21 the IRA was "weakly organized, marginally effective, and by no means in full sympathy, or even contact, with the ordinary people." While the General Headquarters group (GHQ) encouraged minor raids, communication disruption, and individual assassinations that even the weakest local group could carry out, they retained an exaggerated confidence in an eventual physical victory. The "moral attrition of guerrilla warfare"

eventually undermined both the British government and Irish republican volunteers' resolve and led to the 1922 treaty. Baed on memoranda and correspondence between GHQ and the local groups found in Mulcahy and O'Mally papers in the University College, Dublin archives and the Collins papers at the National Library, Dublin as well as War and Colonial Office papers in the Public Record Office; table, 86 notes. R. J. Gromen

260. Tugwell, Maurice. POLITICS AND PROPAGANDA OF THE PROVISIONAL IRA. *Terrorism 1981 5(1-2): 13-40.* Many Northern Irish Catholics supported the Irish Republican Army's violent campaign to abolish the Protestant-dominated Northern Ireland government, but when the IRA rejected the British government's offer to negotiate and adhered to a strategy of uniting Ireland by force, former supporters abandoned it believing its violent approach diminished rather than enhanced the prospects of a united Ireland.

261. VanVoris, W. H. THE PROVISIONAL IRA AND THE LIMITS OF TERRORISM. *Massachusetts Rev. 1975 16(3): 413-428.* Traces the evolution of IRA Provisionals' terrorism and cites its limitations. The terrorist is caught in his own terrorism and its accompanying divisiveness. Ultimately he must face the fact that he is really making war on politics, which demands compromise rather than extremism. Based on primary and secondary sources.
M. J. Barach

262. Vass, Henrik. THE INTERNATIONAL INFLUENCE OF THE HUNGARIAN REPUBLIC OF COUNCILS. *Études Hist. Hongroises [Hungary] 1980 (2): 155-172.* Describes the reception given the Hungarian Soviet Republic in 1919 by the imperialist Great Powers, Social Democrats, and the international revolutionary working-class movement and recounts the new republic's assistance to the rise of the international revolutionary movement in attempting to help the working class of neighboring countries and in showing solidarity with Soviet Russia and the Bavarian Soviet Republic. The Hungarian Soviet Republic was also able to stall armed intervention against Soviet Russia. Under pressure of the overwhelming strength of the imperialist Entente countries, the power of the councils was overthrown in Hungary, and the international movement mobilized to prevent White terrorism in Hungary. 25 notes. Russian summary. S

263. Ventura, Angelo. IL PROBLEMA STORICO DEL TERRORISMO ITALIANO [The historical context of terrorism in Italy]. *Riv. Storica Italiana [Italy] 1980 92(1): 125-151.* Analyzes the historical roots of political terrorism in Italy as a unique phenomenon in contemporary industrial society. 43 notes.
J. J. Renaldo

264. Wagner-Pacifici, Robin. NEGOTIATION IN THE ALDO MORO AFFAIR: THE SUPPRESSED ALTERNATIVE IN A CASE OF SYMBOLIC POLITICS. *Pol. & Soc. 1983 12(4): 487-517.* Negotiation for the release of Aldo Moro, leader of the Christian Democratic Party kidnapped by the Red Brigades on 16 March 1978, posed issues of political legitimacy across the Italian political spectrum. The Italian government, already racked by scandals and political and economic crises, was unable to risk legitimation of the Red

Brigades by negotiating for Moro's release, and like other political participants retreated to a course of "symbolic" action by declaring a no-negotiation policy. 65 notes. D. G. Nielson

265. Walser, Harald. WER STAND HINTER DER NSDAP? EIN BEITRAG ZUR GESCHICHTE VORARLBERGS 1933 UND 1934 [Who stood behind the NSDAP? A contribution to the history of Vorarlberg 1933 and 1934]. *Zeitgeschichte [Austria] 1980 7(8): 288-297.* Outlines Austrian political conditions at the beginning of the 1930's, the aggravation of the conflict with Germany, and the birth of Nazi terrorism in the Vorarlberg. The support of textile industrialists in this part of Austria helped Nazi propaganda derived from Goebbels' to show good results. The ruling classes of Austria, in blind fear of communism, crushed the antifascist workers' movement and thus helped to further the penetration of Nazi ideology. Secondary sources; 45 notes. G. E. Pergl

266. Walsh, Barbara. THE SHAMROCK AND THE MAPLE LEAF. *Can. Dimension [Canada] 1983 17(4): 14-19, 40.* Explores Canadian attitudes toward the liberation struggle being waged by the Irish Republican Army; Canadian antipathy toward the freedom fighters in Northern Ireland results from blind pro-British sentiments, a belief in the righteousness of Western democracy, and contempt for the Irish people.

267. Wasmund, Klaus. THE POLITICAL SOCIALIZATION OF TERRORIST GROUPS IN WEST GERMANY. *J. of Pol. & Military Sociol. 1983 11(2): 223-239.* Deals with the motives of and decisive influences on young terrorists in West Germany. After a brief presentation of the causes and backgrounds of the founding generation of terrorists (the RAF) and its subsequent offshoots, analysis focuses on conditions in the prephase of terrorist organizations that are conducive to a terrorist career, and the recruiting processes. The group is regarded as one decisive factor for a terrorist career, both in the prephase of terrorism and in the terrorist underground itself. Accordingly, the center of this analysis concentrates on the specific dynamics of terrorist groups, including their processes of permanent political socialization, the justification of terrorist activities, the role of personal idols and key experiences, and the reasons for extreme group loyalty. Based on biographical material and oral and published declarations by terrorists and ex-terrorists.
J

268. Weiss, Peter. JOE MCCARTHY IS ALIVE AND WELL AND LIVING IN WEST GERMANY: TERROR AND COUNTER-TERROR IN THE FEDERAL REPUBLIC. *New York U. J. of Int. Law and Pol. 1976 9(1): 61-88.* The fight against terrorism from the Red Army Faction (the "Baader-Meinhof Gang") has led to stringent controls on defense attorneys in political cases, including searches of offices, seizure of documents, exclusion from trials, and criminal proceedings against lawyers. The institutionalization of repression has gone quite far and threatens West German civil liberties. Secondary sources. K. E. Miller

269. Wesseling, H. L. POST-IMPERIAL HOLLAND. *J. of Contemporary Hist. [Great Britain] 1980 15(1): 125-142.* Decolonization had few economic results but caused serious social dislocations in the Netherlands. After the independence of Indonesia, 100,000 military conscripts drafted to serve in the Indies, 250,000 Indonesian Dutch, and 12,000 South Moluccans settled in the Netherlands. Similarly after independence in 1975, Surinam sent about 115,000 Surinamese. While the conscripts and Indonesian Dutch assimilated quickly, the Moluccans and Surinamese assimilated slowly, due to racial and political problems. Loss of empire led to disputes between the Dutch and Indonesians over New Guinea and to Moluccan terrorism over independence. Dutch foreign policy has been noted for pro-Americanism, Europeanism, and development aid. The Dutch have retained an attitude of moral superiority and commercial realism. 24 notes. M. P. Trauth

270. Wickbom, Kaj. DISKUSSION OM NAZISMEN OCH DAGENS TERRORISM I TYSKA FÖRBUNDSREPUBLIKEN. AKTUELLA SPEL- OCH DOKUMENTÄRFILMER [Discussion of Nazism and contemporary terrorism in West Germany: current fictional and documentary films]. *Statsvetenskaplig Tidskrift [Sweden] 1981 84(2): 101-103.* Reviews debates about three recent theater and television films concerning the Nazi period of German history which have become controversial in West Germany. R. G. Selleck

271. Wilamowski, Jacek and Szczepanik, Krzysztof. USTASZE I SEPARATYZM CHORWACKI: PRZYCZYNEK DO BADAŃ NAD CHORWACKIM RUCHEM NACJONALISTYCZNYM [The Ustaše and Croatian separatism: a contribution to the study of the Croatian nationalist movement]. *Przegląd Hist. [Poland] 1983 74(1): 75-94.* Outlines the nature of Croatian separatism in Yugoslavia and analyzes the role played in it by an extreme nationalist organization, the Croatian Liberation Movement (Hrvatski Oslobodilački Pokret). Its Insurgents (Ustaše), led by Ante Pavelić (1889-1959), adopted terroristic tactics seeking the creation of an independent Croatia. In 1929, after the establishment of a Serbian-dominated royalist dictatorship by King Alexander I, 1921-34, they redoubled their activities. In 1934 they succeeded in organizing the king's assassination at Marseilles. In April 1941 Pavelić became the head of "independent" Croatia—in reality a puppet state of the Axis powers, whose hypernationalism led to mass executions of Orthodox Serbians and Jews. Following Germany's defeat in May 1945 and the Communist victory, Pavelić and his supporters fled abroad. In the post-World War II years the Ustaše emigres, operating in various countries, continued to wage a campaign of terror against Tito's Yugoslavia, peaking in 1972. Based on records of the Polish Ministry of Foreign Affairs (vol. 5990), Legation in Belgrade (vol. 42) and Delegation at the League of Nations (vol. 244), in the Archiwum Akt Nowych (Warsaw) and other sources; 92 notes. Russian and French summaries. A. B. Pernal

272. Wilkinson, Burke. ERSKINE CHILDERS: THE BOSTON CONNECTION. *Massachusetts Hist. Soc. Pro. 1974 86: 53-63.* Robert Erskine Childers (1870-1922), author of the suspense novel *The Riddle of the Sands*, led an eventful life the details of which are largely unknown. Despite his upbringing in the British Establishment, he fought and died in the IRA for the freedom of

Ireland. His loyalty to the Irish cause may have sprung from the strong beliefs of his wife, Molly Osborn of Boston, whom he married in 1904. At an early age, Molly learned a hatred of imperial Britain and a love of free Ireland from contact with John Boyle O'Reilly (1844-90); she in turn, being a woman of great inner strength and conviction, influenced Childers. Based on contemporary newspaper accounts, family memoirs, and secondary works; 43 notes, index.

G. W. R. Ward

273. Winston, Colin M. THE PROLETARIAN ROAD TO FASCISM: SINDICALISMO LIBRE. *J. of Contemporary Hist.* [Great Britain] 1982 17(4): 557-585. "Over the past two decades historians have effectively demolished the myth of the fascist character of the Franco regime and the alleged susceptibility of the Spanish right to radical and fascist blandishments." The Carlist faction would substantiate the myth. Although remaining largely premodern and rural, the Carlos ethos bifurcated into a radical group favoring violence and a traditionalist party standing for free trade unions *(sindicatos libres)*. By the early 20th century the *sindicatos libres* had also become radical, republican, and modernist as their centers shifted to more urban areas. The leadership, however, remained moderate. Perhaps this fact accounts for the enduring absence of a real social program. They were anticapitalist, but pro-authoritarian dictatorship. Their ambivalence caused them to be maligned by both Fascists and Communists. By 1980 the conservative Carlist element prevailed. Based on printed primary and archival sources; 85 notes.

M. P. Trauth

274. Woods, Randall B. THE MISS STONE AFFAIR. *Am. Heritage* 1981 32(6): 26-29. America was introduced to 20th-century international political terrorism by the kidnapping of missionary Ellen M. Stone in September 1901. Macedonian revolutionaries, seeking financial support for their revolution against Turkish control, ultimately accepted $66,000 in gold, raised by friends of Stone, after President Roosevelt refused to let the government make the ransom payment. 3 illus.

J. F. Paul

275. Woods, Randall B. TERRORISM IN THE AGE OF ROOSEVELT: THE MISS STONE AFFAIR, 1901-1902. *Am. Q.* 1979 31(4): 478-495. In September 1901, Ellen M. Stone (1846-1927), an American Congregationalist missionary, was kidnapped and held for ransom by a group of Macedonian nationalists called the Internal Macedonian Revolutionary Organization. During her captivity, the Roosevelt administration, the American public, and Stone's organization, the American Board Commissioners for Foreign Missions, struggled with the issues of international political terrorism. A $66,000 ransom raised by public donations was ultimately accepted by the nationalists, who then freed Stone in February 1902. The ransom helped finance a Macedonian rebellion in August 1903 that was quickly suppressed by the Turks. Based on Department of State papers, the Papers of the American Board Commissioners for Foreign Missions, and other primary sources; 69 notes.

D. K. Lambert

276. Xeni, Constantin. PORTRETE POLITICE DIN ANII INTERBELICI: NICOLAE TITULESCU, I. G. DUCA [Political portraits from the

interwar years: Nicolae Titulescu, Ion Duca]. *Magazin Istoric [Rumania] 1975 9(3): 54-60.* Biographies of the Rumanian Secretary-General of the League of Nations and of the Liberal Party leader assassinated by the Iron Guard in 1933. J. M. McCarthy

277. Zaharescu, Vladimir. 1929—IUGOSLAVIA [1929, Yugoslavia]. *Anale de Istorie [Romania] 1979 25(6): 150-162.* Describes the political developments which led from the founding of Yugoslavia in 1918 to the assumption of dictatorial powers by King Alexander I in January 1929 and notes international reaction. Stresses the passivity of public opinion and the political parties with the exception of the Yugoslav Communist Party, which nevertheless failed to rally the masses. After the assassination of King Alexander I in October 1934, the regent Prince Paul attempted to continue the regime against mounting opposition, but internal developments were overtaken by World War II. One of a series on the establishment of fascist regimes in Europe. 49 notes.
R. O. Khan

278. Zakharieva, Iordanka and Petrov, Metodi. MEZHDUNARODNA NAUCHNA KONFERENTSIIA ZA STOGODISHNINATA OT ROZHDENIETO NA ALEKSANDUR STAMBOLIISKI [International conference on the centenary of the birth of Aleksandr Stamboliski]. *Istoricheski Pregled [Bulgaria] 1979 35(4-5): 263-273.* Stamboliski (1879-1923) was the founder of the Agrarian Popular Union and prime minister of Bulgaria until his assassination. The conference, organized by the Bulgarian Academy of Sciences and other scholarly bodies, was held in Sofia on 7-8 June 1979. Summarizes the principal papers, which deal with various aspects of Stamboliski's political theory and practice, including his relations with the Communists.
F. A. K. Yasamee

279. Zincă, Haralamb. PE URMELE UNUI PROCES [After a trial]. *Magazin Istoric [Romania] 1981 15(2): 24-27.* Recounts the police investigations of the murders of the Romanian politicians and scholars Nicolae Iorga and Virgil Madgearu, killed by the Fascist Iron Guard on the night of 27-28 November 1940.

280. —. [GOVERNMENT OPPRESSION AND THE RADICAL LEFT]. *Can. Dimension [Canada] 1983 16(7-8): 41-45.*
Ramirez, Bruno. AFTER MARX—JAIL! *p.41.* Reviews the political background to the 1979 terrorism trials in Italy.
—. THE ITALIAN INQUISITION, *pp. 42-45.* Excerpts from a defendants' statement reviewing the pretrial judicial investigation of leftists arrested on 7 April and 21 December 1979.

281. —. [THE IRISH QUESTION]. *World Survey [Great Britain] 1972 (40): 1-15.*
Grigg, John. THE IRISH QUESTION, *pp. 1-8.* Briefly examines the history of Ireland with special attention to ethnic and religious factors. Emphasizes the recent escalation of events, the role of the Irish Republican Army, and the position of the British Army. Map, biblio.

Critchley, Julian. ULSTER AND THE URBAN GUERILLA, pp. 9-15. Examines the IRA in the context of the global problem posed by urban guerillas. P. J. Beck

282. —. [NAZI TERRORISM AND LAW AND SOCIETY]. *Human Rights Q. 1983 5(2): 151-190.*
Weisberg, Richard. AVOIDING CENTRAL REALITIES: NARRATIVE TERROR AND THE FAILURE OF FRENCH CULTURE UNDER THE OCCUPATION, pp. 151-170. Inquires into literary and legal condoning of Nazi policies in occupied France. Narrative foreshadowed reality. The implication of the 19th- and 20th-century literary insights is that the Holocaust can no longer be considered merely a German, or even predominantly an economic or political, phenomenon.
Richards, David A. J. TERROR AND THE LAW, pp. 171-185. Meditates on the last sentence of American lawyer Telford Taylor's indictment of the Nazi SS lawyers at the Nuremburg war crimes trial: "They, of all Germans, should have understood and valued justice."
Orlow, Dietrich. COMMENTS ON WEISBERG'S "AVOIDING CENTRAL REALITIES" AND RICHARDS' "TERROR AND THE LAW," pp. 186-190. Criticized Richards's and Weisberg's approaches, which demonstrate again the futility of seeking easy and simplistic answers in Holocaust research.

283. —. NEO-NAZIS IN AUSTRIA. *Patterns of Prejudice [Great Britain] 1982 16(1): 13-18.* Discusses the steady integration of far Right and Nazi elements into the major postwar political parties in Austria, a nation which was not so much the victim of Nazi aggression as it was the willing participant in the Third Reich and its programs of anti-Semitism and racial violence. Surveys the organization and influence of neo-Nazi elements in current Austrian politics and society.

3

MIDDLE EAST

284. Ahmad, Naveed. THE LEBANESE CRISIS: THE ROLE OF THE PLO. *Pakistan Horizon [Pakistan] 1976 29(1): 31-46.* The difficulty in maintaining an equilibrium between Christians and Moslems in Lebanon has been further complicated by the presence of Palestinian refugees, who, since the 1950's, have become increasingly militant.

285. Ahmad, Naveed. THE PALESTINE LIBERATION ORGANIZATION. *Pakistan Horizon [Pakistan] 1975 28(4): 81-115.* Describes the Palestine Liberation Organization since its founding in 1964; discusses the PLO's divergent factions, its relations with Arab governments, and its position in international politics.

286. Akhtar, Shameem. PLO IN-FIGHTING. *Pakistan Horizon [Pakistan] 1983 36(3): 100-120.* Eight factions make up the alliance of Palestinian freedom fighters known as the Palestine Liberation Organization (PLO), which has often been strained by its inherent ideological pluralism on the one hand and the external influence of feuding Arab states on the other.

287. Alaolmolki, Nuzar. REVOLUTION AND LEGITIMACY: THE ISLAMIC REPUBLIC OF IRAN. *Australian Outlook [Australia] 1982 36(1): 17-22.* The Ayatollah Khomeini failed to establish a viable and legitimate political system in the process of revolution in Iran. The opposition to Shah Reza Pahlavi had been a coalition not dominated by any single ideological viewpoint, but the revolution was taken over by a religious and theocratic dictatorship. To counter opposition the Khomeini regime tried to gain support by occupying the US Embassy with hostages, attacking the universities, and going to war with Iraq. 2 notes. W. D. McIntyre

288. Al-Dajani, Ahmad Sidqi. THE PLO AND THE EURO-ARAB DIALOGUE. *J. of Palestine Studies [Lebanon] 1980 9(3): 81-124.* Surveys the dialog between the Arabs, including the Palestine Liberation Organization (PLO), and the nine countries of the European Community from 1973 until 1978. The dialog began after the October War when Western Europe issued a communiqué favorable to the Palestinians. Progress was made in these talks, despite US hostility, until the visit of Egyptian President Anwar al-Sadat to Jerusalem in 1977 and the Camp David agreement in 1978 between Egypt and Israel, an agreement which the Europeans supported though they had reservations about its comprehensiveness. The PLO is determined to continue its

diplomatic efforts. The future favors European recognition of the PLO as the representative of the Palestinian people. Based on the minutes of the meetings of the Arab-European dialog, and on Palestinian and western secondary works; 12 notes. P. J. Mattar

289. Alekseev, A. LIVAN: STRASHNYE DNI [Lebanon: days of terror]. *Aziia i Afrika Segodnia [USSR] 1982 (12): 22-24.* Short biography of Talal Naji, member of the executive committee of the Palestine Liberation Organization, including memoirs of battle in Lebanon.

290. Alexander, Yonah. THE LEGACY OF PALESTINIAN TERRORISM. *Int. Problems [Israel] 1976 15(3-4): 57-64.* Examines the origins and development of Arab terrorism against Israel since the 1920's, concentrating on the events of 1947-48.

291. Altman, Israel. THE PALESTINE LIBERATION ORGANIZATION. Legum, Colin and Shaked, Haim, ed. *Arab Relations in the Middle East: The Road to Realignment* (New York: Holmes & Meier, 1979): 35-62. Traces the development of the Palestine Liberation Organization (PLO) from the 1973 October War to 1977, examining internal problems and schisms in the PLO, its relations with Arab governments, the United States, and the USSR.

292. Arafat, Yasser. THE WAY TO RESTORING THE VIOLATED RIGHTS OF THE PALESTINIAN PEOPLE. *World Marxist R. 1975 18(2): 123-132.* "An interview with Yasser Arafat, Chairman of the Executive Committee of the Palestine Liberation Organization" with his analysis of Zionism and imperialism in the 1960's and 1970's. S

293. Ashhab, Naim. TO OVERCOME CRISIS OF PALESTINE RESISTANCE MOVEMENT. *World Marxist Rev. 1972 15(5): 71-78.* Discusses crises in the politics and military operations of guerrillas in the Palestine Liberation Organization in Jordan and the Middle East, 1967-71.

294. Ball, George W. JET PLANES, TELEVISION, AND FOREIGN POLICY. *SAIS Rev. 1981 (1): 5-9.* Discusses how American television has become not simply a reporter but an actor in contemporary diplomatic relations, with special attention to two episodes: the Sinai agreements and the Camp David accords; and the hostage drama in Tehran.

295. Bator, Wolfgang and Bator, Angelika. DER KAMPF DER PALÄSTINENSISCHEN WIDERSTANDSBEWEGUNG [The fight of the Palestinian resistance movement]. *Dokumentation der Zeit [East Germany] 1970 (9): 13-18.* Reviews the history and development of the Palestinian Liberation Organization (PLO) with its groups: Palestinian Liberation Army (PLA), the Al-Fatah, the Al-Saiqa, the Popular Front of Liberation (PFLP), and Arabian Liberation Front (ALF). The Al-Fatah recently developed its own military-political conception. Communist parties in Arab states support the struggle as expressed in international conferences in Berlin and Moscow. 48 notes.
G. E. Pergl

296. Benjelloun, Nadia. L'O.L.P. DANS LE CONCERT DES NATIONS [The Palestine Liberation Organization in the concert of nations]. *Afrique et l'Asie Modernes [France] 1980 (4): 13-38.* Examines the attitude, policies, and actions of the Third World countries, the Arab nations, and other countries—including the United States—toward the Palestine Liberation Organization (PLO) since 1964.

297. Ben-Meir, Alon. THE ARAB PALESTINIANS. *Current Hist. 1978 74(433): 24-28, 41-42.* Examines the Palestine Liberation Organization as separate from the Palestinian people, chronicles the creation of the Israeli state and the lot of dispossessed Palestinians, and reviews events of the 1970's which involve the Arab states, the UN, and the Arab-Israeli conflict.

298. Beres, Louis René. TERRORISM AND THE NUCLEAR THREAT IN THE MIDDLE EAST. *Current Hist. 1976 70(412): 27-29.* Discusses the danger of nuclear arms in the Middle East created by the political terrorism of the Palestine Liberation Organization, 1970-75.

299. Bill, James A. POWER AND RELIGION IN REVOLUTIONARY IRAN. *Middle East J. 1982 36(1): 22-47.* The Iranian revolution was directed and controlled by the Shia religious establishment, and the central and pivotal role played by the religious leaders and Islamic scholars cannot be overemphasized. The revolution exacted a heavy toll in human lives, and the first three years of the revolution were a period of military violence, social uncertainty, disillusionment, and political chaos. The politics of neo-Shi'ism and the political strategy of Ayatollah Ruhollah Khomeini were shaped and influenced by his personality, resulting in a deep personal involvement in violent social and political problems. It will be essential for the mullahs to return to their role as guides and guardians if Iran is to build a new political consensus, and the Shi'a ulema must renew their attacks on oppression rather than being the oppressors. Based on speeches, unpublished papers, and secondary sources; 2 tables, 30 notes. F. A. Clements

300. Bishara, Ghassan. THE POLITICAL REPERCUSSIONS OF THE ISRAEL RAID ON THE IRAQI NUCLEAR REACTOR. *J. of Palestine Studies [Lebanon] 1982 11(3): 58-76.* The attack on the Tammuz reactor was yet another example of the unpunished violation of the terms of the US Foreign Ministry Sales Act by Israel. Examines the terms of the act, the reactions to the raid in America, debates in the US Congress, and deliberations in the UN. No evidence was produced to substantiate the claim of an Iraqi nuclear bomb nor that America will ever place an embargo on the supply of arms to Israel. For the Arabs the case was another lost opportunity due to incompetence. Based on US Official Reports and secondary sources; 3 tables, statistics, 36 notes. F. A. Clements

301. Bormann, Ernest G. A FANTASY THEME ANALYSIS OF THE TELEVISION COVERAGE OF THE HOSTAGE RELEASE AND THE REAGAN INAUGURAL. *Q. J. of Speech 1982 68(2): 133-145.* Explores the usefulness of fantasy theme analysis for the study of live coverage of breaking news events by making a critical analysis of the televised reports of the hostage

release and the Reagan inaugural address of 20 January 1981. Reveals similarities between rhetorical fantasies and televised news by comparing the subliminal impact of the enactment of the transfer of power and end of the crisis by the coverage of the inaugural and hostage release to the way Reagan's speechwriters used the fantasy type of restoration to meet the needs of a conservative political movement in the 1980's. J/S

302. Brenner, Lenni. ZIONIST-REVISIONISM: THE YEARS OF FASCISM AND TERROR. *J. of Palestine Studies [Lebanon] 1983 13(1): 66-92.* The World Zionist Organization had as one of its main leaders Vladimir Jabotinsky (1880-1940), whose ideology, which greatly influenced Menachem Begin, is essential to an understanding of contemporary Israel. The program of revisionism begun in 1923 had as its main platform the creation of a Jewish state in Palestine by any means possible. Although opposed to Hitler and his policies, Jabotinsky was oriented toward Mussolini and aimed at obtaining a national mandate from Great Britain. The role of Jabotinsky in the Arab Revolt, 1936-39, is examined, and Begin's role as a supporter of fascism in the 1930's is related to the present use of state terrorism against the Palestinians. Based on the writings of Jabotinsky, Begin, and secondary sources; 59 notes.
F. A. Clements

303. Browne, Donald R. THE VOICES OF PALESTINE: A BROADCASTING HOUSE DIVIDED. *Middle East J. 1975 29(2): 133-150.* Surveys the origins of Palestinian radio, 1954-65, when the Palestine Liberation Organization finally acquired its own radio voice. Listening has become a symbolic proclamation of support for the revolution, and broadcasts have had a strong impact on those living in refugee camps. The Palestinian radio stations nevertheless remain torn by internal divisions and are pressured by the host governments at whose pleasure the various stations operate. 45 notes.
E. P. Stickney

304. Butenschøn, Nils A. PLO SOM ARABISK AKTØR. SKISSE TIL EN ANALYSEMODELL [The PLO as an Arab actor: a tentative outline for an analytical model]. *Internasjonal Politikk [Norway] 1981 (2): 201-217.* Outlines a possible multidimensional analytical model for the study of the relationship between the Palestine Liberation Organization and the Arab states. Such a model must be macrohistorical to account for the emergence of pan-Arabism and pan-Islamism in the Arab world. It must be system-oriented in order to trace the Palestine problem's specific effects on the Arab regional system. And it must be actor-oriented, analyzing specific interaction between the PLO and the Arab states. The civil war in Lebanon 1975-76 is used to illustrate the strategic dilemmas of the actors involved. J/S

305. Cobban, Helena. THE PLO IN THE MID-1980S: BETWEEN THE GUN AND THE OLIVE BRANCH. *Int. J. [Canada] 1983 38(4): 635-651.* Despite the Israeli invasion of Lebanon in June 1982 and its desire to "root out" the headquarters of the Palestine Liberation Organization (PLO), Israeli actions only led to a hardening of the national resolve of the Palestinian people. In February, 1983, the PLO held the 16th session of its parliament-in-exile, the Palestinian National Council (PNC) in Algiers, and maintained its

support of the Palestinian political leadership. A study of the development of Arab nationalism in Palestine shows the continuity and growth of political awareness, and today the fact and vitality of Palestinian nationhood is incontrovertible. Based on primary and secondary sources, 11 notes.
L. J. Klass

306. Cohen, Michael J. THE BRITISH WHITE PAPER ON PALESTINE, MAY 1939. *Hist. J. [Great Britain] 1976 19(3):* 727-758. Part II. THE TESTING OF A POLICY, 1942-1945. (Continued from a previous article). Winston Churchill opposed the 1939 White Paper on Palestine, considering it a foreign policy mistake of the Chamberlain government. The Middle Eastern military crisis of 1940-42 delayed substitution of any alternative policy, and the Foreign Office was particularly opposed to the pro-Zionist posture of both Churchill and Leo Amery. Zionist terrorism in the form of the assassination in Cairo of Lord Moyne, Minister Resident in the Middle East, on 6 November 1944 delayed further consideration of an alternative to the White Paper, including partition, until World War II was over, and others less favorable to Zionism had replaced Churchill. Clement Attlee and Ernest Bevin never returned to partition as an answer in Palestine before Great Britain pulled out completely in 1947. Based on unpublished documents in the Public Record Office, London, and other archives, published government reports, and secondary sources; 3 maps, 93 notes, appendix.
L. A. McGeoch

307. Cohen, Michael J. THE MOYNE ASSASSINATION, NOVEMBER, 1944: A POLITICAL ANALYSIS. *Middle Eastern Studies [Great Britain] 1979 15(3):* 358-373. Discusses the political background and repercussions of the assassination of Lord Moyne, British Minister Resident, by the Stern Group, an extremist wing of Irgun. The Jewish terrorists thought he was a prime mover in Great Britain's anti-Zionist policy; he was merely symbolic and had, in fact, only recently become part of the government. The assassination and execution of the two terrorists had wide-reaching repercussions: 1) the British withstood pressures to take drastic action—Jewish immigration to Palestine was not suspended and Yishuv was not disarmed; 2) the Jewish Executive Agency gave its full cooperation in hunting terrorists; 3) the British Cabinet postponed consideration of the Palestine Committee Report which recommended the establishment of a Jewish state in Palestine. Based on Foreign Office and Colonial Office papers, Cabinet minutes, Minutes of Agency Executive, and secondary works; 54 notes.
S

308. Cohen, Michael J. WHY BRITAIN LEFT: THE END OF THE MANDATE. *Wiener Lib. Bull. [Great Britain] 1978 31(45-46):* 74-86. Traces negotiations between the British and the Zionists, and the policy debates within the British cabinet. British determination to stay in Palestine was undermined by American pressure, often the result of domestic political considerations, the escalation of illegal immigration after World War II, and Jewish terrorism. The case of the refugee ship *Exodus*, illustrating the Zionist genius for exploiting a situation, put the British in the role of inhuman monsters. Underlying everything was the British concern for their military position in the Middle East. Baffled, the British government decided in 1947 to turn the mandate over to the UN. 82 notes.
R. V. Layton

309. Colebrook, Joan. ISRAEL—WITH TERRORISTS. *Commentary 1974 58(1): 30-39.*

310. Conover, Pamela Johnston and Sigelman, Lee. PRESIDENTIAL INFLUENCE AND PUBLIC OPINION: THE CASE OF THE IRANIAN HOSTAGE CRISIS. *Social Sci. Q. 1982 63(2): 249-264.* Discusses presidential influence on public opinion, focusing on the Iranian hostage crisis responsiveness in Lexington, Kentucky, "varied depending on the nature of the policy which was being pursued" by Jimmy Carter.

311. Dishon, Daniel. THE LEBANESE WAR—AN ALL ARAB CRISIS. *Midstream 1977 23(1): 25-32.* Examines reasons for Syria's intervention in Lebanon and the Lebanese civil war in 1976; Syrian President Hafez al-Assad attempted to use the Palestine Liberation Organization for political and military ascendancy over Egypt in the Arab world, 1968-70's.

312. Diskin, Abraham. TRENDS IN INTENSITY VARIATION OF PALESTINIAN MILITARY ACTIVITY: 1967-1978. *Can. J. of Pol. Sci. [Canada] 1983 16(2): 335-348.* Describes an analysis of terrorist activities that were initiated by various Palestinian organizations. Terrorism is seen as a long-term Palestinian strategy undertaken to support political goals including the dissolution of the Israeli state and the expulsion of most of its citizens. Therefore the frequency of terrorist acts is related to political events and Palestinian aspirations, not just Israeli reprisals. Secondary sources. D. Powell

313. Earl, Robert L. A MATTER OF PRINCIPLE. *US Naval Inst. Pro. 1983 109(2): 29-36.* Analyzes the mission to rescue the US hostages in Iran during April 1980 in terms of the principles of war. Because of the acceptance of a conservative, minimalist plan with its built-in constraints, the operation was fatally inflexible. K. J. Bauer

314. El-Ayouty, Yassin. THE PALESTINIANS AND THE FOURTH ARAB-ISRAELI WAR. *Current Hist. 1974 66(390): 74-78.* The Palestine Liberation Organization in face of the Yom Kippur War and the prospects for diplomatic relations between the PLO and Israel. From an issue on the Middle East, 1974. S

315. Fay, James R. TERRORISM IN TURKEY: THREAT TO NATO'S TROUBLED ALLY. *Military Rev. 1981 61(4): 16-26.* Traces the development of terrorism in Turkey, concentrating on the period between the army coups in 1960 and 1980. Terrorist groups representing both the Left and Right killed freely, protesting against economic, political, and religious trends. This activity was destroying the social and political fabric of the country, but the latest army coup seems to have reversed this trend and restored Turkey's position in NATO. 48 notes. D. H. Cline

316. Furlonge, Geoffrey. THE TRAGEDY OF THE LEBANON. *Asian Affairs [Great Britain] 1978 9(2): 117-134.* Traces the impact of the 1975-76 civil war in Lebanon. This tragic conflict has left over 40,000 dead, over half a million wounded, and another half a million Lebanese in temporary exile.

Throughout its history Lebanon, made up of a mosaic of Moslem and Christian factions, has survived 19 separate conflicts and foreign invasions. Unfortunately, the government failed to develop strong political leadership to fend off problems of agitation by the Palestine Liberation Organization and other factions. A lecture given to the Royal Society for Asian Affairs in London in March 1978. S. H. Frank

317. Garfincle, Adam M. SOURCES OF THE AL-FATAH MUTINY. *Orbis 1983 27(3): 603-640.* Analyzes the causes of the mutiny within the Palestine Liberation Organization (PLO) in June 1983. Although the actual mutiny began as a result of disagreement over a change of two commands in the Bekaa Valley, it had deeper roots that date back to the Israeli invasion of Lebanon in 1982 when the ineptitude of the PLO as a military force was graphically demonstrated. Arafat's seeming willingness to negotiate and Syria's support of the rebels proved to be decisive factors insuring his defeat. Based on published sources; 68 notes. J. W. Thacker, Jr.

318. Giniewski, Paul. LA CHARTE NATIONALE PALESTINIENNE: CE QUE VEUT L'O.L.P. [The Palestinian national charter: what the P.L.O. wants]. *Riv. di Studi Pol. Int. [Italy] 1981 48(1): 33-56.* Examines the four principles underlying the charter of the Palestine Liberation Organization and its relations with the Arab states, the superpowers, and international terrorism; the charter is given in an appendix.

319. Golan, Galia. SOVIET-PLO RELATIONS. *Jerusalem Q. [Israel] 1980 (16): 121-136.* Examines the complexities of the Soviet position regarding the Palestine Liberation Organization and the creation of a Palestinian state, concluding that perils exist for the USSR if that state is established.

320. Goldberg, Giora. HAGANAH, IRGUN AND "STERN": WHO DID WHAT? *Jerusalem Q. [Israel] 1982 (25): 116-120.* Examines new trends in the controversy between the labor movement and the Revisionists in Israel in the 1970's, particularly the impact of three underground organizations Haganah, Etzel, and Lehi.

321. Gordon, Murray. THE SECURITY COUNCIL "DEBATE": THE TANGLE BEHIND IT. *Midstream 1976 22(3): 19-29.* Discusses debate in the UN Security Council over the Middle East in 1975-76, emphasizing the demands of Syria and the Palestine Liberation Organization, and the extent of US support of Israel.

322. Guggenheim, Willy. DIE MACHT DES PARADOXEN. AUGENSCHEIN IN ISRAEL [The power of paradox: surface appearances in Israel]. *Monat [West Germany] 1970 22(260): 45-50.* Israel lives with a paradox of undefined boundaries, half-provisional, half-permanent fortification of occupied areas ruled according to Arab law, while a lively trade moves across the warlike fronts between Israel and the Arab states. Against a successful and highly confident Israeli Army and wise rule of the occupied areas, Arab terrorism has meant only pinpricks and a soothed conscience for Israelis while it is destroying the Arab states. D. Prowe

323. Gunter, Michael M. THE ARMENIAN TERRORIST CAMPAIGN AGAINST TURKEY. *Orbis 1983 27(2): 447-477.* Outraged by the alleged murder of 1.5 million Armenians by the Turks during World War I and the seizure of their homeland, Armenian terrorists have murdered 26 Turkish diplomats between 1972 and 1982. The Armenian question, the current Armenian terrorist campaign, its *modus operandi,* and its connections with other terrorist groups are discussed in detail. Terrorism will continue unless the Armenian community ceases to support the terrorists and the press stops giving them publicity. Based on published sources, mainly newspapers; 146 notes. J. W. Thacker, Jr.

324. Hamid, Rashid. WHAT IS THE PLO? *J. of Palestine Studies [Lebanon] 1975 4(4): 90-109.* Outlines the institutional development of the Palestine Liberation Organization (PLO) from its inception in 1964 as the organization within which all Palestinian organizations meet to work toward Palestinian national goals.

325. Harris, George S. THE LEFT IN TURKEY. *Problems of Communism 1980 29(4): 26-41.* The Left in Turkey claims only a small portion of the popular vote, yet leftist ideas enjoy wide acceptance among students and intellectuals and contribute to political violence. Based on numerous left-wing Turkish language publications; 33 notes. J. M. Lauber

326. Harris, Lillian Craig. CHINA'S RELATIONS WITH THE PLO. *J. of Palestine Studies [Lebanon] 1977 7(1): 123-154.* China's eastern civilization and Communist ideology are fundamental barriers to the development of close foreign relations between China and the Palestinians, who like many modern Moslems identify strongly with the West. On the Palestinian side, the lack of unity is the barrier. Traces the progression of the relationship between China and the Palestinians (and later the Palestinian Liberation Organization—PLO) since the Bandung Conference in 1955. 78 notes. A. Menicant

327. Heradstveit, Daniel. ISRAELSK OPPFATNING AV "FRED" [The Israeli interpretation of "peace"]. *Internasjonal Politikk [Norway] 1973 (2): 425-451.* Analyzes the views of Arab and Israel elites. Arab views range from the elimination of the Israeli state to some form of accommodation. Israelis interpret their role as peaceful and the Arabs as aggressive and terrorist. They are united on goals while the Arabs quarrel among themselves. The Palestinians have no realistic goals. They fear Yassir Arafat and the guerrillas and wish freedom for themselves to choose their future, preferring Israeli methods and regime over Arab control. Most Israelis demand retention of some parts of the territory seized in 1967. Israeli youth are less sympathetic to the Arabs and Palestinians, desiring neither peace with them nor dependence on them. They see peace as something possible in 15 to 20 years based on military strength and development of some form of coexistence. Peace requires a form of neutrality and the lessening of hatred among both Arabs and Jews for each other. R. E. Lindgren

328. Hickman, William F. DID IT REALLY MATTER? *Naval War Coll. Rev. 1983 36(2): 17-30.* In December 1979 a concentrated US naval presence

was established in the Indian Ocean and Arabian Sea in response to the Iranian hostage crisis. Since an immediate rescue attempt was strategically impossible, Carter sought to gain release of the hostages through negotiations backed by the threat of military force. This policy, however, overlooked the tradition of Shia Islam that martyrdom assures immediate entry into heaven. Therefore the Ayatollah Khomeini and his followers were not threatened by the naval presence, but actually welcomed it. Though this military gesture was effective as a signal to the Soviets, it was counterproductive with respect to the fulfillment of American objectives in Iran. Based on interviews, press reports, and other primary sources; 25 notes. J. Powell

329. Hourihan, William J. THE BIG STICK IN TURKEY: AMERICAN DIPLOMACY AND NAVAL OPERATIONS AGAINST THE OTTOMAN EMPIRE, 1903-1904. *Naval War Coll. Rev. 1981 34(5): 78-88.* Missionary societies formed a single issue group in American politics. Their influence, the reported assassination of an American diplomat in Beirut, an impending presidential election, and a Turkish pasha unwilling to receive the American minister because of "important visits to the harem" gave Theodore Roosevelt an opportunity to demonstrate American seapower. If its lessons were lost on the Ottoman Empire, they were not in the capitals of Europe. J/S

330. Hudson, Michael C. THE PALESTINIANS: RETROSPECT AND PROSPECTS. *Current Hist. 1980 78(453): 22-25, 31, 39-41, 48.* Outlines the origins and development of Palestinian identity from the 1970's, with emphasis on the growth and diplomatic influence of the Palestine Liberation Organization during the 1960's-70's.

331. Hudson, Michael C. THE U.S. DECLINE IN THE MIDDLE EAST: CAN IT BE STOPPED? *Orbis 1982 26(1): 19-26.* Analyzes the decline of the US position in the Middle East during 1981, and the failure of the Reagan administration to build a strategic consensus of moderate states to counter the influence of the USSR. The author contends that the Reagan policies are flawed because they are based on four axioms that should be examined closely: the Arabs are more concerned about a Soviet threat than a threat from Israel, Israel is a strategic asset in the region, the Palestinian issue is exaggerated, and the Palestine Liberation Organization is an unacceptable participant in the peace process. J. W. Thacker, Jr.

332. Inglis, Alex I. RECAP OF 29TH GENERAL ASSEMBLY: UNITED NATIONS TURNING-POINT? *Int. Perspectives [Canada] 1976 (3): 25-31.* Discusses the controversial events of the 29th UN General Assembly including the recognition of the Palestine Liberation Organization, the exclusion of South Africa, the questions of Cyprus, Cambodia, and Korea, the special session concerned with the world economic order, disarmament and nuclear proliferation, and the question of peacekeeping.

333. Isaac, Rael Jean. LIBERAL PROTESTANTS VERSUS ISRAEL. *Midstream 1981 27(8): 6-14.* Criticizes the National Council of Churches, whose resolutions since 1974 have uniformly attacked Israel and promoted the Palestine Liberation Organization.

334. Isaac, Rael Jean. THE SEDUCTION OF THE QUAKERS: FROM FRIENDLY PERSUASION TO PLO SUPPORT. *Midstream* 1979 25(9): 23-29. Discusses the pro-Palestine Liberation Organization (PLO) anti-Israeli position of the American Friends Service Committee during the 1970's.

335. Jiryis, Sabri. THE ARABS IN ISRAEL, 1973-79. *J. of Palestine Studies [Lebanon]* 1979 8(4): 31-56. Analyzes the conditions and attitudes of Palestinians with Israeli nationality since the October War. The Palestinians who increased from 160,000 in 1948 to 500,000 in 1978, were oppressed by Israel until 1966 when Israel changed its policy and gave them more rights. But they continued to be second class citizens. The 1973 war led most of them to identify with the Palestinian movement, and increased their support for the Palestine Liberation Organization. Based on Israeli government publications, and Israeli newspapers; 90 notes. P. J. Mattar

336. Johnson, Michael. MIDDLE EAST: IS TIME RUNNING OUT? *World Today [Great Britain]* 1975 31(6): 256-264. Discusses military issues for Israel, Egypt, Syria, and the Palestine Liberation Organization, 1973-75, emphasizing controversies around Israel's control of the Sinai Peninsula and the Golan Heights.

337. Knight, Graham and Dean, Tony. MYTH AND THE STRUCTURE OF NEWS. *J. of Communication* 1982 32(2): 144-161. Crime news in modern society is ideologically presented through myth, as Canadian coverage of the raid by the Special Air Services Regiment of the British army on the terrorists holding hostage the Iranian embassy in London in spring, 1980, shows.

338. Korey, William. THE PLO'S CONQUEST OF THE U.N. *Midstream* 1979 25(9): 10-15. Critically examines the Palestine Liberation Organization's influence at the UN since the creation of the PLO in 1964.

339. Koshelev, V. S. IZ ISTORII TAINYKH ANTIBRITANSKIKH ORGANIZATSII V EGIPTE (1870-1934 GG) [Excerpts from the history of the secret anti-British organizations in Egypt, 1870-1924]. *Narody Azii i Afriki [USSR]* 1980 (1): 111-119. Outlines the different stages in the history of a few anti-British movements in Egypt since the creation of the first societies in the 1870's. Describes the role of these political organizations, their activities in the struggle for independence, and sometimes irresponsible acts of terrorism which gave the British the opportunity to repress the liberation movement. The murder of Sir Lee Stack in Cairo in 1924 marked the end of the most active period of these secret societies. 43 notes. C. Pichelin

340. Kuranov, I. N. V BOR'BE ZA KORENNYE INTERESY TURETSKOGO NARODA [In the struggle for the fundamental interests of the Turkish nation]. *Voprosy Istorii KPSS [USSR]* 1980 (9): 107-110. Commemorates the 60th anniversary of the foundation of the Communist Party of Turkey (CPT). The first Communist organizations were founded in 1918 in major cities and the Party was established in July 1920. Describes the history of the Party's struggle for democracy and social justice and against US imperialism. In recent years the Party has suffered severe terrorist attacks from neofascist

nationalist organizations. The CPT is an important unit of the international Communist movement and has participated in all major events organized by the movement. 13 notes. V. Sobell

341. Kuriyama, Yoshihiro. TERRORISM AT TEL AVIV AIRPORT AND A "NEW LEFT" GROUP IN JAPAN. *Asian Survey 1973 13(3): 336-346.* Studies the activities of the United Red Army, an extreme leftist group in Japan and considers its ties to the Popular Front for the Liberation of Palestine, and the responsibility for the massacre at Lod Airport in 1972. S

342. Landa, R. G. OSVOBODITEL'NAIA BOR'BA ARABOV PALESTINY (1948-1967) [The liberation struggle of the Palestinian Arabs, 1948-67]. *Narody Azii i Afriki [USSR] 1976 (1): 18-32.* Traces the struggle of the Palestinians against Israel from the creation of Israel in 1948 to the 1967 war. Discusses the causes underlying the Arab resistance and liberation movement: the terrorist acts that force the Arabs to leave their lands; the unlawful occupation of these lands by the Israelis, and their refusal to recognize the rights of the Palestinian Arabs, and the Arab refugee problems. The movement is divided into four periods: 1948-54, temporary decline; 1954-57, political activity in Jordan; 1958-64, the emergence of the nationalist Palestinian organizations; 1964-67, the Palestine Liberation Organization program and activities. 53 notes. L. Kalinowski

343. Landa, R. G. [THE PALESTINIAN RESISTANCE MOVEMENT, 1948-71].
IZ ISTORII PALESTINSKOGO DVIZHENIIA SOPROTIVLENIIA (1967-1971 GG.) [The history of the Palestinian resistance movement, 1967-71]. *Narody Azii i Afriki [USSR] 1976 (4): 18-32.* Continued from a previous article in this bibliography. The 1967 Israeli aggression and Arab defeat brought about a strong desire on the part of the Palestinians and other Arabs to improve their armed forces. There was a sudden rise in the ranks of the Palestinian resistance movement, and support for the Palestinian cause became even more widespread among the Arabs. This resulted in commando operations on Jordan's West Bank during August-December 1967 and in the Gaza strip from 1967 to 1971. The author describes the various organizations in the Palestinian resistance movement as well as their differences and internal struggles. Israeli intrigues and Arab mistakes induced the Black September massacres of 1970 and the Palestinian retreat from Jordan in July 1971. Because of the 1970-71 tragedies the leaders of the Palestinian resistance movement reassessed their weaknesses and strengths, and determined to conduct their affairs on a clearer political line and take into account the true interests of the Palestinians. 67 notes.
SOVREMENNYI ETAP BOR'BY PALESTINSKOGO DVIZHENIIA SOPROTIVLENIIA (1971-1976) [The present stage of struggle in the Palestinian resistance movement, 1971-76]. *Narody Azii i Afriki [USSR] 1976 (5): 15-30.* Describes the Palestinian resistance movement from its temporary losses in Jordan in 1971 to the middle of 1976. After withstanding the 1971-73 crisis in Jordan, the movement with the support of the Left in Lebanon defeated the attempt to liquidate it by military

force in May 1973. By the beginning of 1974, terrorism as a tactic of the movement's extremists was quelled. Then came the 1974-75 successes of the movement in the United Nations, widespread recognition, and the increasing effectiveness of the Palestinian National Front formed in 1973 on the West Bank of the Jordan and at Gaza. The movement is continuing the struggle for the rights of the Palestinian Arabs, including the right to form their own state. 70 notes. L. Kalinowski

344. Larson, David L. THE AMERICAN RESPONSE TO THE IRANIAN HOSTAGE CRISIS: 444 DAYS OF DECISION. *Int. Social Sci. Rev. 1982 57(3[i.e., 4]): 195-209.* The Iranian hostage crisis was one of the most difficult episodes in American foreign policy since 1945. The overall strategy of the United States was to achieve the safe release of the hostages without endangering their lives or having the situation spin out of control. As such, the strategy had to be carefully orchestrated, nonprovocative, and nonthreatening. This necessitated the use of a variety of diplomatic, legal, economic, political, and military instruments on both a bilateral and multilateral basis. The consequences of the crisis were quite substantial at the international level, but may have been more substantial at the national level. J/S

345. Legrain, Jean-François. LA "DISSIDENCE" PALISTINIENNE [The Palestinian "dissidence"]. *Esprit [France] 1984 (4): 17-31.* Assesses the impact of events in Lebanon in 1982-83 on the Palestine Liberation Organization and relations between the Palestinians and the Arab states.

346. Lehman-Wilzig, Sam and Goldberg, Giora. RELIGIOUS PROTEST AND POLICE REACTION IN A THEO-DEMOCRACY: ISRAEL, 1950-1979. *J. of Church and State 1983 25(3): 491-505.* Religious problems have existed throughout modern Israel's history, and much of the struggle has taken place outside the parliament and courts. This study is concerned with the reaction to religious protest staged in public. More violence was involved in religious protests than in other types, but the charge of police brutality was less frequently cited in religious protests than in other kinds of demonstrations. Although highly publicized, religious issues are not as important as political and social issues. Based on printed sources; 23 notes, 2 tables.
E. E. Eminhizer

347. Lesch, Ann M. ISRAELI DEPORTATION OF PALESTINIANS FROM THE WEST BANK AND THE GAZA STRIP, 1967-1978. *J. of Palestine Studies [Lebanon] 1979 8(2): 101-131, (3): 80-112.* A short statistical analysis, followed by lists of 1100 Palestinians deported by Israel from the occupied territories. The author analyzes the deportees' towns of origin, ages, occupations, date of deportation, and reasons for banishment. Israeli officials gave several categories of deportees, including infiltrators, terrorist infiltrators, inciters and migrants, even though Article 49 of the Fourth Geneva Convention of 12 August 1949 prohibits deportation, regardless of the motive. Based on Jordanian police records, the list of Rouhi al-Khatib (ex-mayor of East Jerusalem), *al-Quds* newspaper, other newspapers, and secondary sources; 4 tables, 31 notes, list of deportees. P. J. Mattar

348. Lesch, Ann M. THE PALESTINE PROBLEM. *World Pol. 1982* 34(4): 560-573. The contradiction between Israeli and Palestinian goals and Israel's refusal to negotiate with the Palestine Liberation Organization have caused a profound diplomatic impasse. Moreover, the PLO's dependence on Arab hosts has embroiled it in secondary-level conflicts with Arab states. Although the PLO has gained their moral, diplomatic, and financial support, it has posed a threefold challenge: rulers resent the military cost of confronting Israel; Palestinian raids precipitate Israeli retaliatory actions against host territories; and the presence of autonomous Palestinian political and military forces undermines the host regimes' sovereignty and legitimacy. The author explores the ramifications of these Palestinian-Israeli and Palestinian-Arab dilemmas and assesses the likelihood of a compromise settlement by creating a Palestinian state on the West Bank and the Gaza Strip. J

349. Lewis, Bernard. THE PALESTINIANS AND THE PLO: A HISTORICAL APPROACH. *Commentary 1975* 59(1): 32-48. Defines groups of people comprising Palestinians, follows the development of the Palestine Liberation Organization from 1964, and discusses obstacles to a peaceful solution of the Arab-Israeli conflict.

350. Litani, Yehuda. LEADERSHIP IN THE WEST BANK AND GAZA. *Jerusalem Q. [Israel] 1980* (14): 99-109. Discusses the local political situation in the West Bank and Gaza, the interaction of the political leaders of Israel, the Palestine Liberation Organization, and Jordan in the local politics of the region, and the possibilities for political accommodation in the future.

351. Lorch, Netanel. A COMPARATIVE HISTORY OF THE ARAB-ISRAELI CONFLICT. *Rev. Int. d'Hist. Militaire [France] 1979* (42): 148-162. Discusses Israel's War of Independence, 1947-49; the Sinai Campaign of 1956; the Six-Day War of 1967; the War of Attrition 1968-70; and the Yom Kippur War of 1973 and its subsequent War of Attrition with respect to Arab and Israeli objectives, initiative, the attitudes of the USSR and the United States, the number of fronts, the weaponry, the balance of forces, the duration, casualties, the terms of termination, and terrorism. J. Powell

352. Macintyre, Ronald R. THE PALESTINE LIBERATION ORGANIZATION: TACTICS, STRATEGIES AND OPTIONS TOWARDS THE GENEVA CONFERENCE. *J. of Palestine Studies [Lebanon] 1975* 4(4): 65-89. Examines the alternatives facing the Palestine Liberation Organization since its inception in 1964; emphasizes the difficulty of an Arab revolutionary movement's seeking entry into the institutional system of international relations with the intention of displacing Israel, an existing member state.

353. Mantovani, Giovanni. I PALESTINESI DOPO RABAT; OPPORTUNITÀ E LIMITI [The Palestinians after Rabat: opportunity and limits]. *Civitas [Italy] 1974* 25(12): 45-59. "The Arab summit in Rabat (26-28 October) was the turning point in Middle East politics, that gave a new asset to the prospects of the crisis and also to those of the diplomatic negotiations. The summit has chosen 'the Palestinian way' thus making Arafat's PLO [Palestine Liberation Organization] the only valid interlocutor for Israel. There is also a

tendency of the Arab countries to keep their single diplomatic activities intact, while Arafat could face some difficulties in the control of the extremist guerrilla wing. After Rabat the key problem of future peace is if and how Israelis and Palestinians may and will live together in Palestine." J

354. Mead, James M. LEBANON REVISITED. *Marine Corps Gazette 1983 67(9): 64-73.* Describes the experiences of the US 22d Marine Amphibious Unit in Beirut, Lebanon, during February-May 1983, including military exercises with the Lebanese army, rescues of civilians, and the terrorist bombing of the US embassy.

355. Milson, Menahem. HOW TO MAKE PEACE WITH THE PALESTINIANS. *Commentary 1981 71(5): 25-35.* Reviews the history of the negotiations between Israel, Egypt, and the United States concerning the autonomy plan for the West Bank and Gaza from 1978 to 1981, especially the Palestine Liberation Organization's rejection of the Camp David accords, and suggests that the solution is freeing the population of the territories from the grip of the PLO.

356. Mishael, I. MEDINIUT HATAGMUL UPLITEI ARAV [The policy of retaliation and the Arab refugees]. *Bitzaron 1966 55(2): 100-103.* Traces the history and development of night retaliatory raids in response to Arab attacks on Israeli life and property since the British Mandate period. Deals extensively with the moral and political implications of a regular army's need to respond in the manner of scattered bands of terrorists. Illustrates the better-known incidents, many caused by Israel's lax defense due to international and UN criticism.   T. Z. Herman

357. Mishal, Shaul. NATIONALISM THROUGH LOCALISM: SOME OBSERVATIONS ON THE WEST BANK POLITICAL ELITE. *Middle Eastern Studies [Great Britain] 1981 17(4): 477-491.* Despite changes caused by incorporation into Jordan, Israeli occupation, and the increasing involvement of the PLO in internal politics, the political elite on the West Bank did not change in power structure or political behavior. Despite radical external changes it continued to draw power from a local base and its behavior was more moderate than its declared position. This moderation was not a result of Jordanian or Israeli forces as local political conditions were paramount in forming the behavior of the elite. The West Bank political elite was a local power element forced to adapt its political views to satisfy the demands of multiaffiliation and cooperation but with local interests still the determining factor. The success of PLO supporters in the 1976 municipal elections has not meant a complete change as allowances are still made for local interests and old loyalties. Expansion of a paper given at a conference "Israel: A Society in Formation" Tel Aviv University, 10-11 April 1978; 32 notes.
F. A. Clements

358. Muradov, G. A. NOVYI ETAP APREL'SKOI REVOLIUTSII V AFGANISTANE [A new stage in the April Revolution in Afghanistan]. *Narody Azii i Afriki [USSR] 1981 (2): 14-25.* Examines the cultural, industrial, technological, and educational backwardness and inequalities in pre-April

1978 Afghanistan and the rise of the Popular Democratic Party as a result of proletarian antagonism to the ruling class. The negative consequences of Hafizullah Amin's terrorist government and the near breakup of the country are examined. The new era began on 28 December 1979 when Babrak Karmal became prime minister, determined to strengthen national unity, religious freedom, democratic centralism, and the security forces and to redistribute wealth. The Soviet people will continue to give the Afghan people military and economic support. The two countries share a common world view. Soviet and Afghan press and government sources; 30 notes. A. J. Evans

359. Muslih, Muhammad Y. MODERATES AND REJECTIONISTS WITHIN THE PALESTINE LIBERATION ORGANIZATION. *Middle East J.* 1976 (2): 127-140. Since the 1973 October War, the Arab world has been divided on the issue of reaching a political settlement in the Arab-Israeli conflict. The recognition of Israel has been vaguely implied by the Palestine Liberation Organization. The ideology of the Democratic Front for the Liberation of Palestine (DFLP) seems to center its vision on Arab unity and on an Arab nation, revealing its rejection of conciliation with Israel. The author emphasizes the representative nature of the PLO, and fears the overthrow of moderate Arab regimes, which could be accompanied by a fifth Arab-Israel confrontation. 48 notes. E. P. Stickney

360. Nesterov, N. TURTSIIA: STARYE I NOVYE PROBLEMY [Turkey: old and new problems]. *Aziia i Afrika Segodnia [USSR]* 1979 (6): 17-19. Analyzes the economic, political, and international position of Turkey which is now facing a number of serious problems. Turkey's foreign debt has mounted to a sizable sum, the government has failed to put an end to the terrorist raids of right-wing extremists and their Maoist accomplices, and inflation has reached a menacing level. It is in these conditions that the United States last August lifted an embargo on the delivery of its arms to Turkey. J

361. Nimrod, Yoram. REFLECTIONS ON PALESTINIAN HISTORY. *Jerusalem Q. [Israel]* 1982 (25): 31-53. A review of Yehoshua Porath's *The Emergence of the Palestine-Arab Movement 1918-1929* (1974) and *The Palestinian Arab National Movement 1929-39: From Riots to Rebellion* (1977). These volumes are not only the first systematic study of the emergence of the Palestinian movement, but, the author maintains, they are free from both accusation and apologetics. The author also considers the discussions that took place between Arabs and Jews in the political sphere during this period.

362. O'Neill, Bard E. TOWARDS A TYPOLOGY OF POLITICAL TERRORISM: THE PALESTINIAN RESISTANCE MOVEMENT. *J. of Int. Affairs* 1978 32(1): 17-42. Following Richard Shultz's typology, concludes that capability reduction is critical in explaining Palestinian terrorism. Attributes the capability reduction to the combination of the effectiveness of counterinsurgency with bad strategy, a poor environment, organizational defects, low active popular support in the target area, and limited means for conducting guerrilla warfare. 48 notes. V. Samaraweera

363. Orlow, Dietrich. POLITICAL VIOLENCE IN PRE-COUP TURKEY. *Terrorism 1982 6(1): 53-71.* Discusses the contributions of Kemalist modernization from 1920 to 1945 in Turkey to the political violence in the country from the end of World War II to the military coup of September 1980.

364. Perry, Victor. TERRORISM INCORPORATED. *Midstream 1982 28(2): 7-10.* Discusses the terrorist activities of the Palestine Liberation Organization, its alliance with other terrorist organizations such as the Baader-Meinhoff group, and its continuing contribution to instability in the Middle East.

365. Piotrowski, Jerzy. THE PALESTINIAN QUESTION: EVOLUTION OF THE PLO STANCE. *Studies on the Developing Countries [Poland] 1979 (10): 37-56.* Examines the positions of Israel, Egypt, and the Great Powers on the establishment of an independent Palestinian state and the development of the Palestine Liberation Organization.

366. Pryce-Jones, David. HOW TO MISLEAD A PEOPLE AND RUIN A CAUSE. THE RISE AND FALL OF THE PLO. *Encounter [Great Britain] 1984 63(1): 61-64.* Reviews Jillian Becker's *The PLO: The Rise and Fall of the Palestine Liberation Organization* (1984) on the history of the PLO, Israel, and the Arab states between 1967 and 1983.

367. Rana, Swadesh. THE OBJECTIVES AND STRATEGY OF THE PALESTINE LIBERATION ORGANIZATION. *India Q.: J. of Int. Affairs [India] 1976 32(2): 153-168.* Examines the strategies of the Palestine Liberation Organization in terms of the objectives attained. In the 1930's, opposition to both Zionism and British rule provided the twin objectives of Palestinian nationalism; problems of political leadership and organization were partly responsible for the inability of Palestinians to prevent the establishment of the nation of Israel in 1947. For almost two decades thereafter, Egypt, Syria, and Jordan led the Palestinian cause. Their changing relations with each other and with the major powers inhibited the evolution of a coordinated strategy. The policy of Arab confrontation with Israel produced situations wherein Palestinian objectives assumed the character of ultimate goals, even though the more immediate issues of cease-fire, disengagement, and Israeli withdrawal from Arab lands commanded the attention of political leaders. Secondary sources; 38 notes. S. H. Frank

368. Reid, Donald M. POLITICAL ASSASSINATION IN EGYPT, 1910-1954. *Int. J. of African Hist. Studies 1982 15(4): 625-651.* An analysis of all Egyptian attempted political assassinations between 1910 and 1954. There were two distinct waves of activity, 1919-24 and 1945-49. These waves of assassinations paralleled worldwide political patterns. Based on Egyptian government records; 3 tables, 83 notes. R. T. Brown

369. Rekhess, Elie and Avidan, Dan. THE WEST BANK AND GAZA STRIP. Legum, Colin and Shaked, Haim, ed. *Arab Relations in the Middle East: The Road to Realignment* (New York: Holmes & Meier, 1979): 65-80. Analyzes the rivalry between the Palestine Liberation Organization (PLO) and

Jordan in capturing the allegiance of the inhabitants of the West Bank and the Gaza Strip; the changing fortunes of the PLO and Jordan in these areas correspond directly with the changes in their relative recognition internationally and by Arab nations.

370. Rokach, Livia. ISRAELI STATE TERRORISM: AN ANALYSIS OF THE SHARETT DIARIES. *J. of Palestine Studies [Lebanon] 1980 9(3): 3-29.* Analyzes the diaries of Moshe Sharett (Shertok), first foreign minister of Israel and prime minister, 1954-55. The diaries show that Sharett, a moderate, was constantly at odds with Prime Minister David Ben-Gurion's methods in dealing with the Arab countries in the 1950's. P. J. Mattar

371. Rondot, Pierre. PALESTINE: PEACE TALKS AND MILITANCY. *World Today [Great Britain] 1974 30(9): 379-387.* "Since this article was written, the split in the Palestinian guerrilla movement has widened again. In Moscow at the end of July, Yasser Arafat secured renewed Soviet approval of the PLO's participation in the Geneva conference; but the extreme militants have accused him of selling out." J

372. Rondot, Pierre. QUELQUES ASPECTS DU PROBLEME PALESTINIEN [Some aspects of the Palestinian problem]. *Etudes [France] 1982 356(5): 581-594.* Examines the legitimacy of the Palestinian cause, the problem of defining Palestinian nationality and Palestinians' relationship with the land, the Palestinian resistance, the Palestine Liberation Organization and its charter, and the future of negotiations between the PLO and Israel.

373. Root, Anthony. SETTLEMENT OF THE IRANIAN HOSTAGE CRISIS: AN EXERCISE OF CONSTITUTIONAL AND STATUTORY EXECUTIVE PREROGATIVE IN FOREIGN AFFAIRS. *New York U. J. of Int. Law and Pol. 1981 13(4): 993-1048.* Examines the settlement of the Iranian hostage crisis, ended by an agreement signed on 19 January 1981 by the United States, exchanging Iranian assets frozen under Executive Order 12170 for the release of American hostages, concluding that although the action was legal, litigation will persist.

374. Rouleau, Eric. THE WANDERING PALESTINIANS. *Can. Dimension [Canada] 1973 9(6): 46-47, 62-63.* Examines the political strategy and ideology of Palestinians' guerrilla organizations since 1967, particularly the terrorism of the Black September group.

375. Rubinstein, C. L. THE LEBANON WAR: OBJECTIVES AND OUTCOMES. *Australian Outlook [Australia] 1983 37(1): 10-17.* National survival was not at stake in Israel's attack on the PLO in southern Lebanon in 1982; "Operation Galilee" was designed to remove the PLO from Lebanon as a prelude to negotiations over the Palestinians in Gaza and the West Bank. Considering the PLO's activities over the preceding 15 years and Arab insistence that Israel should not exist, the Israeli operation in 1982 was successful because it created opportunities for autonomous Palestinian units in Gaza and the West Bank, with Jordanian cooperation. Based on newspapers and secondary sources; 37 notes. W. D. McIntyre

376. Sayegh, Fayez A. THE CAMP DAVID AGREEMENT AND THE PALESTINE PROBLEM. *J. of Palestine Studies [Lebanon] 1979 8(2): 3-40.* Analyzes how the Camp David agreement of September 1978 dealt with the Palestinian problem. The agreement was a separate peace between Egypt and Israel, in which Palestinian national rights were ignored despite declarations to the contrary. The Camp David formula excluded three main Palestinian national rights recognized by the UN: the right of self-determination and independence; the right to appoint representatives (the Palestine Liberation Organization) to negotiate on their behalf; and the right of dispossessed and displaced people to return to their property. Therefore, the formula has condemned Palestinians to permanent exile and to permanent separation from each other. Based on the text of the Camp David agreement and press reports; 72 notes. P. J. Mattar

377. Sayeh, Mai; Aulas, Marie-Christine and Gadant, Monique, interviewers; Toelle, Heïdi, transl. CHOISIR LA REVOLUTION... [Choosing the revolution..]. *Mediterranean Peoples [France] 1983 (22-23): 149-155.* Summarizes a December 1982 interview with Mai Sayeh, member of the Union of Palestinian Women. Reviews the purpose of this organization and the personal history of Mai Sayeh, who was born in Gaza, studied in Cairo, lived with her husband and four children in Jordan and chose to join the revolution, the Palestinian Liberation Organization, in 1970 when the Palestinian refugees were cruelly repressed by King Hussein and his army.

378. Schachter, Oscar. SELF-HELP IN INTERNATIONAL LAW: U.S. ACTION IN THE IRANIAN HOSTAGES CRISIS. *J. of Int. Affairs 1984 37(2): 231-246.* The Iranian hostage crisis raises the question of whether unilateral retaliatory action against violators of international law becomes justified in law and policy when international institutions are unable to provide an adequate remedy.

379. Seikaly, Samir. PRIME MINISTER AND ASSASSIN: BUTRUS GHĀLĪ AND WARDĀNĪ. *Middle Eastern Studies [Great Britain] 1977 13(1): 112-123.* Traces the career, beginning in 1875, of Egypt's Coptic prime minister, Boutros Pasha (d. 1910); examines Coptic-Moslem antagonism, British policy and influences, and Boutros and Ibrahim Nasif al-Wardani as political symbols; and explains the evolution of Wardani from student to political assassin within the immediate political context of Anglo-Egyptian relations. The realization of Great Britain's monopoly of force elicited the antithesis of Egyptian violence, with Wardani the agent and Boutros Pasha the victim of assassination. 60 notes. R. B. Mendel

380. Sela, Abraham. THE PLO, THE WEST BANK AND THE GAZA STRIP. *Jerusalem Q. [Israel] 1978 (8): 66-77.* Discusses the emergence of new Palestinian organizations after 1967, the Palestine Liberation Organization's stress on political activism in the territories after 1970, and the impact of the establishment of the Palestine National Front in 1973.

381. Shapira, Anita. THE DEBATE IN MAPAI ON THE USE OF VIOLENCE: 1932-1935. *Zionism [Israel] 1981 2(1): 99-124.* Turmoil between

Revisionist Jewish workers and those of the Histadrut caused ugly and violent clashes repeatedly between 1932 and 1935. Mapai, a political body, was led by Histadrut members, forcing Mapai into the fray. By late 1934 much of the Mapai leadership was convinced that constant unrest and violence were not in the interests of Zionism, and conciliatory advances were offered. The Revisionists scoffed at these measures and militant Mapai and Histadrut members repudiated their leaders' positions. Several rising party leaders, including Golda Meyerson (Meir) and Berl Katznelson, decried the use of violence and warned of a fascist tendency in Israeli Jewish youth if continued. By 1935 the labor movement began to restrain its members. Such restraint allowed the labor movement to gain respect and regain its position as a central force in the Yishuv. Based primarily on documents of the Mapai Central Committee.

T. Koppel

382. Sharif, Regina. THE UNITED NATIONS AND PALESTINIAN RIGHTS, 1974-79. *J. of Palestine Studies [Lebanon] 1979 9(1): 21-45.* Examines the decisions and actions of the UN—particularly the Security Council, General Assembly, and Economic and Social Council, including subsidiaries such as the Commission on Human Rights, and specialized agencies such as the International Labor Organization—on the Palestine question. Since it gave observer status to the Palestine Liberation Organization (PLO) in 1974, the UN has repeatedly reaffirmed that the PLO is the sole representative of the Palestinian people and that the Palestinians should have the right of self-determination and national independence. Israel continues to obstruct these resolutions. Based on UN documents; 4 tables, 59 notes. P. J. Mattar

383. Shattan, Joseph J. ISRAEL, THE UNITED STATES, AND THE UNITED NATIONS. *World Affairs 1981 143(4): 335-345.* Describes anti-Zionist UN resolutions from 1975 to 1980, the role of the Palestine Liberation Organization, and President Ronald Reagan's resolution to bring an end to UN scapegoating of Israel.

384. Shuaibi, Issa al-. THE DEVELOPMENT OF PALESTINIAN ENTITY-CONSCIOUSNESS. *J. of Palestine Studies [Lebanon] 1980 9(2): 50-70, (3): 99-124.* Part 1. The Palestinian Arabs developed both a particularist nationalism and a more general Arab nationalism. They demanded an independent Palestinian state and, because of their common background with other Arabs, joined Arabs in their struggle for independence. The Palestinians found themselves stateless in 1948 but maintained their identity because they hoped to return to Palestine, and because the Arab countries were unable to absorb them. As hope for a return began to fade so did their identity, until after the 1956 war when a new organiation called Fatah (Palestinian Liberation Movement) began to remind the Palestinians of their identity. Based on the works of historian Izzat Darwaza, the journal *Filastinuna,* Fatah internal pamphlets, and other primary sources; 39 notes. Part 2. The establishment of the Palestine Liberation Organization (PLO) in 1964 heralded a fundamental stage in the political life of the Palestinians because the PLO embodied Palestinian national consciousness. As a consequence of the Arab defeat in the 1967 war, the PLO became more active militarily. The war evoked Palestinian consciousness on the East and West Bank of the Jordan river, where

Palestinians sought a Palestine state and where the PLO received widespread support. Part 3. Palestinian consciousness underwent important changes after the October War in 1973. The Palestinian resistance in 1974 set clearly defined goals and came close to accepting the concept of a Palestine entity on the West Bank. The PLO was recognized by the Arab countries, including Jordan, as the representative of the Palestinian people at Rabat in 1974. Few in Israel were convinced that the PLO represented the West Bank until 1976, when supporters of the PLO won municipal council elections in 24 towns of the West Bank. Such support for the PLO gave it more influence and credence in its demand for authority over the West Bank. Based on PLO documents, memoirs, and Palestinian, Israeli, and Arab press reports; 83 notes.

P. J. Mattar

385. Sisco, Joseph J. MIDDLE EAST: PROGRESS OR LOST OPPORTUNITY? *Foreign Affairs* 1983 61(3): 611-640. Discusses events in the Middle East during 1982. The Soviet presence in Afghanistan continued. The war between Iran and Iraq was unresolved, with Iran regaining most of its territory and assuming an offensive posture. Fighting broke out in Lebanon between Israeli and PLO forces, resulting in the withdrawal of PLO troops from Lebanon. The United States proposed a peace initiative to deal with the political future of the West Bank and Gaza. 2 notes.　　　　A. A. Englard

386. Smirnov, V. Iu. POLITICHESKIE PARTII IZRAILIA I NATSIONAL'NOE SAMOOPREDELENIE ARABSKOGO NARODA PALESTINY [Political parties of Israel and the national self-determination of the Arab people of Palestine]. *Narody Azii i Afriki [USSR]* 1980 (5): 40-51. Focuses on the desire of the Palestine Liberation Organization to create an independent state for the Palestinian Arabs, examining the views of other political parties, including the National Religious Party, the Labor Party, Likud, and the Israeli Communists on this issue. The Israeli Communists see themselves as the only party able to evaluate the situation correctly. They see a resolution of the Palestine problem by acknowledging the legal rights of the Palestinian Arabs as the only key to peace. Cites the 17th and 18th conferences of the Communist Party of Israel and other primary sources; 44 notes.　　　　S. J. Talalay

387. Sofer, Naim. THE POLITICAL STATUS OF JERUSALEM IN THE HASHEMITE KINGDOM OF JORDAN, 1948-1967. *Middle Eastern Studies [Great Britain]* 1976 12(1): 73-94. Jerusalem was not raised to an equal administrative status with Amman until 1955, and King Hussein did not establish his palace in Jerusalem until 1963, apparently because 1) it continued to be the center of foreign activities, e.g., the proclamation of Jerusalem as Israel's capital, establishment of Arab states' consulates, the meeting place of various Arab committees and organizations, etc.; 2) many Arab states supported internationalization; 3) it continued to be the center of opposition groups, including the Palestine Liberation Organization; 4) it continued to be the religious and cultural center of the West Bank; 5) it became a symbol of Palestinian demands in a kingdom where Palestinians outnumbered Jordanians two to one; and 6) because it symbolized the assassination of Hussein's grandfather, King Abdullah, which made Hussein hostile to the city (he was standing beside Abdullah when the latter was killed). Based on Jerusalem

newspaper accounts, some government documents, and secondary works; 85 notes, biblio. K. M. Bailor

388. Spiegel, Steven L. THE MIDDLE EAST: A CONSENSUS OF ERROR. *Commentary 1982 73(3): 15-24.* Examines the development of support in American political circles for Israeli accommodation of the Palestine Liberation Organization, and argues that this arises from a basically inaccurate perception of reality.

389. Starchenkov, G. TERRORIZM V TURTSII [Terrorism in Turkey]. *Aziia i Afrika Segodnia [USSR] 1981 (11): 39-41.* Discusses the social and economic causes of terrorism in Turkey.

390. Stein, Ted L. CONTEMPT, CRISIS, AND THE COURT: THE WORLD COURT AND THE HOSTAGE RESCUE ATTEMPT. *Am. J. of Int. Law 1982 76(3): 499-531.* Discusses legal basis and ramifications of the censure of the United States by the World Court for undertaking the 1980 military operation to liberate American diplomatic hostages held by Iran.

391. Stoakes, Frank. THE CIVIL WAR IN LEBANON. *World Today [Great Britain] 1976 32(1): 8-17.* Since Lebanon's independence in 1943, conflicts between Christians and Moslems, between the Palestine Liberation Organization and the rightist Kata'eb Party, and between social classes have been building and have resulted in the 1975 civil war.

392. Stoakes, Frank. THE SUPERVIGILANTES: THE LEBANESE KATAEB PARTY AS BUILDER, SURROGATE AND DEFENDER OF THE STATE. *Middle Eastern Studies [Great Britain] 1975 11(3): 215-236.* A former paramilitary youth movement, now comprised mostly of middle- and lower-class Maronites, constitutes Lebanon's largest and best organized party, with approximately 60,000 members. Since 1952, it has methodically pursued five means of preserving the state and advancing society, all dependent upon the incredible persistence, flexibility, and discipline of the party members: 1) improving the state machinery by total party support of its few cabinet ministers and members of parliament; 2) fostering public devotion to the state by "increasing and advertising" the benefits which the state supplies and by teaching these same benefits in the public schools; 3) neutralizing political confessionalism by economic and social reforms which will benefit all Lebanese; 4) consolidating relations with sympathetic foreign nations and convincing others of Lebanist Lebanon's good intentions, as well as its ability and determination to defend itself; and 5) protecting "the authority and reputation of the state from suspicion or attack by street demonstrations, party newspaper editorials, and by supporting the army with the party militia or, if necessary, by taking the army's place in maintaining a "Fortress Lebanon." This last self-appointed duty has, of course, involved the Kataeb militia in all of Lebanon's civil strife, including operations against the PLO. Based on fieldwork in Lebanon; 3 notes. K. M. Bailor

393. Stylianou, Petrou APOKALYPTIKA STOICHEIA KAI MARTYRIES GIA TĒ MACHĒ TOU NOSOKOMEIOU LEUKŌSIAS [Revealing

ghosts and martyrs in the fight of the Leukosia Hospital]. *Kypriakos Logos* [Cyprus] 1980 12(67-68): 157-166. Relates details concerning the murder of several members of the Cypriote terrorist organization EOKA during the night of 30-31 August 1956 in the main hospital of Leukosia. Provides details from the official transcript and from EOKA documents investigating these murders. Accuses the Special Branch from the British forces on Cyprus of unexplained intrigues concerning these particular murders. Based on published EOKA archival sources and newspaper accounts. W. D. Wrigley

394. Stylianou, Petrou. HĒ APOPEIRA APELEUTHERŌSĒS TŌN THANATOPOINITŌN KOUTSOFTA MAUROMMATĒ PANAGIDĒ CHOIROPOULĒ KAI HĒ APELEUTHERŌSĒ TOU HELLADITĒ "POLITIKOU KATADIKOU" AR. KARADĒMA [The emancipating trial of capital punishment for Koutsofta, Maurommates, Panagides, Choiropoules, and the emancipation of the Greek political prisoner Argeres Karademas]. *Kypriakos Logos* [Cyprus] 1980 12(67-68): 175-180. Describes the acts and trial of accused Cypriote terrorists Michael Koutsoftas, Stelios Maurommates, Andreas Panagides, Paraskeuas Choiropoules, and Argeres Karademas. Relates the details and chronological events of their last conspiracy against the British authorities in Cyprus on 14-15 August 1956. Based on published EOKA archival sources and newspaper accounts. W. D. Wrigley

395. Stylianou, Petrou. ME HYDROCHLŌRIKO OXY KAIONTAN TA KORMIA TŌN AGŌNISTŌN STA PHYLAKISMENA MNĒMATA [The hydrochloric acid regulation: the bodies of the fighters in the prisoners' tombs]. *Kypriakos Logos* [Cyprus] 1980 12(67-68): 131-136. Briefly relates the execution of Cypriot terrorists and the subsequent decay of their corpses in hydrochloric acid by the British authorities during the Cypriot struggle for independence in the 1950's. Provides a brief biography of the executed prisoners associated with the EOKA [Ethnike Organosis Kypriakou Agonos] terrorist organization. Secondary sources. W. D. Wrigley

396. Stylianou, Petrou. NEŌTERA DEDOMENA GIA TĒN HISTORIKĒ MACHĒ TOU LIOPETRIOUS [Modern facts concerning the historical fight of Liopetrios]. *Kypriakos Logos* [Cyprus] 1980 12(67-68): 137-144. Describes the terrorist ambush near the village of Liopetrios fought between the British forces and the Cypriot terrorists of Ethnike Organosis Kypriakou Agonos (EOKA) from 30 August to 2 September 1958. Relates the organization of the participating forces of EOKA and provides the names of the Cypriot commanders involved. Based on published archival sources of the terrorist organization EOKA. W. D. Wrigley

397. Susser, Asher. EMDAT HUSAYN B'SHEILAT ATID HAGEDA HA MA'ARAVIT [King Hussein's position on the future of the West Bank]. *Hamizrah Hehadash* [Israel] 1979 28(3-4): 239-243. King Hussein of Jordan is in an uncomfortable position. His power base in Amman is vulnerable if the Palestine Liberation Organization (PLO), recognized in 1974 as the "sole legitimate representative" of the Palestinian people, is to succeed at creating its own power base. Hussein's 1972 plan of federation for the two banks of the Jordan river called for an autonomous Palestinian region, but left the Amman

government dominant. This would preserve Hussein's power as well as his claims to be the last member of the Hashemite dynasty. Hussein believes that Palestinian self-determination should be decided by referendum, hoping that the population will decide against the PLO and for his own rule. Secondary sources; 32 notes. T. Koppel

398. Suudi, M. HET PALESTIJNSE CONFLICT [The Palestinian conflict]. *Spiegel Hist. [Netherlands] 1973 8(6): 366-373.* In spite of considerable Jewish migration to Palestine before and after World War II, the Arabs still had about 94% of the land in 1957. The Israelis deliberately planned the expulsion and pauperization of the Palestinian Arabs, through Plan Dalet, which was finally successfully implemented in 1967. The Palestine Liberation Organization will attempt to correct the injustices of the past and create a free and democratic Palestinian state. Biblio. G. D. Homan

399. Syrkin, Marie. HOW LONG THE PLO CAMPS? *Midstream 1982 28(7): 53-56.* Discusses the role of UNRWA in supporting Palestinian Arab refugee camps and questions to what degree the long-term support of a given group of refugees is the responsibility of the international community.

400. Syrkin, Marie. ISRAEL'S BORDERS: A SECRET PENTAGON MEMORANDUM. *Midstream 1983 29(5): 54-56.* Summarizes the consensus of opinion of the US Joint Chiefs of Staff regarding the possible expansion of Israel's boundaries in 1967, in order to permit effective defense against possible Arab attack and terrorist raids.

401. Tadayon, K. M. THE CHANGING IMAGE OF IRAN IN THE UNITED STATES: OPEN-ENDED-FORMAT SURVEYS BEFORE AND AFTER THE HOSTAGE CRISIS. *Gazette: Int. J. for Mass Communication Studies [Netherlands] 1982 30(2): 89-95.* In 1976 and again in 1981 an open-ended survey administered to college students asked them to complete the sentence, "When I think of Iran I think of...." Comparative content analysis of the responses shows that the respondents were deeply influenced by media coverage of the hostage crisis. Open-ended polls are less biased than closed-ended polls, such as the Gallop poll. 6 notes. J. Powell

402. Taylor, Alan R. THE PLO IN INTER-ARAB POLITICS. *J. of Palestine Studies [Lebanon] 1982 11(2): 70-81.* The Palestine Liberation Organization's relation to the Israeli conflict is as involved and complex as its relationship with the Arab world in general and with the superpowers. Analyzes the motives of the superpowers in their dealings with the PLO, the attitudes of the Arab states, and interregional rivalries and conflicts. In the regional sense the PLO has the major problem that it stands for change, whereas, in territorial matters, the Arab states support the status quo. Other difficulties are the attempts by various Arab regimes to influence or control the PLO and the resentment felt by some Arabs, such as the Lebanese, at the use of their lands as guerrilla bases for activities against Israel. Based on documentary sources, press reports, and secondary sources; 21 notes.
F. A. Clements

403. Thauby García, Fernando. CONFLICTO DEL SUR DEL LÍBANO [The conflict in southern Lebanon]. *Rev. de Marina [Chile] 1980 97(5): 420-426.* Reviews the political and military aims of the various factions active in southern Lebanon: the UN peacekeeping group, the Christian militias, Israel and the Palestine Liberation Organization, all acting on Lebanese territory not under Syrian control.

404. Toubi, Jamal. SOCIAL DYNAMICS IN WAR-TORN LEBANON. *Jerusalem Q. [Israel] 1980 (17): 83-109.* Discusses the socioeconomic organization of modern Lebanon and the strains placed on the cohesive pluralism of Lebanese society by the 1975-77 civil war between traditionalists and the forces supported by the Palestine Liberation Organization.

405. Turki, Fawaz. ARAFAT'S PLO ADOPTS NEW LOOK FOR THE PALESTINIAN MOVEMENT. *Int. Perspectives [Canada] 1975 (3): 11-14.* Describes the importance of the Palestine Liberation Organization in the lives of Palestinians, its recent rise to respectability, and the internal politics of its turn from terrorism to politics and diplomacy.

406. Turki, Fawaz. THE PASSIONS OF EXILE: THE PALESTINE CONGRESS OF NORTH AMERICA. *J. of Palestine Studies [Lebanon] 1980 9(4): 17-43.* Reports and analyzes the proceedings of the founding meeting of the Palestine Congress of North America which was held in 1979 in Washington, D.C. The meeting, attended by Palestinians living in North America, reflected the sentiments of several Palestinian political groups, but its policies were dominated by al-Fatah, the largest body in the Palestine Liberation Organization. Despite emotional protests, supporters of al-Fatah were able to change the wording of the preamble in the constitution from a call for independence and sovereignty "in all of Palestine" to "in Palestine," and they beat back an attempt to condemn "Arab reaction." The Congress was democratic and united against Zionism and for national self-determination. Based on the author's notes of the 1979 meeting. P. J. Mattar

407. Tzur, Daniel. LA GUERRA DEL LÍBANO: BUSCANDO LAS RAÍCES DEL CONFLICTO ÁRABE-ISRAELÍ [The war in Lebanon: searching for roots of the Arab-Israeli conflict]. *Estudios Centroamericanos [El Salvador] 1982 37(407-408): 879-896.* Examines the positions of the principal actors in the Arab-Israeli conflict and their strategic and tactical concepts. Maintains that the roots of the war in Lebanon are found in the basic problem of the Middle East since 1948, the question of the Palestinians. The Camp David Agreements, rather than a plan for peace in the zone, in reality represent part of the US strategy of confrontation with the Soviet Union and prepared the way for the Israeli invasion of Lebanon. Concludes with a list of implications of the conflict for Israel, the PLO, the United States, the USSR, Western Europe and the Arab countries. A chronology of events in the Middle East for 1947-82 is appended. R. L. Woodward, Jr.

408. Ullman, Richard H. AFTER RABAT: MIDDLE EAST RISKS AND AMERICAN ROLES. *Foreign Affairs 1975 53(2): 284-296.* The emergence of the Palestine Liberation Organization (PLO) from the Arab summit conference

in October 1974 as a Palestinian national entity was a destabilizing influence in the already tangled web of Middle Eastern politics. The risks of war are much greater, and with that, the time for American ambiguity in its Middle East policy is past. "Since the United States finds it politically impossible to wash its hands of Israel (one type of certainty), an overt and explicit commitment to Israel's defense—including even the stationing of U.S. military contingents in Israel—remains the most logical choice for those who would prevent a new war.... Beneath the umbrella of deterrence, regional political wounds have healed, and peace has been preserved." 3 notes. C. W. Olson

409. Varon, Benno Weiser. YESTERDAY'S WORLD TODAY: A REFLECTIVE MEMOIR. *Midstream 1976 22(2): 18-27*. Reviews the changing world power-bloc scene during 1942-75 regarding US and USSR attitudes toward Israel, the Arabs, and the Palestine Liberation Organization.

410. Vashitz, Joseph. TOWARDS CHANGES IN THE MIDDLE EAST. *Int. Problems [Israel] 1980 19(1-2): 18-20*. Discusses the dilemma confronting the Palestine Liberation Organization leadership over the establishment of an Arab Palestinian state since 1974 especially after President Anwar Sadat's journey to Jerusalem in 1977.

411. Walters, Ronald W. THE BLACK INITIATIVES IN THE MIDDLE EAST. *J. of Palestine Studies [Lebanon] 1981 10(2): 3-13*. The resignation of Andrew Young as US Ambassador to the UN in 1979 led to a backlash from the black community in the United States. The leaders of the Southern Christian Leadership Conference, Joseph Lowery and Walter Faintroy, accepted an invitation from Yasir Arafat of the Palestine Liberation Organization to meet with him in September 1979. Arafat made a favorable impression on the black leaders. Israel's snubbing these leaders, as well as Jesse Jackson, and Zionist support for the racist regimes will increase support for the Palestinians because blacks identify with victims of Western oppression. Secondary works; 6 notes. P. J. Mattar

412. Wasserstein, Bernard. NEW LIGHT ON THE MOYNE MURDER. *Midstream 1980 26(3): 30-38*. Briefly discusses the circumstances surrounding the assassination of Walter Edward Guinness, Lord Moyne, British Minister Resident in the Middle East, shot by two young Palestinian Jews 6 November 1944 in Cairo, and asks why the murder occurred, what Moyne's views on Jews and the Palestine problem were, and what the political consequences of his murder were.

413. Whitteridge, Gordon. AFGHANISTAN: BACKGROUND FOR THE VISITOR. *Asian Affairs [Great Britain] 1972 59(2): 147-152*. Presents a brief analysis of the history, economics, and social and political climate of Afghanistan. Details the principal events in the political history of a country of "autocracy tempered by assassination." S. H. Frank

414. Wilkinson, Paul. AFTER TEHRAN. *Contemporary Rev. [Great Britain] 1981 238(1385): 281-290*. Examines American and other diplomatic reactions to the Iranian hostage crisis of 1979-80.

415. Wolf, John B. BLACK SEPTEMBER: MILITANT PALESTINIANISM. *Current Hist.* 1973 64(377): 5-8, 37. Examines terrorism and the attention it has drawn to Arab Palestinian refugees.
P. J. Adler

416. Wright, Jeffrey W. TERRORISM: A MODE OF WARFARE. *Military-Rev.* 1984 64(10): 35-45. The October 1983 bombing of the marine headquarters in Beirut, Lebanon, has brought about changes in the US Army's doctrine of war. The Long Commission report of the incident found that the attack was both tactically and strategically effective while employing a minimum of force. Because such terrorist acts are capable of achieving the same objectives conventionally assigned to much larger forces, they should be classified as acts of war. Terrorism against the United States is increasing, particularly by Middle Eastern nations and groups. These acts pose a worldwide threat to US forces. The US Army should put as much emphasis on the study and prevention of terrorism as it does on other forms of warfare. Based on the *Report of the Department of Defense Commission on Beirut International Airport Terrorist Act, October 23, 1983* and newspaper reports; 64 notes.
J. Powell

417. Yodfat, Arieh. BERIT HAMO'ATSOT VEHA'IRGUNIM HAPALESTINIIM [The USSR and the Palestinian organizations]. *Hamizrah Hehadash [Israel]* 1975 25(4): 273-292. The USSR rejected the Palestine Liberation Organization (PLO) in 1964, but in 1969 began taking an interest in the Palestinian organizations. In 1974 the first official PLO delegation visited Moscow, but since 1969 Soviet policy has been to support a Palestinian state, with Israel's frontiers being redrawn according to the 1949 Armistice. Primary sources; 64 notes.
T. Sassoon

418. Yodfat, Arieh Y. TURKIYAH—MEDINIYUT, BA'AYOT WE-SIHSUHIM [Turkey: policy, problems, and conflicts]. *Int. Problems [Israel]* 1980 19(3-4): 8-18. Discusses the problems and crises Turkey faces on the way to modernization and development, such as high inflation, unemployment, economic recession, terrorism, violence, political instability, and the conflict with Greece.

419. Younger, Sam. THE SYRIAN STAKE IN LEBANON. *World Today [Great Britain]* 1976 32(11): 399-406. Examines strategic and territorial reasons for Syria's intervention in Lebanon against the Palestine Liberation Organization in 1976; asserts that Syria's national self-image and desire to form an alliance with Jordan against Israel were key factors.

420. Zabih, Sepehr. ASPECTS OF TERRORISM IN IRAN. *Ann. of the Am. Acad. of Pol. and Social Sci.* 1982 (463): 84-94. Traces the composition and ideological orientation of violent groups in Iran from the early 1900's. Describes the change from religious to Marxist-Islamic actors, the realignments of the forces of terrorism during and after the 1979 revolution and their international links.
J/S

421. Zamir, Meir. POLITICS AND VIOLENCE IN LEBANON. *Jerusalem Q. [Israel]* 1982 (25): 3-26. Traces the origin of the violence in Lebanon since

1975, examining not only the struggle between Muslims and Christians, but also the deep divisions that exist within both the Muslim and Christian communities.

422. —. A DISCUSSION WITH YASSER ARAFAT. *J. of Palestine Studies [Lebanon] 1982 11(2): 3-15.* Interview on the 18th anniversary of the Palestine Liberation Organization (PLO). Discusses the motivation for its establishment and reviews its progress. Centers on the international recognition now accorded to the PLO, the national unity of the Palestinians, and the changing attitude of Israel. Recognition of Israel is raised and rejected and future patterns of struggle assessed. Considers the role of France in the Middle East, the image of the Palestinian people, and Arafat's optimism. A translation from the Arabic of the main parts of an interview originally given for the *Revue d'Etudes Palestiniennes;* 5 notes. F. A. Clements

423. —. IRAN: CONSEQUENCES OF THE ABORTIVE ATTEMPT TO RESCUE THE AMERICAN HOSTAGES. *Conflict 1981 3(1): 55-77.* Discusses the impact of the unsuccessful 1980 attempt to rescue the hostages held in Iran on US relations with its allies, the position of Iranian moderates such as Bani-Sadr, Iran's relations with the USSR, and the US image in the Third World; outlines the planning of the rescue attempt from 1979.

4

ASIA AND THE PACIFIC REGION

424. Alpern, Stephen I. THE THAI MUSLIMS. *Asian Affairs 1974 1(4): 246-254.*

425. Baker, Edward J. POLITICS IN SOUTH KOREA. *Current Hist. 1982 81(474): 173-174, 177-178.* Discusses the assassination of South Korean President Park Chung-hee in 1979, his replacement by General Chun Doo-hwan, and US-Korean relations since the incident.

426. Beckert, Siegfried. REVOLUTIONÄR AN DER SEITE LENINS: WLADIMIR MICHAILOWITSCH SAGORSKI [A revolutionary at Lenin's side: Vladimir M. Zagorski]. *Beiträge zur Gesch. der Arbeiterbewegung [East Germany] 1982 24(6): 912-919.* Traces the life, career, and political activities of Zagorski (Lubotski, 1883-1919), who was killed by a bomb probably destined for Lenin. Sentenced to imprisonment for distributing leaflets in 1902, he escaped to Geneva, where he met Lenin. Traces his political activities with Lenin after 1904, his attachment to the Bolsheviks, his return to Moscow, his illegal activities for the Bolsheviks, and his arrest as a Russian spy in Karlsruhe in 1914. He was sent to a prisoner-of-war camp near Leipzig, where he remained until 1918, continuing his political activities within the camp. He returned to Moscow in 1918, was reunited with Lenin, and continued to work for the Party until his death. Based on letters and documents held in Moscow and secondary sources; 48 notes. G. L. Neville

427. Bergeron, Francis. ITINÉRAIRE D'UN "TERRORISTE" SOVIÉTIQUE [Itinerary of a Soviet terrorist]. *Écrits de Paris [France] 1979 (389): 64-68.* Tells the story of Vasili Sosnovski, a Soviet citizen constantly persecuted and frequently imprisoned by the KGB between 1958, when he was arrested for strolling near the Polish frontier, and 1977, when in desperation he hijacked an airplane to Stockholm, Sweden, where he is serving a four-year term.

428. Bergman, Jay. VERA ZASULICH, THE SHOOTING OF TREPOV AND THE GROWTH OF POLITICAL TERRORISM IN RUSSIA, 1878-1881. *Terrorism 1980 4(1-4): 25-51.* Analyzes the trial of Vera Zasulich for the shooting of the governor of St. Petersburg, Fëdor Trepov, which initiated a wave of political terrorism culminating in the assassination of Tsar Alexander II; the author corrects the interpretation of Trepov's shooting as political and explores Zasulich's motives for it.

429. Blackton, Charles S. SRI LANKA'S MARXISTS. *Problems of Communism 1973 22(1): 28-43.* Traces the history and development of the Marxist parties of Sri Lanka. In 1971 terrorist insurgency of the radical Marxist People's Liberation Front found the established Marxist leadership backing the government in its suppression of the uprising. This has created a dilemma for the Marxists that has not been resolved. Map, 47 notes. J. M. Lauber

430. Chakravarty, S. R. BENGAL REVOLUTIONARIES IN BURMA. *Q. Rev. of Hist. Studies [India] 1979-80 19(1-2): 42-49.* Before World War I Bengali revolutionaries initiated activities in Burma. After the war, branches of Bengali terrorist organizations, including the Anusilan Samities of Eastern Bengal and the Chittagong Samity, were established in Burma and in the 1920's and 1930's were vitally important to the anti-imperialist movement in Burma, although their impact declined in the late 1930's. Based on primary sources; 33 notes. W. T. Walker

431. Chakravarty, S. R. BHIKHU U. OTTAMA—AN ADVOCATE OF INDO-BURMESE FRIENDSHIP. *Q. Rev. of Hist. Studies [India] 1977-78 17(1): 36-42.* A review of the activities of Bhikhu U. Ottama, Burmese revolutionary. Ottama worked closely with Indian revolutionaries, for he knew that Burma could not achieve independence alone. He preferred the extremist, terrorist wing of the revolutionary group. As his activities increased, the British sought to capture him, but were unsuccessful. Ottama stayed on the move, moving from country to country. He opposed the separation of Burma from India until the British were overthrown. V. L. Human

432. Congdon, Lee. LUKÁCS, CAMUS, AND THE RUSSIAN TERRORISTS. *Continuity 1980 (1): 17-36.* While a comparison of contemporary world terrorists with Russian terrorists at the turn of the century demonstrates many similarities, the two groups differ substantially in terms of morality. The latter seemed less inclined to kill innocent people. They recognized that overthrowing the government was a noble end, but murder of uninvolved and harmless individuals was never a justifiable means. To support these conclusions, one can carefully analyze the writings of Georg Lukács *(The Theory of the Novel)* and Albert Camus *(The Just Assassins).* W. A. Wiegand

433. Diokno, José; Falk, Richard, interviewer. ON THE STRUGGLE FOR DEMOCRACY. *World Policy J. 1984 1(2): 433-445.* Presents the text of an interview of 26 October 1983 with José Diokno, a leader of the constitutional opposition to Ferdinand Marcos in the Philippines; the assassination of Benigno Aquino, Jr., has enlarged the base of opposition to the Marcos government, which will inevitably fall, creating a new political climate in which major changes in relations with the United States can be effected.

434. Fëdorov, V. "LEVYI" EKSTREMIZM V POLITICHESKOI ZHIZNI STRAN VOSTOKA [Left extremism in the political life of the Eastern countries]. *Aziia i Afrika Segodnia [USSR] 1983 (5): 13-16.* Describes the specific revolutionary groups, their typical desire to carry out immediate revolution, and their terrorist tactics.

435. Gibian, George; Naimark, Norman M., (commentary). TERROR IN RUSSIAN CULTURE AND LITERARY IMAGINATION. *Human Rights Q.* 1983 5(2): 191-198. Discusses Russian literature's reaction to terrorism.

436. Giffin, Frederick C. ALEXANDER PELL. *Social Sci.* 1976 51(2): 86-90. Alexander Pell was for a decade (1898-1908) one of the most popular academicians on the faculty of the University of South Dakota. A professor of mathematics and founding dean of the College of Engineering, he was described by one of his students as "one of the most humane men I have ever known." Neither Pell's students nor colleagues were aware that his real name was Sergei Degaev and that he was an exiled Russian terrorist who had fled to the United States after first betraying his revolutionary comrades and then taking part in the murder of the police official who had prompted his treachery. J

437. Gregor, A. James and Chang, Maria Hsia. TERRORISM: THE VIEW FROM TAIWAN. *Terrorism* 1981 5(3): 233-264. Describes the conditions that have faced the government of Taiwan since 1949, its beleaguered fortress mentality, emergency legislation, and antiterrorist measures, including restrictions on political and civil rights, taken in a period of protracted crisis.

438. Grigorenko, Petro. THE GHOST OF STALIN. *Freedom at Issue* 1979 (50): 14-16. In January 1979, after a secret trial, the USSR executed three citizens of Soviet Armenia accused, but undoubtedly innocent, of having caused the deaths of seven people by exploding a bomb in the Moscow subway in 1977. The KGB was clearly guilty of the blast, which was used for antidissident propaganda.

439. Gupta, Maya. A REVIEW OF REVOLUTIONARY TERRORISM IN INDIA, 1927-29. *J. of Indian Hist.* [India] 1977 55(3): 189-204. Reviews the activities of revolutionary terrorists in India conducted by the *Samitis* (secret societies). Although the leadership of India's independence movement was dedicated to nonviolence, a few young fanatics attempted to bring about political change by murder and intimidation. Recounts episodes of bombings, sabotage, and other attacks in Assam, Bengal, Bihar, Punjab, and Uttar Pradesh. Secondary sources; 53 notes. S. H. Frank

440. Hashmi, Tajul Islam. NEHRU AND SOCIALISM IN INDIA: A CRITICAL APPRAISAL. *Dacca U. Studies Part A* [Bangladesh] 1980 (32): 84-101. Examines the record of Jawaharlal Nehru (1889-1964), independent India's first prime minister, to ascertain whether he was a socialist, in the sense intended by Marx, Engels, and Lenin, rather than that of Bernard Shaw and the Webbs. Nehru was an admirer of Gandhi, who rejected socialism because of its emphasis on violence. He was a political leader in the Congress Party who cultivated the rich landholders for contributions to the party. He seemed to be sympathetic to the peasants and the proletariat but disinclined to be one of them. In power, Nehru appointed only Brahmins and wealthy persons to his cabinet. In short, Nehru was a social reformer, not a social revolutionary. 68 notes. J. V. Groves

441. Hildemeier, Manfred. ZUR SOZIALSTRUKTUR DER FÜHRUNGS-GRUPPEN UND ZUR TERRORISTISCHEN KAMPFMETHODE DER SOZIALREVOLUTIONÄREN PARTEI RUSSLANDS VOR 1917 [On the social structure of leadership groups and terrorist methods of struggle in the Social Revolutionary Party of Russia before 1917]. *Jahrbücher für Geschichte Osteuropas [West Germany] 1972 20(4): 516-550.* Examines how and why the Russian Social Revolutionary Party was defeated in the crucial months between March and October 1917. This party, composed largely of intellectuals, became isolated in its struggle for power, and its individual terror methods were too archaic to cope with the Bolshevist revolutionary system. Based on published sources; 158 notes. G. E. Pergl

442. Holler, Lyman E. "THEY SHOOT PEOPLE DON'T THEY?" A LOOK AT SOVIET TERRORIST MENTALITY. *Air U. Rev. 1981 32(6): 83-88.* Examines the cultural attitudes that affect the Russian perception and use of terrorism from the time of Ivan IV to the Revolution of 1917.

443. Holtzappel, Coen. THE 30 SEPTEMBER MOVEMENT: A POLITICAL MOVEMENT OF THE ARMED FORCES OR AN INTELLIGENCE OPERATION? *J. of Contemporary Asia [Sweden] 1979 9(2): 216-240.* Considers whether the Indonesian Army was correct in denying responsibility for the deaths of six top generals arrested on 30 September 1965. The responsibility for the generals' murder lies with unidentifiable members of the Indonesian Intelligence Services, who were perhaps collaborating with former members of one or more of the forbidden Indonesian political parties. 67 notes.
R. H. Detrick

444. Horielov, M. Ie.; Kamins'kyi, Ie. Ie.; and Koval'ov, V. V. POHLYBLENNIA KRYZY EMIHRANTS'KYKH ORHANIZATSII UKRAINS'KOHO BURZHUAZNOHO NATSIONALIZMU [The deepening crisis of Ukrainian bourgeois nationalist emigre organizations]. *Ukrains'kyi Istorychnyi Zhurnal [USSR] 1981 (8): 29-38.* Discusses the aims and activities of several Ukrainian emigre organizations, which still present a danger to the socialist brotherhood of nations, due to their propaganda, underground activities, and terrorist attacks against Soviet citizens and representatives abroad. L. Djakowska

445. Horner, Charles. THE FACTS ABOUT TERRORISM. *Commentary 1980 69(6): 40-45.* Discusses the involvement of governments with international terrorism, especially the role of the USSR in training, arming, and supporting international terrorists.

446. Indorf, Hans H. INSURGENCY PROBLEMS IN MALAYSIA DURING THE POST-VIETNAM ERA. *Asian Thought and Soc. 1976 1(2): 171-188.* Discusses patterns of Communist terrorism in Malaysia since 1930, its augmentation since 1974 due to the fragmented organization of indigenous Communists, and government repression which has aggravated racial tensions.

447. Islam, Syed Nazmul. THE CHITTAGONG HILL TRACTS IN BANGLADESH: INTEGRATIONAL CRISIS BETWEEN CENTER AND PE-

RIPHERY. *Asian Survey 1981 21(12): 1211-1222*. Since 1976, the law enforcement agencies in different parts of the Chittagong Hill Tracts (CHT) in Bangladesh have come under repeated attacks by the so-called Shanti Bahini [peace corps]. Among the complex reasons for this violence and the factors that have led to the emergence of the militant Shanti Bahini as a dissident force demanding full autonomy for the CHT, are accumulated grievances plus the resistance of aspiring tribal leaders to attempts by the national leadership to integrate the culturally divergent CHT with the otherwise homogeneous society of Bangladesh. Based on interviews, newspapers, and government documents.

M. A. Eide

448. Ivansky, Zeev. INDIVIDUAL TERROR: CONCEPT AND TYPOLOGY. *J. of Contemporary Hist. [Great Britain] 1977 12(1): 43-63*. Discusses three different types of terrorism in the modern era: those associated with anarchism, with social revolution, and with national liberation movements. The anarchist tends to act as lone wolf without organization. The social rebels and national liberals use violence as a milder substitute for mass revolution. In each case, Russian history furnishes a prototype. What has not been realized by the terrorist is that his actions usually have served only to inaugurate a reign of terror, not the vaunted liberation. Secondary sources; 36 notes.

M. P. Trauth

449. Ivansky, Zeev. PROVOCATION AT THE CENTER: A STUDY IN THE HISTORY OF COUNTER-TERROR. *Terrorism 1980 4(1-4): 53-88*. The Russian secret police had its origins in the French Revolution's Joseph Fouché, whose Third Republic heir, Louis Andrieux, advised the tsar on the use of agents provocateurs and counterrevolutionaries; the Okhrana under Minister of Interior Vyacheslav Plehve, while aiming at curtailing terrorism, perpetuated it.

450. Kahin, George McT. POLITICAL POLARIZATION IN SOUTH VIETNAM: U.S. POLICY IN THE POST-DIEM PERIOD. *Pacific Affairs [Canada] 1979-80 52(4): 647-673*. Analyzes the political levels of US intervention in South Vietnam from the overthrow of Ngo Dinh Diem to American disengagement. The US military and political leaders in Southeast Asia found it necessary to replace the key officials in Vietnam as each government in turn sought a viable political accommodation with the Viet Cong. The assassination of Ngo Dinh Diem was followed in November 1963 by the removal of General Duong Van Minh, then General Nguyen Khanh in February 1965 was followed by a government led by Marshall Ky and Nguyen Van Thieu, who retained American favor from mid-1965 to 1975. Each of these new governments was deemed necessary to maintain progress in hostilities against the government in North Vietnam. Secondary sources; 71 notes. S. H. Frank

451. Keep, John. EMANCIPATION BY THE AXE? PEASANT REVOLTS IN RUSSIAN THOUGHT AND LITERATURE. *Cahiers du Monde Russe et Soviétique [France] 1982 23(1): 45-61*. Contrary to widespread opinion, a continuous thread runs from the 17th- and 18th-century Russian peasant revolts to the agrarian revolutions of 1905 and 1917. The Razin legendary cycle, distorting Christian teaching, presents the "liberator" as

an avenging apostle. Russian writers from Pushkin on, and later social theorists, took up the theme of agrarian violence but were shocked by the brutal events of 1917-18. Early Soviet writers offered a critical portrait of the peasant revolutionaries, but the theme has since been neglected. A comparison of two novels on the Razin revolt illustrates changes in the offical ideology and Soviet literary taste; popular mythology is now manipulated for mundane political ends. J/S

452. Kelly, William E. SOVIET INTELLIGENCE SINCE WORLD WAR II, A SURVEY OF LITERATURE. *New Rev. of East European Hist.* [Canada] 1976 15-16(3-4, 1): 67-78. Works about the operation of the Committee of State Security (KGB) tend to cluster around the memoirs of intelligence chiefs or the autobiographies of defectors. Western intelligence officers such as John Barron or Lyman Kirkpatrick put more emphasis on the KGB's terrorist activities while defectors such as Kim Philby or Peter Deriabin dwell on the daily happenings of the intelligence business. 46 notes. W. L. Olbrich

453. Knight, Amy. FEMALE TERRORISTS IN THE RUSSIAN SOCIALIST REVOLUTIONARY PARTY. *Russian Rev.* 1979 38(2): 139-159. An analysis of the women terrorists among the Socialist Revolutionaries, who advocated terrorism as a means of overthrowing the tsarist state. Between 1905 and 1908, Socialist Revolutionary women carried out 11 acts of terrorism. They were totally committed to the revolutionary cause; their capacity for self-sacrifice was limitless. They often considered the revolution in personal terms. Their intense emotional faith in the cause and their will to martyrdom prevented them from analyzing their terrorist activities in terms of rational political objectives. 59 notes. M. R. Yerburgh

454. Kodikara, S. V. THE SEPARATIST EELAM MOVEMENT IN SRI LANKA: AN OVERVIEW. *India Q.* [India] 1981 37(2): 194-212. Tamil leaders have demanded a separate state, denominated Eelam, for Tamils in Sri Lanka since 1976 under the aegis of the Tamil United Liberation Front. They have also been concerned with the legal status of the Tamil language and citizenship requirements. Though Sinhala was the official language in 1956, in 1966 Tamil gained greater official status in the northern and eastern provinces. In 1975 the Tamil movement was split between the TULF's Gandhian approach and youthful terrorists organized as the Tiger Movement. In 1978 the republican constitution declared Sinhala the official language but accorded Tamil the title of national language. In 1980 government administration was decentralized, giving more power to the Tamil districts. Based on newspaper accounts and debate records of the House of Representatives and Constituent Assembly of Sri Lanka; 33 notes. J. Powell

455. Kowalewski, David. PROVINCIAL VIOLENCE IN POSTREVOLUTIONARY CHINA: A QUANTITATIVE STUDY. *Asian Survey* 1981 21(8): 885-900. Political violence seems as woven into the fabric of postrevolutionary China as into that of traditional China. Provincial violence is directly related to certain factors; for example, provinces in which the People's Liberation Army (PLA) played an influential role in civilian politics tended to experience greater levels of violence. Furthermore, the magnitude of violence

both during 1966-68 and during 1969-78 revealed that China's provinces seemed to learn violent or nonviolent lessons from events in the immediately preceding period. Based on newspapers and secondary sources; 15 notes, 8 tables.
M. A. Eide

456. Krahenbuhl, Margaret. THE TURKISH COMMUNISTS: SCHISM INSTEAD OF CONCILIATION. *Studies in Comparative Communism 1973 6(4): 405-413.* Irreconcilable differences within the Turkish Communist Party have continued. In the 1920's, rightists associated themselves with the Kemalist revolution and were ousted from the party. During the years of illegality, the party avoided splits. But in the 1960's, the party split into those pledged to evolutionary change and leftists who adopted terrorism. The split continued until a military coup in Turkey in 1971 cracked down on the leftists. 10 notes.
D. Balmuth

457. Krebs, Edward S. ASSASSINATION IN THE CHINESE REPUBLICAN REVOLUTIONARY MOVEMENT. *Pro. and Papers of the Georgia Assoc. of Hist. 1981: 111-134.* Studies two phases of assassination activity by the revolutionary movement in China, 1903-07 and 1910-12. Describes the political theory used to justify assassination. After the republic was established, the use of assassination as a political tactic declined, even among those advocating radical social change. Reprinted from *Ch'ing-shih wen-t'i (Ching Studies)* 1981 4(December) and presented in modified form at the 1981 meeting of the Southern Historical Association. 2 tables, 64 notes.
R. Grove

458. Lefort, Claude. D'UN DOUTE A L'AUTRE [From one doubt to another]. *Esprit [France] 1982 (6): 23-30.* Examines Maurice Merleau-Ponty's views of the USSR and the nature of Marxism in his *Humanisme et Terreur* and discusses his criticism of liberal humanism, or "abstract humanism," which accommodates violence in the occidental democracies and condemns it in societies that glorify violence and use it for the emancipation of the oppressed.

459. Lesure, Michel. LES MOUVEMENTS RÉVOLUTIONNAIRES RUSSES DE 1882 À 1910 D'APRÈS LES FONDS F7 DES ARCHIVES NATIONALES [Russian revolutionary movements from 1882 to 1910 according to source F7 in the Archives Nationales]. *Cahiers du Monde Russe et Soviétique [France] 1965 6(2): 279-326.* Classifies by subject and chronology documents amassed by the Sûreté Générale in Paris in 1882-1910. The diverse material includes letters, leaflets, programs of meetings, police reports, and resumés of informers' reports. Topics are anti-czarist demonstrations; the assassination of General Seliverstoff; explosives; Russian revolutionaries in the provinces; the congress of revolutionaries at Chen; and revolutionaries in Paris. Describes also activities in Switzerland; conferences and general activities of the revolutionaries; England 1887-1908; the revolutionary movement in Russia; underground press and propaganda; and translations of documents. Primary source; index, appendix.
P. T. Herman

460. L'vunin, Iu. A. IZ ISTORII SOZDANIIA I PERVYKH LET DEIATEL'NOSTI SOVETSKOI SEKTSII MEZHDUNARODNOI ORGANIZAT-

SII POMOSHCHI BORTSAM REVOLIUTSII (1922-1928) [The founding and early activities of the Soviet section of the International Organization for Aid to Fighters for Revolution, 1922-28]. *Vestnik Moskovskogo U., Seriia 9: Istoriia [USSR] 1973 28(1): 3-21.* Takes issue with the views of J. Martin Ryle's "International Red Aid and Comintern Strategy, 1922-1926," in *Int. Rev. of Social Hist. 1970 15(1): 43-68,* and cites some 50 Soviet and East European studies on this subject published between 1960 and 1972. The functions of the International Red Aid (MOPR) were to support revolutionaries jailed in capitalist countries; provide them and their families with moral, material, and legal aid; give refuge to dissidents fleeing to the USSR; and organize campaigns against bourgeois terrorism and reactionary forces fighting revolutionary movements. The author includes selected statistical data on the International Red Aid. 136 notes. N. Frenkley

461. Lyon, Peter. BANGLADESH SINCE MUJIB. *World Survey [Great Britain] 1976 (89/90): 1-15.* Discusses the political developments in Bangladesh since approximately 1945, the 1975 assassination of President Mujibur Rahman, and subsequent coups d'etat and analyzes the effects of the political unrest on Bangladesh foreign policy.

462. Marchese, Stelio. ALLE ORIGINI DEL TERRORISMO STRATEGICO [Origins of strategic terrorism]. *Storia e Pol. [Italy] 1982 21(2): 257-275.* It is difficult to distinguish the Chinese and Soviet influence on terrorism in the Near East after 1967, but it is certain that this influence sharpened the crisis in those places and underlined the international aspects of the question. Secondary sources; 17 notes. A. Canavero

463. Mitrokhin, L. V. and Raikov, A. V. TIUREMNYE ZAPISKI BKHAGAT SINGKHA [Bhagat Singh's prison notes]. *Narody Azii i Afriki [USSR] 1980 (3): 88-95.* Discusses the political evolution of Bhagat Singh (executed 23 March 1931) from Indian freedom fighter to a follower of Marxism-Leninism. A 200-page notebook shows Singh's growing absorption with ideals of a worldwide socialist revolution, abolition of capitalism, and establishment of people's control over the economy and natural resources. He came to reject the superficial nationalistic aspirations of his former coconspirators, condemned individual acts of terrorism, and endorsed Lenin's thesis that dialog with the enemy and compromise were acceptable tools in the early stages of revolution. 24 notes. N. Frenkley

464. Morell, David and Samudavanija, Chai-anan. THAILAND'S REVOLUTIONARY INSURGENCY: CHANGES IN LEADERSHIP POTENTIAL. *Asian Survey 1979 19(4): 315-332.* Among the many coups in Thailand since 1932, the 1976 military coup was the most significant in terms of violence and political implications. In response to it, students from varied class backgrounds, labor union members, farmer leaders, intellectuals, and some former government officials joined the Communist Party of Thailand, giving the revolutionary movement new leaders capable of sustained, disciplined action and thus enhancing the potential of the communist movement. 23 notes.
M. A. Eide

465. Mukherjee, Kalyan and Yadav, Rajendra Singh. FOR REASONS OF STATE: OPPRESSION AND RESISTANCE. A STUDY OF BHOJPUR PEASANTRY. *J. of Peasant Studies [Great Britain] 1982 9(3): 119-147.* Records the attempts by the state government, landlords, and the village upliftment movement to stamp out rural insurgency in the plains of Bhojpur, a district of south Bihar, between 1967 and 1977. The examples show how a political problem with socioeconomic roots was defined by the upper castes as a law and order problem, leading to inter-caste violence and atrocities by the police and upper-caste leaders with state connivance. Despite the belated admission of injustice by the state, the war in the plains was still continuing in 1979. A chapter from the authors' *Bhojpur: Naxalism in the Plains of Bihar;* biblio.
D. J. Nicholls

466. Nevada, Yosef. SOME ASPECTS OF INDIVIDUAL TERRORISM: A CASE STUDY OF THE SCHWARTZBARD AFFAIR. *Terrorism 1979 3(1-2): 69-80.* Examines the case of Shalom Schwartzbard, who assassinated Simon Petliura, chief Ataman in the Ukrainian Republican Army, in Paris in 1926 because of the latter's role in the murder of 1,500 Jews.

467. Perrie, Maureen. THE RUSSIAN PEASANTRY IN 1907-1908: A SURVEY BY THE SOCIALIST REVOLUTIONARY PARTY. *Hist. Workshop J. [Great Britain] 1977 4: 171-191.* Discusses the mood of the Russian peasantry, 1907-8, whose most militant elements were the middle and poor peasants who were in conflict with landowners over wages and rents. Examines peasant political attitudes to revolution, to the policies of the Socialist Revolutionaries, and to the use of violence and terrorism. Based on a political survey conducted by the central committee of the Socialist Revolutionaries which documents the political consciousness of the Russian peasantry, 1905-17; 16 notes.
C. A. McNeill

468. Plimak, E. G. and Khoros, V. G. "NARODNAIA VOLIA": ISTORIIA I SOVREMENNOST' [People's Will (Narodnaia Volia): its history and relationship to the present]. *Voprosy Filosofii [USSR] 1981 (5): 97-112.* Shows the negative consequences of the policy of terrorism pursued by both the authorities and the revolutionaries, analyzes the political doctrines of the Narodniks [Populists], discusses modern terrorism and some common features between it and the Russian prototype, the differences between today's terrorism and the policy of People's Will, and the absence of any justification for terror as a method of political struggle.

469. Pomper, Philip. NEČAEV, LENIN AND STALIN: THE PSYCHOLOGY OF LEADERSHIP. *Jahrbücher für Geschichte Osteuropas [West Germany] 1978 26(1): 11-30.* A study in comparative psychobiography and a critical review of some historians' attempts to link the methods of V. I. Lenin and Joseph Stalin on their way to power in Russia with those of Sergei Nechaev and his terrorist strategy in 1869-72. A paranoid leadership presents and will present an everpresent danger in eras of crisis. 58 notes.
G. E. Pergl

470. Raikov, A. V. M. K. GANDI I NATSIONAL'NYE REVOLIUTSIONERY [M. K. Gandhi and the national revolutionaries]. *Narody Azii i Afriki [USSR] 1976 (1): 59-72.* Analyzes the relations between Mahatma Gandhi and the national revolutionaries during the most difficult period in the national liberation movement, the 1920's. Gandhi viewed tactics of violence as impractical, developed principles of nonviolent struggle, and felt that it was India's mission to bring nonviolence to the world. Gandhi's party, the Indian National Congress, supported Gandhi, but in 1924 many of its members did not condemn the terrorist actions of the national revolutionaries. Due to this, polemics between Gandhi and the leaders of the national revolutionaries began in the newspaper *Young India,* in which Gandhi accused the revolutionaries of not having the support of the masses, criticized their violent actions as impractical and futile, and preached nonviolence. At the end of the 1920's national revolutionaries moved toward an interest in Communism, and their arguments with Gandhi switched from tactics to ideology. 50 notes.
L. Kalinowski

471. Reddy, N. Subba. CRISIS OF CONFIDENCE AMONG THE TRIBAL PEOPLE AND THE NAXALITE MOVEMENT IN SRIKAKULAM DISTRICT. *Human Organization 1977 36(2): 142-149.* Lying in the northeastern corner of Andhra State in India is the administrative unit called Srikakulam District, a hinterland inhabited by a tribal people numbering about 200,000. This area was the scene of an armed rebellion which lasted for two and a half years from the beginning of 1968 to the middle of 1970. The author analyzes the socioeconomic bases and the ethnopolitical aspects of the revolt of the tribal people that took the form of a guerrilla movement characterized by isolated acts of terrorism.
J

472. Rohlen, Thomas P. VIOLENCE AT YOKA HIGH SCHOOL: THE IMPLICATIONS FOR JAPANESE COALITION POLITICS OF THE CONFRONTATION BETWEEN THE COMMUNIST PARTY AND THE BURAKU LIBERATION LEAGUE. *Asian Survey 1976 16(7): 682-699.* Examines the effects which a split in the Buraku Liberation League (partially supported by the Socialists and partially supported by the Communists) had on national politics, especially the withdrawal of candidacy of Tokyo's leftist governor, Ryokichi Minobe, and the eruption of violence in a high school in Tajima in 1974 over the rights of Burakumin students.

473. Romaniecki, Leon. THE SOVIET UNION AND INTERNATIONAL TERRORISM. *Soviet Studies [Great Britain] 1974 26(3): 417-440.* Examines the evolution of the Soviet attitude to terrorism, considers some aspects of terrorism in relation to the modern concept of force and the self-determination of peoples, and relates the modern Soviet approach to terrorism to early Bolshevik revolutionary theory. From the beginning terrorism has been a part, though not always a significant part, of the "technique of action for the seizing and holding of power" for Bolsheviks. Refers particularly to international agreements on terrorism. Primary and secondary sources; 102 notes.
L. Brown

474. Sarkar, Tanika. POLITICS AND WOMEN IN BENGAL—THE CONDITIONS AND MEANING OF PARTICIPATION. *Indian Econ. and Social Hist. Rev. [India] 1984 21(1): 91-101.* The late 1920's and early 1930's saw the growth of a rich and highly complex spectrum of political experience in Bengal, including strikes, union building, peasant movements, civil disobedience, and terrorist activities. Women were active in all but union building and peasant movements. However, women's participation in civil disobedience and terrorist movements did not result in an increase of leadership roles because women's participation was thought to be temporary and an extension of their traditional role of religious service and sacrifice. Government reports and secondary works; 43 notes. J. V. Groves

475. Senn, Alfred Erich and Goldberg, Harold J. THE ASSASSINATION OF COUNT MIRBACH. *Can. Slavonic Papers [Canada] 1979 21(4): 438-445.* The assassination of Count Wilhelm von Mirbach, German ambassador to Soviet Russia, 6 July 1918, marked the final split between the Left Socialist Revolutionaries (SR's) and the Bolsheviks. The event is significant although the actual purpose and reasons for the murder remain undefined. Central to the event is the Bolshevik-supported Treaty of Brest-Litovsk, opposed by the Left SR's, who carried out the assassination, apparently hoping to disrupt German-Soviet relations and thereby negate the treaty. However, the Left SR's failed to generate an attempt to seize power, finding less Bolshevik opposition to the treaty than estimated. Lacking support and organization, the Left Socialist Revolutionary Party was weakened, violence increased, and the development of a one-party system strengthened. Secondary sources; 36 notes. French abstract. S

476. Shillony, Ben-Ami. PATTERNS OF VIOLENCE: POLITICAL TERRORISM IN PREWAR JAPAN. *Asian and African Studies [Israel] 1979 13(3): 242-263.* An analysis of 25 political assassinations in Japan between the Meiji Restoration and Pearl Harbor. These murders had little direct effect on politics until the late 1930's, and the terrorists themselves never obtained power. Based on Japanese sources; 2 tables, 88 notes. R. T. Brown

477. Shultz, Richard. THE LIMITS OF TERRORISM IN INSURGENCY WARFARE: THE CASE OF THE VIET CONG. *Polity 1978 11(1): 67-91.* Viet Cong terrorist tactics were employed with restraint and were secondary in importance to its military strategy of ideological and organizational restructuring of the countryside. J/S

478. Singh, Pakir. THE POLITICS OF COERCION: THE AKALI AGITATION OF 1960 AND 1961. *J. of the Hist. Soc. U. of Singapore 1969/70: 29-41.* A consideration of the political goals and methods of the Akali Dal Party in India. The Akali wanted a Sikh state with a comfortable Sikh majority and political control, not merely a distinct region. The Akali turned to violence because peaceful methods had not proved efficacious. The process took too long; the Indian government had time to plan and implement a considered response. Akali leader Tara Singh reacted by fasting, but Prime Minister Jawaharlal Nehru held firm, causing Singh to break his fast. Both

Singh and the Akali Dal consequently lost prestige. Based on secondary sources, 47 notes.
V. L. Human

479. Steinhoff, Patricia G. PORTRAIT OF A TERRORIST: AN INTERVIEW WITH KOZO OKAMOTO. *Asian Survey 1976 16(9): 830-845.* Psychological profile of Kozo Okamoto, a Japanese student who participated in a terrorist attack in a crowded Israeli airport, 1972; examines his heroes, thoughts on terrorism, and the background which led to his involvement with a radical organization, the Red Army Faction.

480. Takagi, Masayuki. RIGHT WING DRAWS PUBLIC ATTENTION. *Japan Q. [Japan] 1980 27(4): 479-486.* Recent reactionary tendencies in Japan have brought rightist groups back to public attention. There are about 600 organizations of this type in Japan, with a membership of about 120,000, of which active members total not more than 21,000. Their ultimate goal is the return to absolute power of the emperor and the revival of ultranationalism, including the resurrection of state Shinto. They also demand the return of the Northern territories. There is, however, little cooperation among these groups, many of them being parasitic, supported by corporations. They are anti-Communist, and direct their activities especially against the Japan Teachers' Union, resorting frequently to terrorist measures.
F. W. Iklé

481. VanderKroef, Justus M. INDONESIA'S POLITICAL PRISONERS. *Pacific Affairs [Canada] 1976-77 49(4): 625-647.* Analyzes the Orde Baru [new order] of General T. N. J. Suharto who replaced Achmed Sukarno as President of Indonesia in 1965. Under a rationale of unrelenting domestic anti-Communism, the new government ordered arrests, imprisonment, torture, and assassination of over a million political enemies. The treatment of "B" category prisoners on the remote island of Baru was inhumane. The author criticizes the inadequacies of food, poor medical service, severe overcrowding, and deprivation of legal rights suffered by enemies of the Suharto regime. Secondary sources; 49 notes.
S. H. Frank

482. Veber, Václav. ÚVAHY NAD MLÁDÍM J. V. STALINA [Thoughts about J. V. Stalin's youth]. *Dějiny a Součastnost [Czechoslovakia] 1969 11(5): 28-31.* Attempts to shed more light on the obscure youth of J. V. Stalin to see how these years influenced his character. Stalin had a very harsh adolescence, being the fourth son of an authoritative Georgian father and a pious mother. From 1901, when Stalin became an active revolutionary, until 1917, when he was liberated by the revolution, he exprinced prison, exile, escapes, terrorism and political struggle. Based on secondary sources.
G. E. Pergl

483. Veerathappa, K. MYSORE CHALO PALACE SATYAGRAHA (SEPTEMBER-OCTOBER, 1947). *J. of Indian Hist. [India] 1980 58(1-3): 233-251.* Narrates carefully the progress of the Mysore Chalo movement in attaining responsible government, a constitution, and the release of political prisoners through the use of satyagraha in September and October of 1947. Under the initial leadership of K. C. Reddy, satyagraha took on far more violence than was associated with Gandhi-led satyagraha. His opponent, the Diwan of the Maharaja of Mysore, Arcot Ramaswamy Mudaliyar, applied the familiar

tactics of bloodshed used by the British during the Quit India movement. The 41-day satyagraha's success hinged on the consistent and massive support of the people of the state of Mysore. 54 notes. J. F. Riddick

484. VonLaue, Theodore H. STALIN IN FOCUS. *Slavic Rev. 1983 42(3): 373-389.* Assesses Stalinist political terror, to put a humane, yet realistic and more complete face on events, personalities, and policies that reflect the turbulence of the Soviet body politic. Based on secondary sources; 21 notes.
R. B. Mendel

485. Weatherbee, Donald E. COMMUNIST REVOLUTIONARY VIOLENCE IN THE ASEAN STATES. *Asian Affairs: An Am. Rev. 1983 10(3): 1-17.* Surveys the Communist Party and its activities in Thailand, Malaysia, Singapore, Indonesia, and the Philippines. Determines that the most capable Communist Party is that in the Philippines. Attributes this to its isolation, self-reliance, leadership, and the dysfunction of Ferdinand Marcos's administration. Concludes that "urban terrorism" is the face of the future in the Association of Southeast Asian Nations (ASEAN) countries. 18 notes. R. B. Mendel

486. Wickramanayake, D. HARIJAN TERROR IN INDIA. *Plural Societies [Netherlands] 1975 6(3): 17-20.* Recent crimes of violence committed by Harijan (Untouchable) terrorists organized under the Naxalite movement in India, are an expression of their continued persecution despite state and federal government efforts to eradicate untouchability.

487. Yin Ch'ing-yao. A STUDY OF MAO'S THEORY "POLITICAL POWER GROWS OUT OF THE BARREL OF A GUN." *Issues & Studies [Taiwan] 1973 9(4): 48-56.* Describes the development of Communist theories of violent revolution for the overthrow of capitalism from ca. 1850 to Mao Tse-tung's thought in the 1970's.

488. Zasloff, Joseph J. and Brown, MacAlister. THE PASSION OF KAMPUCHEA. *Problems of Communism 1979 28(1): 28-44.* Investigates the nature of the radical Cambodian regime overthrown by a Vietnamese invasion force in January 1979. Analyzes the background and training of its leaders in an attempt to discover why the regime imposed deadly work camp conditions upon the Cambodian people and pursued a defiant, disastrous foreign policy toward its powerful Vietnamese neighbor. In all likelihood, Cambodian society will continue to confront political instability, violence, and social dislocation in the foreseeable future. Based on Cambodian and Western sources; 52 notes.
J. M. Lauber

489. —. THE KGB ABROAD: "WET AFFAIRS": SOVIET USE OF ASSASSINATION AND KIDNAPPING. *Survey [Great Britain] 1983 27: 68-79.* The Soviet Committee of State Security (KGB) has long resorted to "abduction and murder to combat what are considered to be actual or potential threats to the Soviet regime. These techniques, frequently designated as 'executive action' and known within the KGB as 'wet affairs' *(mokrye dela)*, can be and are employed abroad as well as within the borders of the USSR. They have been used against Soviet citizens, Soviet emigres and even foreign

nationals." Currently, the executive action component of the Soviet government is located in the Thirteenth Department of the KGB intelligence directorate (First Chief Directorate). Reprint of a declassified CIA report to J. Lee Rankin, General Counsel of the President's Commission on the Assassination of President Kennedy. L. J. Klass

490. —. MATERIALS ON MASSACRE OF KOREAN OFFICIALS IN RANGOON. *Korea & World Affairs [South Korea] 1983 7(4): 735-764.* The terrorist bombing in the national shrine of Burma in Rangoon on 9 October 1983 killed 17 high officials of the Republic of Korea, including four cabinet ministers; official statements and reports are reprinted from *Massacre in Rangoon: North Korean Terrorism* (1983), compiled by the Korean Overseas Information Service, the *Korea Times,* and other international newspapers and magazines.

5

LATIN AMERICA AND THE WEST INDIES

491. Aguilera Peralta, Gabriel. EFECTOS CUANTITATIVOS DE LA POLÍTICA DEL TERROR DEL ESTADO GUATEMALTECO EN RELACIÓN AL MOVIMIENTO POPULAR [Quantitative effects of state political terror in Guatemala in relation to the popular movement]. *Estudios Sociales Centroamericanos [Costa Rica] 1980 9(27): 217-249.* Violence in Guatemala is related to the matter of state political terror as a means of social control. Especially since 1966, this violence is linked to the lack of legitimacy which the elite requires to conserve itself. This tactic of very violent repression via institutional mechanisms has taken on the permanent stamp of counterinsurgency. Political violence is exercised principally against the popular sectors of the population. Based on Guatemalan newspapers, other primary and secondary printed sources; 11 tables, 31 notes. T. D. Schoonover

492. Alba, Carlos. NATIONALISM IS CONTRARY TO NATIONAL INTERESTS. *World Marxist Rev. [Canada] 1973 16(7): 75-83.* Analyzes the present Bolivian Nationalist Popular Front government terrorist tactics. Continuing series on "Political Portrait of Latin America."

493. Anderson, Thomas P. THE AMBIGUITIES OF POLITICAL TERRORISM IN CENTRAL AMERICA. *Terrorism 1980 4(1-4): 267-276.* Considers the difficulty of labeling Central American terrorism as either right or left, a situation complicated by international factors such as connections with the Palestine Liberation Organization or Cuban exile groups.

494. Angell, Alan. THE CHILEAN ROAD TO MILITARISM. *Int. J. [Canada] 1974 29(3): 393-411.* Explains the unexpected brutality of the counterrevolution following the long-expected fall of the Allende government. 15 notes. R. V. Kubicek

495. Asencio, Diego C.; Livingstone, Susan Morrisey, interviewer. TERRORISM: "THE ORIGINAL CHEAP SHOT." *World Affairs 1983 146(1): 42-53.* An interview with US ambassador to Colombia Diego C. Asencio on the impact of terrorism on the conduct of diplomacy, the adequacy of US counterterrorism policies, and his own experience as a terrorist victim; Asencio was one of 50 hostages when the Colombian terrorist group, M-19, captured the Dominican Embassy in Bogota on 27 February 1980.

496. Barkey, David W. and Eitzen, D. Stanley. TOWARD AN ASSESSMENT OF MULTI-NATIONAL CORPORATE SOCIAL EXPENDITURES IN RELATION TO POLITICAL STABILITY AND TERRORIST ACTIVITY: THE ARGENTINE CASE. *Inter-American Econ. Affairs 1981 34(4): 77-90.* Describes the reactions of multinational corporations to terrorist harrassment in Argentina, 1955-80, focusing on corporate social welfare programs during and after terrorist activity. The social expenditures of corporations do not necessarily increase in response to terrorism.

497. Bicheno, H. E. ANTI-PARLIAMENTARY THEMES IN CHILEAN HISTORY: 1920-70. *Government and Opposition [Great Britain] 1972 7(3): 351-388.* Discusses assassinations and political conspiracies against parliamentary institutions of Chile, 1920-70, emphasizing social class issues.

498. Booth, John A. A GUATEMALAN NIGHTMARE: LEVELS OF POLITICAL VIOLENCE, 1966-1972. *J. of Interamerican Studies and World Affairs 1980 22(2): 195-225.* By 1971 perhaps 50 persons per month were meeting violent politically related deaths in Guatemala, perhaps the peak in a long, continuing nightmare of political violence. Areas of Guatemala which seem to have balanced left- and right-wing political factions have experienced the highest levels of violence. Social change as measured did not contribute in a major way to the level of violence. Until competing elites develop institutional solutions for conflict, which seems unlikely, peace will probably elude Guatemala. Based on newspapers, magazines, and US State Department documents; 5 tables, 2 fig., 12 notes, ref.   T. D. Schoonover

499. Booth, John A. LA VIOLENCIA RURAL EN COLOMBIA: 1948-1963 [Rural violence in Colombia, 1948-63]. *América Latina [Brazil] 1972 15(1-4): 58-74.* Rural violence in Colombia has peaked when the Conservative and Liberal parties share equal electoral strength. Changes in the socioeconomic levels also produce violence, and the more change, the more intense and prolonged the violence. The period of *La Violencia* after 1958 was a period of pronounced rural socioeconomic change, with the concomitant establishment of the unique Frente Nacional, alternating government leadership between the two parties. Secondary sources; 4 charts, 25 notes.
C. B. Fitzgerald

500. Bourdillat, Nicole. DICTATURE ET OPPOSITION AU SALVADOR (25 JANVIER 1961-15 OCTOBRE 1979) [Dictatorship and opposition in El Salvador: 25 January 1961-15 October 1979]. *Problèmes d'Amérique Latine [France] 1980 57(4579-4580): 7-28.* Discusses the context and phases of the political situation in El Salvador which have led to the present civil war: the establishment of a military regime in 1961, the victory of the opposition in legislative elections in 1972, and the military's use of violence which has increased since the last military coup in 1979.

501. Brockman, James R. OSCAR ROMERO: PARADIGM OF THE NEW LATIN AMERICAN CHURCH. *Thought 1984 59(233): 195-204.* Oscar Romero became Archbishop of San Salvador, capital of El Salvador, on 22 February 1977. He was murdered by assassins of the Right on 24 March

1980. The author chronicles his development from a discreet, spiritually-oriented pastor into a champion of social change and human rights within the Catholic Church and in the relations of the Church to the government. 33 notes. R. Grove

502. Cabrer i Pallas, R. EL CAS DEL LÍDER ASSASSINAT [The case of the murdered leader]. *Xaloc [Mexico] 1979 (101): 36-43.* Analyzes the background and new tactics leading to Leon Trotsky's assassination in Mexico in 1940 and the political situation in Barcelona at that time.

503. Campbell, Trevor A. THE MAKING OF AN ORGANIC INTELLECTUAL: WALTER RODNEY (1942-1980). *Latin Am. Perspectives 1981 8(1): 49-63.* Traces the career of Walter Rodney, historian and leader of the Marxist opposition party, the Working People's Alliance in Guyana, who was killed in a bomb blast in 1980. 13 notes, biblio. J. F. Vivian

504. Centro Universitario de Documentación e Información (CUD). LA VIOLACION DE LOS DERECHOS HUMANOS EN EL SALVADOR [The violation of human rights in El Salvador]. *Estudios Centroamericanos [El Salvador] 1982 37(403-404): 543-556.* Presents statistical data on violation of human rights in El Salvador during the period 1980-82. The figures on deaths, tortures, and missing persons are based on proven and declared facts. The real numbers could be significantly higher. The authors comment on the legislation and juridical system that allowed widespread violation of human rights in the period and conclude that violations of human rights have reached a magnitude hitherto unknown in the history of the country. Despite the recognition of the problem by the US Congress, the US government has supported these violations. Based on primary sources; biblio., 9 tables, graph, 4 photos.
R. L. Woodward, Jr.

505. Chandisingh, Rajendra. THE STATE, THE ECONOMY, AND TYPE OF RULE IN GUYANA: AN ASSESSMENT OF GUYANA'S "SOCIALIST REVOLUTION." *Latin Am. Perspectives 1983 10(4): 59-74.* The People's National Congress (PNC) has failed to deliver the promised "socialist revolution" in Guyana, although it has exercised a monopoly of power since 1970. The assassination in 1980 of Walter Rodney, leader of the Working People's Alliance (WPA), has strengthened opposition groups and driven the government to depend on police and the recently created military forces. 5 notes, 2 tables, biblio. J. F. Vivian

506. Deiner, John T. RADICALISM IN THE ARGENTINE CATHOLIC CHURCH. *Government and Opposition [Great Britain] 1975 10(1): 70-89.* Discusses the political doctrines of the Argentine Catholic Church and the Movement of Priests for the Third World, particularly focusing on the violence which has occurred in Argentina since 1969.

507. Ellner, Steve. POLITICAL PARTY DYNAMICS IN VENEZUELA AND THE OUTBREAK OF GUERRILLA WARFARE. *Inter-American Econ. Affairs 1980 34(2): 3-24.* Examines the relations between the leftists (Venezuelan Communist Party and Movimiento de Izquierdo Revolucionaria)

and the moderates in Venezuela from General Marcos Pérez Jiménez's forced departure in 1958 to President Rafael Caldera's fulfillment of an election promise in 1969 to legalize the two leftist parties and to grant amnesty to leftists not involved in terrorist activities; explains why the attempts to unite leftist and moderate political parties of the opposition failed.

508. Fleurant, Gerdes. THE PRESENT SITUATION IN HAITI AND ANTI-DUVALIER STRUGGLE. *Pan-African J. [Kenya] 1975 8(4): 355-370.* The period 1957-74 was marked by sinister political repression, violence, and corruption in Haiti under the dictatorship of the Duvalier family. This situation conforms to the existence of a feudal socioeconomic structure dating from the colonial period, and to the growing US influence in the economic and political life of Haiti. Thousands of people have been imprisoned, and large numbers of Haitians have fled the country. An anti-Duvalier political opposition has developed among the one million Haitian emigrés. The aim of the struggle is not only the overthrow of Duvalierism but the complete liberation of the Haitian people. R. G. Neville

509. Galich, Manuel. NICARAGUA 1933-1936: GESTACIÓN Y NACIMIENTO DE LA DINASTÍA [Nicaragua 1933-36: gestation and birth of the dynasty]. *Casa de las Américas [Cuba] 1979 20(117): 65-75.* A study of Anastasio Somoza's rise to power from the death of Augusto César Sandino to his occupation of the presidency. Key factors in his rise to power were the control of the National Guard, trained by US marines; US-supervised elections in 1928 and 1932, and the assassination of Sandino. By means of instigated internal disorders, Somoza and his National Guard removed Juan Bautista Sacasa in 1936 and took over the presidency on 1 January 1937. Based on writings of Juan Bautista Sacasa, Anastasio Somoza, and contemporary journal articles; 6 notes. H. J. Miller

510. Gerlach, Allen. EL SALVADOR: BACKGROUND TO THE VIOLENCE. *Contemporary Rev. [Great Britain] 1981 239(1386): 1-7.* Discusses the socioeconomic problems which are the underlying causes of the political violence in El Salvador in 1980.

511. Gilhodès, Pierre. LA VIOLENCE EN COLOMBIE, BANDITISME ET GUERRE SOCIALE [La Violencia in Colombia, banditry and social war]. *Cahiers du Monde Hispanique et Luso-Brésilien [France] 1976 26: 70-81.* A critical study of *La Violencia* in Colombia as a peasant uprising and harsh interparty competition, comparing it to the Zapatista revolution in Mexico or the Vietnamese civil war. Defines *La Violencia* as a confused accumulation of thefts, rapes, assassinations, tortures, forced migrations, arrests, and military occupations within the indefinite dates of about 1946-64. The assassination of liberal leftist leader Jorge Eliécer Gaitán (1948) marked one of the first stages. Conservative pressure and police activity to control popular mobilization ensued, but the new government of General Gustavo Rojas Pinilla had difficulty handling the growing Communist activity, 1953-58. Outlines the final degeneration of the guerrilla warfare into banditry in the early 1960's. Concludes that the *Violencia* brought important social effects, such as accelerated urbanization, liberalization of the labor force, and a rise in peasant

consciousness and effectiveness in national political affairs. 2 charts, 8 notes.

S. Sevilla

512. Goodsell, James Nelson. GUATEMALA: EDGE OF AN ABYSS? *Current Hist.* 1972 62(366): 104-108. Discusses political instability, leftism, terrorism, and the suppression of dissent in the military government of President Carlos Manuel Araña in Guatemala in 1971.

513. Govea, Rodger M. and West, Gerald T. RIOT CONTAGION IN LATIN AMERICA, 1949-1963. *J. of Conflict Resolution* 1981 25(2): 349-368. Discusses contagion as a model for explaining political violence and finds that it explains the frequency of riots in six out of 20 Latin American countries studied.

514. Janke, Peter. TERRORISM IN ARGENTINA. *J. of the Royal United Services Inst. for Defence Studies [Great Britain]* 1974 119(3): 43-48. Describes and analyzes the activities of the Trotskyist People's Revolutionary Army (ERP) and its guerrilla warfare in Argentina since 1968. ERP's tactics have included kidnapping for ransom or propaganda effect and minor military actions. The aim of the ERP's terrorist policies is "to provoke the government into over-reacting so as to drive the country's left wing generally into a common policy of violence."

D. H. Murdoch

515. Johnson, Kenneth F. ON THE GUATEMALAN POLITICAL VIOLENCE. *Pol. and Soc.* 1973 4(1): 55-82. A case study that explores the variables in the relationship between land tenure and political violence in Guatemala. The elite's assumption of an "amoral" position in asserting their right to use violence to suppress all challenges to their regime and control of the land evoked terrorist tactics by the challengers. Both sides have accepted violence as a way of life. The role of the United States in the institutionalization of violence in Guatemala and its psychological effects upon its citizens also is examined. Primary and secondary sources; 61 notes, appendix.

D. G. Nielson

516. Kirichenko, V. SSHA I VOENNO-DIKTATORSKIE REZHIMY V LATINSKOI AMERIKE [The United States and military dictatorships in Latin America]. *Voenno-Istoricheskii Zhurnal [USSR]* 1981 23(5): 54-58. Recent strengthening of liberation and democratic movements in Latin America seriously threatens American imperialism and its regional representatives. Political awareness has been raised by the success of socialism in Cuba. Mexico, Colombia, and Ecuador remain bourgeois-democracies; Chile, Paraguay, Guatemala, and others remain military-fascist dictatorships due to long and damaging economic dependence on the United States, which purports to stand on the side of human rights while employing in Latin America the terrorist methods it condemns. Historical experience shows that such colonialism inevitably leads to national liberation from within. Based on articles in *Pravda, El Tiempo,* the *New York Times,* and other newspapers; 20 notes.

L. Smith

517. Klette, Immanuel J. U.S. ASSISTANCE TO VENEZUELA AND CHILE IN COMBATTING INSURGENCY, 1963-1964: TWO CASES. *Conflict 1982 3(4): 227-244.* Discusses US military aid sent to Venezuela and Chile during 1963-64 to insure peaceful elections in Venezuela in response to the activities of Fidel Castro's Fuerzas Armadas de Liberacion Nacional (FALN), and to insure peaceful elections in Chile in 1964 because Castro had supported Dr. Salvador Allende, leader of the leftist Popular Action Front.

518. LeBot, Yvon. GUATEMALA: LUTTES SOCIALES SUR HORIZON DE GUERRE (1973-1982) [Guatemala: social struggles on the brink of war, 1973-82]. *Problèmes d'Amérique Latine [France] 1983 (67): 93-113.* Focuses on the revival of trade unions in Guatemala after 1973 and their campaign for workers' rights, which has become increasingly political, especially since the massacres of Indian peasants and the widespread assassination of union leaders after 1979-80.

519. Lefever, Ernest W. MURDER IN MONTEVIDEO: THE AID/MITRIONE STORY. *Freedom At Issue 1973 (21): 14-16.* Defense of the U.S. Agency for International Development's "public safety program" against criticisms from Uruguayan leftists. S

520. Leich, Marian Nash. CONTEMPORARY PRACTICE OF THE UNITED STATES RELATING TO INTERNATIONAL LAW. *Am. J. of Int. Law 1983 77(4): 875-877.* Examines US interpretation of international law on the issue of deporting Cuban refugees who are ineligible to remain in the United States, and on the problem of obtaining information on the fate of persons who hijack airplanes to Cuba.

521. Levine, Daniel H. REVIEW ESSAY: RELIGION AND POLITICS, RECENT WORKS. *J. of Inter-Am. Studies and World Affairs 1974 16(4): 497-507.* A number of recent books on the relationship of politics and religion in Latin America conclude that individual Christians cannot avoid involvement in the political activities of their countries. Consequently, many difficult questions have arisen such as the relationship of Catholic lay groups to the institutionalized church and the relation of Catholics to Marxism. Further, Catholics are confronted with the dilemma of whether to use force and violence to attain political objectives. Based on the five books reviewed and secondary works; 11 notes, biblio. J. R. Thomas

522. Livingstone, Neil C. DEATH SQUADS. *World Affairs 1983-84 146(3): 239-248.* Since the 1950's, anti-Communist terrorism in Latin America has been characterized by the appearance of death squads that have often been allied to conservative governments.

523. Livingstone, Susan Morrisey. TERRORISM: "THE ORIGINAL CHEAP SHOT." *World Affairs 1983 146(1): 42-53.* Prints an interview with US Ambassador Diego C. Asencio on 5 August 1983. Covers his personal perspectives on the impact of terrorism on the conduct of diplomacy, his comments on the adequacy of US counterterrorism, and his reflections on his own experience as a terrorist victim, when the Colombian terrorist group M-19

captured the Dominican Embassy in Bogotá on 27 February 1980 and with it 50 hostages, including Ambassador Asencio and the ambassadors of 14 other nations.

524. López Vallecillos, Italo. REFLEXIONES SOBRE LA VIOLENCIA EN EL SALVADOR [Reflections on violence in El Salvador]. *Estudios Centro Americanos [El Salvador] 1976 31(327-328): 9-30.* Gives social, political, and economic antecedents to institutional violence in El Salvador since 1900, focusing particularly on government violence since the 1930's.

525. Maechling, Charles, Jr. THE ARGENTINE PARIAH. *Foreign Policy 1981-82 (45): 69-83.* Traces 30 years of political chaos and four years of terrorism and repression in Argentina and examines its serious economic problems, political strife, and repressive military government, which give the Argentine military regime of the early 1980's little future and provide little common ground for US-Argentine friendship. The attempts of President Ronald Reagan's administration to bridge the gap bring no benefit to the United States, and the United States should instead keep relations on a "cool, correct, and impersonal plane." M. K. Jones

526. Maingot, Anthony P. OPTIONS FOR GRENADA: THE NEED TO BE CAUTIOUS. *Caribbean Rev. 1983 12(4): 24-28.* An analysis of the political events in Grenada leading up to the assassination of Prime Minister Maurice Bishop, the US invasion, and reflections on the future.

527. Martín-Baró, Ignacio. EL LIDERAZGO DE MONSEÑOR ROMERO (UN ANÁLISIS PSICO-SOCIAL) [The leadership of Monsignor Romero: a psychosocial analysis]. *Estudios Centroamericanos [El Salvador] 1981 36(389): 151-172.* Neither his personality nor his previous experience as a priest and bishop adequately explain the extraordinary leadership of Archbishop Oscar Romero of San Salvador. Confrontation with historic events and demands brought out his distinctive characteristics. In the face of public disunity engendered by the authorities, Romero served as a social unifier at both the spiritual and political levels. Opposing oppression, Romero became a revolutionary symbol, challenging the dominant ideology and, by his example and words, promoting radical social changes. His assassination assured his influence, which continues to animate the struggle of the Salvadoran people for liberty and justice. Biblio. R. L. Woodward, Jr.

528. McDonald, Ronald H. ELECTORAL POLITICS AND URUGUAYAN POLITICAL DECAY. *Inter-Am. Econ. Affairs 1972 26(1): 25-45.*

529. McDonald, Ronald H. THE RISE OF MILITARY POLITICS IN URUGUAY. *Inter-Am. Econ. Affairs 1975 28(4): 25-43.* Traces the military's rise and route to political power in Uruguay, emphasizing the role of Tupamaro violence and the political deinstitutionalization of Uruguay by its military. Primary and secondary sources; table, 31 notes. D. A. Franz

530. Millett, Richard. ANASTASIO SOMOZA GARCÍA, FUNDADOR DE LA DINASTÍA SOMOZA EN NICARAGUA [Anastasio Somoza Gar-

cía, founder of the Somoza dynasty in Nicaragua]. *Estudios Centro Americanos [El Salvador] 1975 30(326): 725-741.* Discusses the influence in Nicaragua of the dynasty founded by Anastasio Somoza García (1896-1956), showing that the political power of the Somoza family did not end with the assassination of Anastasio Somoza García in 1956.

531. Millett, Richard. THE POLITICS OF VIOLENCE: GUATEMALA AND EL SALVADOR. *Current Hist. 1981 80(463): 70-74, 88.* Traces the causes of past and present political violence in El Salvador and Guatemala, and analyzes the politics of the successive governments in the 1970's in their attempts to alleviate economic and social problems, commenting also on US involvement in these countries.

532. Mottet, George J. EL URUGUAY Y LAS GUERRILLAS URBANAS [Uruguay and urban guerrillas]. *Lock Haven R. 1973 (14): 21-35.* Presents a brief history of the Tupamaros, their motives and ideology. S

533. Navarro, Vicente. GENOCIDE IN EL SALVADOR. *Monthly Rev. 1981 32(11): 1-16.* Describes the reign of terror being carried on by the current military junta in El Salvador, including widespread murder and torture of citizens and agrarian reforms designed to control the peasantry, the US role in providing military and economic aid to the terrorists, and the efforts of armed struggles of liberation in El Salvador since the early 1970's.

534. Oliveira, Sergio L. d'. URUGUAY AND THE TUPAMARO MYTH. *Military R. 1973 53(4): 25-36.* Describes the development of Uruguay's subversive Tupamaro movement. The Tupamaros reached their peak strength in 1971 and then declined as a result of their own vulnerabilities and effective government antisubversive measures. These measures included assignment of the principal antisubversive mission to the armed forces, adequate legislation, and creation of functional organizations to cope with subversive activity. 4 illus., table. J. K. Ohl

535. Pastorino, Enrique. STOP THE TERROR! *World Marxist R. [Canada] 1974 17(7): 108-110.* In 1974 Uruguay's rulers used terror to defeat the Communist Party and the revolutionary movement. S

536. Pecaut, Daniel. LA PHÉNOMÈNE DE "LA VIOLENCE" EN 1945-53 [The phenomenon of La Violencia in 1945-53]. *Cahiers du Monde Hispanique et Luso-Brésilien [France] 1976 26: 55-67.* Studies the social and political consequences of the first part of *La Violencia*, the civil war in Colombia. Attempts to align the violence with the process of national modernization, offering an explanation behind the development resulting from the movement. Points out that the cities were mainly involved in the battle, and that the systematic offensive of the dominant class in blocking popular mobilization was strongest in cities such as Rio Magdalena, Bogota, and Cali, (ca. 1945-47). Examples of cohesion to block *La Violencia* were efforts by industrialists to maintain the agrarian structure, the counter-reform law of 1944, and the dislocation of the government resulting from the adoption of a

new economic policy. Based largely on G. Guzman's *La Violencia en Colombia* (1962); note.   S. Sevilla

537. Péronne, Louis-P. EL SALVADOR: QUI ASSASSINE? [El Salvador: who is assassinating?]. *Études* [France] 1981 354(5): 607-619. Discusses the political crisis in El Salvador, the injustices it is suffering, the violence of the Junta, US involvement in the right-wing government's attempt to thwart the efforts of the militant left.

538. Premdas, Ralph R. GUYANA: VIOLENCE AND DEMOCRACY IN A COMMUNAL STATE. *Plural Soc.* [Netherlands] 1981 12(3-4): 41-63. Created by Dutch and British colonists, Guyana has experienced violence from its inception when European settlers required slaves, then indentured laborers, uprooted from Africa and Asia, to serve on cotton and sugar plantations. The struggle for self-determination over a century later was also marked by violence, and the post-independence period continued the tradition that culminated in June 1980 with the assassination of Dr. Walter Rodney.

539. Premo, Daniel L. POLITICAL ASSASSINATION IN GUATEMALA: A CASE OF INSTITUTIONALIZED TERROR. *J. of Interamerican Studies and World Affairs* 1981 23(4): 429-456. Guatemalan terror is related in part to the general uncertainty in Central America. Guatemalan officials believe their country to be the target of an international Communist conspiracy. The government's creation of a climate of terror is aimed at paralyzing mass activity. Public assassinations are intended to show the state's vulnerability and its inability or unwillingness to guarantee personal safety. In few countries in the world is it as dangerous to struggle for individual self-improvement or democratic rights as in Guatemala. The rules of the game have changed drastically in Guatemalan politics in recent decades. Based on Guatemalan newspapers, Amnesty International reports, and other printed primary and secondary sources; 12 notes, table, ref.   T. Schoonover

540. Radu, Michael S. TERROR, TERRORISM, AND INSURGENCY IN LATIN AMERICA. *Orbis* 1984 28(1): 27-41. Examines recent trends in Latin American terrorism and explores the increasingly close ties between Latin American guerrilla groups and similar groups in Western Europe and the Middle East. The roles of the universities and the church are discussed in detail. The author also analyzes the failure of Castro-style guerrilla movements in Latin America. Based on published sources; 15 notes.   J. W. Thacker, Jr.

541. Ranis, Peter. POST POPULIST MODELS OF THE LATIN AMERICAN POLITY. *Polity* 1980 13(1): 126-133. The liberal prescriptions of the early 1960's gave way to economic structuralist and neo-Marxist analyses of Latin American polity which, in turn, have helped shape the works under review: Ernest Halperin, in *Terrorism in Latin America* (Beverly Hills: Sage Publ., 1976), Robert R. Kaufman, in *Transition to Stable Authoritarian-Corporate Regimes: The Chilean Case?* (Beverly Hills: Sage Professional Papers in Comparative Politics, 1976), Gustavo Lagos and Horacio H. Godoy, in *Revolution of Being: A Latin American View of the Future* (New York: Free Pr., 1977), and Candido Mendes, in *Beyond Populism* (Albany: State U.

of New York, 1977), having witnessed the failure of populist experiences in Chile, Argentina, Uruguay, and Brazil, see a consensual model of political development, based on a general will as opposed to the competing demands of a democratic-pluralist society, as leading to political and economic stability in Latin America.

542. Rock, David. REVOLT AND REPRESSION IN ARGENTINA. *World Today [Great Britain] 1977 33(6): 215-222.* Examines events in Argentina, including guerrilla and terrorist activities, the Peronist revival, and the decline of the populist government, 1973-77.

543. Rodney, Walter. PEOPLE'S POWER, NO DICTATOR. *Latin Am. Perspectives 1981 8(1): 64-78.* Reprint of pamphlet published in 1979, the last political statement written by Walter Rodney (assassinated, 1980) for Guyana's Working People's Alliance (WPA). J. F. Vivian

544. Russell, Charles A. LATIN AMERICA: REGIONAL REVIEW. *Terrorism 1980 4(1-4): 277-292.* A statistical survey of the incidents of terrorism in Latin America, 1970-78; Latin America with 24.5% is second only to Europe with 47.2% in worldwide terrorist activity.

545. Sánchez Gómez, Gonzalo. EL GAITANISMO Y LA INSURRECCION DEL 9 DE ABRIL EN PROVINCIA [Gaitanism and the insurrection of 9 April in the provinces]. *Anuario Colombiano de Hist. Social y de la Cultura [Colombia] 1982 (10): 191-229.* Examines the role played by Jorge Eliécer Gaitán in the events preceding his assassination on 9 April 1948 and the subsequent wave of violence (the Bogotazo) and compares and contrasts the events in the principal Colombian cities with events in the provinces. The situation which led to the insurrection is reviewed and details of the actions in Bogotá, the western provinces, el Tolima, and Santander are described. Both the nature of the leadership and the characteristics of the rebellion varied greatly between the cities and the provinces, and this influenced the course of events in 1948 and in later years. Based on newspaper articles and primary sources; 39 notes. J. Gasco

546. Silva, Geraldo Eulálio do Nascimento e. OCUPAÇÃO DA EMBAIXADA AMERICANA EM BOGOTA [Occupation of the American embassy in Bogotá]. *Rev. do Inst. Hist. e Geog. Brasileiro [Brazil] 1981 (330): 187-198.* In February 1980, terrorists of the M-19 movement occupied the embassy of the Dominican Republic in Bogotá, where the national feast day was being celebrated. The terrorists held 57 hostages, among them 14 ambassadors, and occupied the embassy for 61 days. The author provides an eye-witness account of the episode. J. V. Coutinho

547. Sofer, Eugene F. TERROR IN ARGENTINA: JEWS FACE NEW DANGERS. *Present Tense 1977 5(1): 19-25.* Discusses the birth, development, and renascence of Peronism, focusing on Jewish contributions and repercussions for the Jewish community. Describes the current atmosphere of intimidation, violence, and terrorism; the suspension of constitutional law; the extension of martial law; and the official tolerance of overt anti-Semitism.

Details the David Graiver case, the American Jewish Committee's difficulties, the efforts of the *Delegación de Asociaciones Israelitas de la Argentina* to combat anti-Semitism, the legacy of Isabel Peron, the impact of the Montoneros (left Peronistas) and the para-militarists (right-wing Nationalists), and the policies of Lopez Rega. Incorporates a reprint of Kathleen Teltsch's "Jewish Group Closes Argentine Office, Cites Threats" *(New York Times,* 8 July 1977). 4 photos. R. B. Mendel

548. Solberg, Mary. EL SALVADOR. *Migration Today 1982 10(2): 6-12.* Presents background on El Salvador's political situation since 1979, and focuses on the human toll of the recent violence, and, particularly, on the thousands of would-be refugees; discusses US policy regarding the refugees.

549. Suarez, Alberto. THE OLIGARCHY OF THE PEOPLE. *World Marxist R. [Canada] 1973 16(2): 77-85.* The revolution of socialism is being assisted by Uruguay's Communist Party. Part of the continuing series "Political Portrait of Latin America." S

550. Taylor, Robert W. and Vanden, Harry E. DEFINING TERRORISM IN EL SALVADOR: "LA MATANZA." *Ann. of the Am. Acad. of Pol. and Social Sci. 1982 (463): 106-118.* Explores the various actors and motives operating in El Salvador in an attempt to clarify the meaning of terrorism. A case study approach is employed to analyze the evolutionary incidents, the hidden agendas, and the critical issues that characterize terrorism as an activity defined in regard to the perspectives of different political groups. J/S

551. Watson, G. Llewellyn. PATTERNS OF BLACK PROTEST IN JAMAICA: THE CASE OF THE RAS-TAFARIANS. *J. of Black Studies 1974 4(3): 329-343.* The Ras-Tafarians—poor, black, lower-class Jamaicans who advocate the overthrow of the current Jamaican government—combine violence with Marxism and religion. 4 notes, biblio. K. Butcher

552. Wohlstetter, Roberta. KIDNAPPING TO WIN FRIENDS AND INFLUENCE PEOPLE. *Survey [Great Britain] 1974 20(4): 1-40.* A discussion of a mass kidnapping engineered by Raul Castro in Cuba in 1958. It was done for publicity, but the rebels were unprepared for the unfavorable press. The hostages were released when the United States threatened to renew arms shipments to the Batista government. The publicity the revolutionaries wanted had to be sympathetic publicity. But with modern communications, they were competing with mere bandits for air time. Based on interviews, newspaper accounts and secondary sources; 77 notes. R. B. Valliant

553. Zaïd, Gabriel. UNE GUERRE DE CHEFS. LECTURE DE LA TRAGÉDIE SALVADORIENNE [A war among leaders: the tragedy of El Salvador]. *Esprit [France] 1981 (12): 26-38.* An account of political events in El Salvador since 1972, centering on the evolution of the civil war, which is actually a personal war among the country's leadership. The author recommends a cessation of violence and a withdrawal of US interference. A partial translation of an article in *Vuelta* [Mexico] 1981.

554. —. ON THE TRANSFER OF WEAPONS. *Inter-American Econ. Affairs 1979 33(1): 85-90.* Reprints a correspondence between Congressman Eldon Rudd and Secretary of State Cyrus Vance on the request for permission to sell armaments to Costa Rica after many of the arms had already been transferred; raises questions about the possession of American-made weapons by Nicaraguan terrorists; March 1979.

555. —. STATEMENT BY THE CUBAN PARTY AND REVOLUTIONARY GOVERNMENT ON THE EVENTS IN GRENADA. *Black Scholar 1984 15(1): 30-32.* Reprints the Cuban government's statement of 20 October 1983 made in response to the killing of Maurice Bishop during the political crisis in Grenada.

556. —. SUBVERSION IN THE ARGENTINE. *Patterns of Prejudice [Great Britain] 1975 9(4): 13-17.* Discusses political subversion, terrorism, and anti-Semitism in Argentina in 1975, including the role of the Roman Catholic Church.

6

NORTH AMERICA

557. Bell, Robert G. THE U.S. RESPONSE TO TERRORISM AGAINST INTERNATIONAL CIVIL AVIATION. *Orbis 1976 19(4): 1326-1343.* In recent years, aviation has been "a natural target for terrorist attack." Between 1960 and 1975, for example, "there were 439 hijacking attempts on American and foreign aircraft." Because it has "the most comprehensive aviation network in the world... the United States assumed leadership of the international response to aerial terrorism." The US effort "was in no way perfect," but all in all its effort worked. Still, "unless the broad and fundamental causes of terrorism themselves are addressed, governments will remain one step behind the terrorists." 45 notes. A. N. Garland

558. Blumberg, Janice Rothschild. THE BOMB THAT HEALED: A PERSONAL MEMOIR OF THE BOMBING OF THE TEMPLE IN ATLANTA, 1958. *Am. Jewish Hist. 1983 73(1): 20-38.* The wife of Jacob M. Rothschild, rabbi of Atlanta's Hebrew Benevolent Congregation at the time their temple was bombed by neonazis in October 1958, recounts events, thoughts, and feelings from the time of the bombing through the trial of the accused. Suggests that the event had positive outcome, including the orderly desegregation of Atlanta's public schools and greater public respect across religious and racial lines. Based on the Rabbi Jacob M. Rothschild papers. R. A. Keller

559. Cherne, Leo. INTELLIGENCE CANNOT HELP A NATION FIND ITS SOUL. IT IS INDISPENSABLE, HOWEVER, TO HELP PRESERVE THAT NATION'S SAFETY WHILE IT CONTINUES THE SEARCH. *Freedom at Issue 1976 35: 6-11.* Argues the need for intelligence services in combatting political terrorism, and in establishing realistic international economic guidelines for US foreign policy in the 1970's.

560. Clark, Lorne S. CANADA'S INITIATIVES TO COMBAT THE LATEST SCOURGE OF THE SKIES. *Int. Perspectives [Canada] 1973 (1): 47-51.* Traces Canada's attempts to establish a new convention to combat hijacking through the International Civil Aviation Organization. The goal was to implement the enforcement of the Tokyo Convention (1963), the Hague Convention (1970), and the Montreal Convention (1971). The subcommittee report from the Washington Conference of 15 September 1972 provided measures to determine if a country had defaulted on its international legal obligations and for deciding on joint action measures. L. S. Frey

561. Clutterbuck, Richard. AIR PIRACY: A GLEAM OF HOPE FOR THE WORLD. *Army Q. and Defence J. [Great Britain] 1974 104(4): 402-408.* The recent decline in air piracy began with its virtual elimination in the United States, 1971-73. Examines incidents to show that the only effective countermethods involve rigorous search on the ground, as practiced in the United States. Final solutions would involve an international Air Crimes Commission using internationally approved sanctions. D. H. Murdoch

562. Daniels, Stuart. THE WEATHERMEN. *Government and Opposition [Great Britain] 1974 9(4): 430-459.* Analyzes the political and cultural roots of the Weathermen (1962-71), tracing the use and decline of terrorism in the Weathermen's attempt to institute revolution in the most advanced nation in the world.

563. Decter, Midge. NOTES FROM THE AMERICAN UNDERGROUND. *Commentary 1982 73(1): 27-33.* Key members of the Weather Underground, the Black Liberation Army, and other fugitive groups involved in terrorist activities in the late 1960's and early 1970's, including Kathy Boudin, were captured in October 1981, and only recently has the Left disassociated itself from these terrorist groups, whose revolutionary activity was previously viewed as innocent idealism or insanity.

564. Dudley, J. Wayne. "HATE" ORGANIZATIONS OF THE 1940S: THE COLUMBIANS, INC. *Phylon 1981 42(3): 262-274.* A wave of racial violence followed World War II. A number of racist organizations emerged to promote patriotism, faith, and the white community. In 1946, several white men chartered the Columbians in Atlanta, Georgia. To join, one had to hate Blacks and Jews and have three dollars. While the Columbians stirred up Atlanta for several months, the city and state governments, local politicians, and the city's newspapers attacked the group until it was legally disbanded, June 1947. A. G. Belles

565. Fenello, Michael. TECHNICAL PREVENTION OF AIR PIRACY. *Int. Conciliation 1971 (585): 28-41.* Describes technical apsects of prevention programs effective in the United States, including physical detection devices, behavioral profiles, and air security teams. Because the motives and methods of hijackers are changing, newer programs must be developed such as a uniform ground security program for airport personnel and more sensitive detection devices. Based on secondary sources; table, 12 notes. C. A. Gallaci

566. George, Paul S. COLORED TOWN: MIAMI'S BLACK COMMUNITY, 1896-1930. *Florida Hist. Q. 1978 56(4): 432-447.* The early 20th century marked the nadir of race relations in Florida and especially Colored Town, the northwest section of Miami. Blacks were subject to Jim Crow legislation, inadequate municipal services, cramped housing, a dual system of justice, and white terrorism. Nevertheless, black citizens formed church and fraternal organizations, established a business and professional community, and played a vital role in the economic growth of Miami. The black community's troubles worsened in later decades. Based mainly on newspapers, government records, and secondary sources; 3 illus., map, 58 notes. P. A. Beaber

567. Gleason, John M. A POISSON MODEL OF INCIDENTS OF INTERNATIONAL TERRORISM IN THE UNITED STATES. *Terrorism 1980 4(1-4): 259-265.* Quantitative studies of terrorism are lacking; for international terrorism in the United States, 1968-74, the Poisson model is suggested.

568. Ivanian, E. A. POLITICHESKII TERROR—NEOT"EMLIMAIA CHAST' AMERIKANSKOGO OBRAZA ZHIZNI [Political terror is an inseparable part of the American way of life]. *Voprosy Istorii [USSR] 1982 (3): 91-104.* In the 20th century, violence has become a common feature of American politics, as the high number of political murders indicates. There have been assassination attempts on six of the 15 presidents who have held office since 1900. Repeated campaigns have been launched to ban the sale of weapons, but the arms lobby has the support of the military-industrial complex and thwarts efforts at gun control. Secondary sources; 48 notes.

G. Dombrovski

569. Jaros, Dean; Sigelman, Lee; and Conover, Pamela Johnston. SOPHISTICATION & FOREIGN-POLICY PREFERENCES: THE IRANIAN HOSTAGE CRISIS. *Polity 1982 15(1): 151-155.* In Lexington, Kentucky, during the crisis caused by the Iranian seizure of American hostages, the relationship between sophistication and opinion, with reference to foreign policy, was a function of the stance of the American government. When the government took a definite policy, either hawkish or conciliatory, the more sophisticated person looked less sophisticated. In the event of a government policy that was not clear cut, the differences between the more and less sophisticated emerged. Under these conditions, the less sophisticated tended to favor simplistic solutions, whether hawkish or dovish, while the more sophisticated favored less clear-cut solutions. Based on a telephone survey; table, 5 notes. J. Powell

570. Jeffreys-Jones, Rhodri. VIOLENCE IN AMERICAN HISTORY: PLUG UGLIES IN THE PROGRESSIVE ERA. *Perspectives in Am. Hist. 1974 8: 465-583.* The Progressive Era exhibited marked bourgeois anxieties concerning potential class conflict between capital and labor, but this concern was unjustified, as the United States' size and scattered population prevented any real threat to national security. Statistics reveal the Progressive era experienced no more violence than any other period in American history, yet Progressive reformers and politicians, including those on the US Commission on Industrial Relations, translated isolated incidents of violence into the illusion of potential revolution. In addition, conspiracy theories led to increased numbers of armed guards and labor spies, who tended to distort the threat of industrial violence. Appendix. W. A. Wiegand

571. Kelley, Don Quinn. WHAT PRICE FREEDOM IN AMERICA? *Monthly Rev. 1982 34(6): 24-39.* Recounts the history of racist repression and black terrorism in America from the colonial period, concentrating on events of the 20th century.

572. Landes, William M. AN ECONOMIC STUDY OF U.S. AIRCRAFT HIJACKING, 1961-1976. *J. of Law and Econ. 1978 21(1): 1-31.* Increases in the probability of apprehension and punishment have significantly reduced

domestic hijacking; foreign hijacking is not much affected. The cost of screening passengers just offsets the expected hijacking losses. Primary and secondary sources; 10 tables, 56 notes. C. B. Fitzgerald

573. Monti, Daniel J. THE RELATION BETWEEN TERRORISM AND DOMESTIC CIVIL DISORDERS. *Terrorism 1980 4(1-4): 123-141.* Examines 300 years of civil disturbances in New York City, pointing out the essentially conservative nature of collective violence and the conditions which might change it into political terrorism.

574. Ofri, Aric. INTELLIGENCE AND COUNTERTERRORISM. *Orbis 1984 28(1): 41-52.* Analyzes the political role of terrorism and the best methods for the United States to counter its effectiveness. The problems of deterrence, intelligence and early warning, defense, and retaliation are discussed in detail. The author concludes with a series of recommendations to increase US effectiveness against terrorism. J. W. Thacker, Jr.

575. Richmond, Douglas W. LA GUERRA DE TEXAS SE RENOVA: MEXICAN INSURRECTION AND CARRANCISTA AMBITIONS, 1900-1920. *Aztlán 1980 11(1): 1-32.* Traces efforts by the Mexican government, under the leadership of President Venustiano Carranza, to foment revolt among the Mexicans living in Texas. Since 1848 Mexicans, numerically the vast majority of the population of south Texas, had endured discrimination and exploitation. Prompted by American reluctance to give legitimacy to his movement and by anger over Anglo mistreatment of Texas Mexicans, Carranza supported the Plan of San Diego in 1915, an effort designed to recapture Texas for Mexico through a coalition of Mexicans, Negroes, and Indians. The scheme failed to attract widespread support, but for over a year Mexican raids over the border resulted in numerous outbreaks of violence and created political turmoil in south Texas. Tensions between Mexico and the United States increased with the Pershing Expedition to chase Pancho Villa in Mexico in 1916, and a point short of war was reached in 1919 as Texas conservatives advocated armed intervention in Mexico. As long as Carranza remained in power, he continued to support revolutionary agitation in Texas. 94 notes.
A. Hoffman

576. Schlaefer, Cindy Verne. AMERICAN COURTS AND MODERN TERRORISM: THE POLITICS OF EXTRADITION. *New York U. J. of Int. Law and Pol. 1981 13(3): 617-643.* Examines the judicial response to the modern wave of politically motivated terrorism, both in terms of the purposes underlying the political offense exception and the unique characteristics of modern international terrorism.

577. Shannon, Kristin and Regenstreif, Peter. HANGING TOGETHER. *Wilson Q. 1982 6(3): 44-59.* Reviews the past decade's tumult in Canada, partly due to its geographical mass with its resultant isolation, reinforced by ethnic differences; many of these distinct regional cultures have undergone sporadic outbreaks in the 1970's, such as militant separatism, chronic political squabbling, and acts of terrorism.

578. Swearingen, Rodger. REAGAN AND RUSSIA: THE NEW COURSE. *Korea & World Affairs [South Korea] 1982 6(2): 292-311.* Supporting President Ronald Reagan's condemnation of detente as an instrument of foreign policy, discusses the president's foreign policy during 1981-82 and looks at improving US military power, limiting Cuba's influence, and controlling terrorism.

579. Yerbury, J. C. THE "SONS OF FREEDOM" DOUKHOBORS AND THE CANADIAN STATE. *Can. Ethnic Studies [Canada] 1984 16(2): 47-70.* A small radical group of Doukhobors in British Columbia, the "Sons of Freedom," are well-known to state authorities for their nihilistic activities. Explanations of their depredations by politicians, lawyers, and journalists include the belief that Freedomite activities were an organized and enduring terrorist conspiracy against the Canadian government and populace. Other explanations have included the notion that the depredations of the Sons of Freedom were the acts of lunatics and criminals. Adequate explanations for Doukhobor and Sons of Freedom activities can only be achieved through an understanding of the Doukhobors as a revivalistic movement. The term *revitalization* embraces all those beliefs and rituals sometimes referred to as nativistic, millenarian, or messianic, and it is a process of interaction between a depressed, subordinate religious minority like the Doukhobors and a superordinate system such as the Canadian state. Proper consideration of Doukhobor revitalizing processes and the matrix of state systems is of theoretical importance to an understanding of the discordance, disharmony, or conflict between the Doukhobors and the legal and social norms of Canadian society. J

580. —. [ANTITERRORISM LEGISLATION]. *Terrorism 1984 7(2): 213-231, 233-239.*
Smith, Brent L. ANTITERRORISM LEGISLATION IN THE UNITED STATES: PROBLEMS AND IMPLICATIONS, pp. 213-231. Compares proposed federal legislation to combat terrorism and existing state legislation; probes the effectiveness and potential abuse of such legislation.
Paust, Jordan J. TERRORISM AND "TERRORISM-SPECIFIC" STATUTES, pp. 233-239. Rejects Smith's recommendation that "terrorism-specific" legislation be abandoned.

581. —. THE QUEBEC QUESTION: TWO VIEWS. *North Am. R. 1971 256(3): 9-33.*
Marshall, Peter. QUEBEC: AFTER THE ENGLISH CONQUEST, pp. 10-23. Considers the past, present, and future of French Canada, noting that "only in Ulster can be found a[nother] region of the Western world where the past enjoys so active and political a role."
LaPierre, Laurier. QUEBEC: OCTOBER, 1970, pp. 23-33. A separatist argument that the events of October 1970 have made the independence of Quebec a certainty. Argues that the real terrorists were not the kidnappers, but the government. Questions whether or not the people of Quebec have any genuine liberty under the Canadian federal system of government. Claims that the governmental terror instituted in reprisal over the kidnappings has unified the people of Quebec on the issue of independence from Canada. 3 photos. E. P. Costello

7

AFRICA

582. Cherkasov, P. P. FRANTSUZSKII INOSTRANNYI LEGION [The French Foreign Legion]. *Voprosy Istorii [USSR] 1979 (11): 184-188.* The Foreign Legion was created in 1831 by King Louis Philippe (1773-1850) to neutralize potentially subversive foreign mercenaries living in France and to pacify newly colonized Algeria. Except for rare military intervention outside Africa in the 19th century and the war in Indochina (1946-54), the Legion stayed mostly in Algeria. In 1961, some units took part in the abortive anti-Gaullist coup and some Legion deserters joined the terrorist Organization of the Secret Army (OAS). In 1978, the Foreign Legion, now serving the interests of international reactionaries, helped suppress the Shaba Province uprising against Zaire's president Mobutu Sese Seko and continues to fight against the National Liberation Front in Chad. 13 notes. N. Frenkley

583. Cherkasov, P. P. KRAKH OAS [Collapse of the OAS]. *Voprosy Istorii [USSR] 1974 (9): 133-149.* The Organisation de l'Armée Secrète (OAS) was formed in April 1961 by ultra-rightist French underground groups to combat the Algerian Front de Libération Nationale. Arising during the Algerian war of 1954-62, the OAS defended the French colonial hold on Algeria and used terrorism to oppose General Charles de Gaulle's reversal of policy and his decision to grant independence to Algeria. The last important terrorist act of the OAS was the abortive assassination attempt on de Gaulle on 22 August 1962. 88 notes. N. Frenkley

584. Friedland, Elaine A. SOUTH AFRICA AND INSTABILITY IN SOUTHERN AFRICA. *Ann. of the Am. Acad. of Pol. and Social Sci. 1982 (463): 95-105.* In southern Africa, anti-governmental organizations operating in Mozambique, Angola, and Zimbabwe depend on financial and military assistance from the South African regime, which utilizes these organizations as one component of its strategy to destabilize these governments. Demonstrates that these anti-governmental organizations, such as União Nacional de Independencia Total de Angola (UNITA) and the Movimento de Resistência Nacional de Moçambique, by their tactics, conform to the definition of a terrorist organization; they could not survive without their linkages to the South African regime, and the South African regime's objective in promoting these anti-governmental organizations is to attempt to continue the status quo inside South Africa. J/S

585. Glentworth, Garth and Hancock, Ian. OBOTE AND AMIN: CHANGE AND CONTINUITY IN MODERN UGANDA POLITICS. *African Affairs [Great Britain] 1973 72(288): 237-255.* Idi Amin's brutal and inconsistent behavior is in many ways an extension of the system he inherited in 1971. Post-independence political maneuvering, the massive role of the military, the 1971 coup, and Amin's violent behavior since taking power may bequeath his successor a pattern of violence in government. 30 notes.
H. G. Soff

586. Kirk, Tony. POLITICS AND VIOLENCE IN RHODESIA. *African Affairs [Great Britain] 1975 74(294): 3-38.* Traces nationalist politics in Rhodesia from 1963 to the guerrilla raids of 1972 led by the Front for the Liberation of Zimbabwe (FROLIZI). Analyzes the FROLIZI movement which was designed to terrorize white Rhodesians, and the government response to this sabotage. Also refutes several propositions of Kenneth Good (see *African Affairs* 1974 73(290): 20-36). Although the blacks might have been just in taking up arms, their leadership was interested in selfish goals and not national deliverance. 39 notes.
H. G. Soff

587. Koerner, Francis. LE MOUVEMENT NATIONALISTE ALGÉRIEN (NOV. 1942-MAI 1945) [The Algerian nationalist movement, November 1942-May 1945]. *Rev. de l'Hist. de la Deuxième Guerre Mondiale [France] 1974 24(93): 44-64.* Although the Algerian nationalist movement can be traced back to 1880, the return of Algeria to Free France in November 1942 provoked Moslem Algerians to call for a new political, economic, and social statute as the price for their support in the war. Pressure from Americans, disputes between the supporters of Henri Girard and Charles de Gaulle, and the interaction of nationalist groups led to confusion and violence. In May 1945 Algerian Moslems rioted and killed about 100 Europeans in the department of Constantin. In retaliation the civil population was attacked and bombed by the Foreign Legion and the Air Force, causing between 1,000 and 45,000 deaths. This left bitter memories that were revived in the 1954 revolt. Based on archival and published documents, newspapers, and secondary sources; 110 notes.
G. H. Davis

588. Lever, Évelyne. L'OAS ET LES PIEDS-NOIRS [The OAS and the *pieds noirs*]. *Histoire [France] 1982 (43): 10-23.* A relation, with illustrations, a chronological table, and a short bibliography, of the political and military events that after 1954 led to Algeria's independence from France in July 1961, centering on the rebellion of the *pied noirs* (Algerian-born descendants of French settlers), and the terrorist actions of the Secret Army Organization (OAS).

589. Menarchik, E. Douglas. STRIKE AGAINST TERROR! THE ENTEBBE RAID. *Air U. Rev. 1980 31(5): 65-76.* Surveys international terrorist activities and specifically analyzes the Israeli raid on Entebbe.

590. Mittelman, James H. THE UGANDA COUP AND THE INTERNATIONALIZATION OF POLITICAL VIOLENCE. *Munger Africana Lib. Notes 1972 (14): 2-36.*

591. Mushkat, Marion. BERIT HAMO'ATSOT VEHAMAAVAK BIF'EULOT GARILA VETEROR [The USSR and the struggle against guerrilla warfare and terrorism]. *Int. Problems [Israel] 1978 17(2): 16-26.* While the Soviet attitude toward terrorism has traditionally been ambivalent, it has supported such activities in Africa, to extend Soviet influence there without provoking Western reaction.

592. Parsons, Q. N. SHOTS FOR A BLACK REPUBLIC? SIMON RATSHOSA AND BOTSWANA NATIONALISM. *African Affairs [Great Britain] 1974 73(293): 449-458.* The colonial period saw a resurgence, not a reduction, in the threat of revolt by Westernized Africans. Two assassination plots in the period 1916-26 were led by educated Africans, particularly the Ratshosa brothers. The author analyzes the political ideology of Simon Ratshosa after 1926, focusing on his ideas on a unified state, the economic status of peasants, and democratization of local governments. 30 notes.
H. G. Soff

593. Pribytkovski, Lev Naumovich. NIGERIIA V PERIOD VOENNYKH REZHIMOV [Nigeria under military governments]. *Narody Azii i Afriki [USSR] 1980 (6): 45-57.* Examines the positive aspects of reforms introduced by Yakubu Gowon and his successors. Nationalization, trade, taxation of foreign oil revenues, and closer economic ties with the USSR strengthened Nigeria's national economy. However, Gowon's inability to check corruption and refusal to grant political freedom caused his ouster in 1975. The dynamic domestic and foreign policy of Brig. Gen. Murtala Muhammed, treacherously assassinated in 1976, was continued under Lt. Gen. Olusegun Obasanjo who restored a multiparty system and saw a president elected in 1979. 22 notes.
N. Frenkley

594. Rich, Paul. INSURGENCY, TERRORISM AND THE APARTHEID SYSTEM IN SOUTH AFRICA. *Pol. Studies [Great Britain] 1984 32(1): 68-85.* Discusses the development of guerrilla insurgency in South Africa, 1976-84, and the government response centered around the concept of "total strategy." After distinguishing analytically between the notions of terrorism and guerrilla warfare, the insurgent campaign is seen to have a threefold impact in terms of loss of economic confidence, sapping of white morale, and a mobilization of black political consciousness. The resulting response of "total strategy" effectively represents an escalation of previous efforts to entrench a black middle class as a factor to enhance political stability. The political isolation of South Africa from close Western support makes it difficult for the South African government to avoid pursuing a strategy of full-scale counterterrorism in response to the increased insurgency threat. Based on newspaper reports, primary, and secondary sources; 65 notes.
G. L. Neville

595. Rochat, Giorgio. L'ATTENTATO A GRAZIANI E LA REPRESSIONE ITALIANA IN ETIOPIA NEL 1936-37 [The attempt on Graziani's life and the Italian repression in Ethiopia, 1936-37]. *Italia Contemporanea [Italy] 1975 26(118): 3-38.* On 19 February 1937 seven or eight small fragmentation bombs were hurled at Marshal Rodolfo Graziani, Viceroy of Abyssinia. About 30 persons were wounded but only one seriously. A bloody

massacre followed, and for several days hastily organized Fascist units committed innumerable acts of terror. In addition to summary executions (324) over 1,000 people were rounded up and herded into concentration camps. In addition, Graziani ordered the total liquidation of all those associated with sorcery or soothsaying. The severity of the measures reveals the shocking cruelty of Fascist colonial rule. H. W. L. Freudenthal

596. Salomone, Franck A. ETHNICITY AND THE NIGERIAN CIVIL WAR. *L'Afrique et L'Asie modernes* [France] 1976 4(111): 5-12. Outlines theories of ethnicity and their relationship to the formation of a nation, applying these theories to the Nigerian civil war, 1966-67, in an attempt to discover the causes of the political crises and violence of the Biafran breakaway.

597. Southall, Aidan. SOCIAL DISORGANISATION IN UGANDA: BEFORE, DURING, AND AFTER AMIN. *J. of Modern African Studies* [Great Britain] 1980 18(4): 627-656. Assesses political turmoil and later eventual economic and social chaos in independent Uganda. The marginal role of the Nubi in Ugandan society and the problem of Buganda continued after independence in 1962, leading to the use of violence as public policy by the Obote government and the rise of Idi Amin. The decline and fall of Amin, 1976-79, resulted from the total economic disarray and universal corruption associated with control of Amin's military and police. Its effects have continued to disorient society and prolong violence and political instability in the post-Amin period. Based on personal communications, newspapers, and secondary sources; note. L. W. Truschel

598. Welch, Claude E. WARRIOR, REBEL, GUERRILLA, AND PUTSCHIST. *J. of Asian and African Studies* [Netherlands] 1977 12(1-4): 82-98. Analyzes the development of four types of political violence in Africa. Includes a list of military coups in Africa to 1975. Table, 35 notes.
R. T. Brown

SUBJECT INDEX

Subject Profile Index (ABC-SPIndex) carries both generic and specific index terms. Begin a search at the general term but also look under more specific or related terms. This index includes selective cross-references.

Each string of index descriptors is intended to present a profile of a given article; however, no particular relationship between any two terms in the profile is implied. Terms within the profile are listed alphabetically after the leading term. The variety of punctuation and capitalization reflects production methods and has no intrinsic meaning; e.g., there is no difference in meaning between "History, study of" and "History (study of)."

Cities, towns, and other small geographical subdivisions are listed following their respective countries, e.g., "USA (Kentucky; Lexington)." Terms beginning with an arabic numeral are listed after the letter Z. The chronology of the bibliographic entry follows the subject index descriptors. In the chronology, "c" stands for "century"; e.g., "19c" means "19th century."

The last number in the index string, in italics, refers to the bibliographic entry number.

A

Action Française. Fascism. France. Italy. 1919-26. *143*
Adler, Friedrich. Assassination. Austria. Socialism. 1900-17. *126*
Adolescence. Russia. Stalin, Joseph. 1879-1917. *482*
Affiche Rouge. France. Psychological Warfare. Resistance. Trials. World War II. 1944. *203*
Afghanistan. Amin, Hafizullah. Karmal, Babrak. Revolution. USSR. 1979-81. *358*
—. Political history. 1947-72. *413*
Africa. Coups d'Etat. Violence. 19c-20c. *598*
—. Foreign Legion. France. Intervention. 1961-78. *582*
—. USSR. 20c. *591*
Africa, southern. Foreign Policy. South Africa. 1970's-82. *584*
Agca, Mehmet Ali. Assassination. Bulgaria. Italy (Rome). John Paul II, Pope. Secret service. 1979-81. *220*
—. Assassination. Bulgaria. Italy (Rome). John Paul II, Pope. USSR. 1979-81. *174*
Agency for International Development. Mitrione, Dan A. Tupamaros. Uruguay. USA. 1969-73. *519*
Airplanes. *See also* Civil Aviation.
—. Cuba. Deportation. Hijacking. International law. Refugees. USA. 1983. *520*
—. Economic Conditions. Hijacking. USA. 1961-76. *572*
—. Hijacking. International Civil Aviation Organization. 1963-80. *37*
—. Hijacking. International law. 1930-73. *1*
—. Hijacking. International law. 1950-70. *32*
—. Hijacking. International law. 1970-73. *109*
—. Hijacking. International Law. USA. 1971-74. *561*
—. Hijacking. Montreal Agreement. Victims. Warsaw Convention. 1929-73. *89*
Akali Dal Party. India. Nehru, Jawaharlal. Separatist Movements. Sikhs. Singh, Tara. 1960-61. *478*
Albania. Assassination. Demi, Ahmet. Revolution. Rustem, Avni. Zog I. 1924. *155*
—. Gurakuqi, Luigj. Nationalism. Politics. 1911-25. *232*
Alexander I. Dictatorship. Fascism. Yugoslavia. 1918-39. *277*
Algeria. Front de la Libération Nationale (FLN). Strategy. 1950's-72. *56*
—. France. Secret Army (OAS). 1961-62. *583*

—. French. Independence Movements. Secret Army (OAS). 1954-61. *588*
—. Nationalist movements. World War II. 1942-45. *587*
Amendola, Giovanni. Assassination. Fascism. Italy. 1920-25. *237*
American Board Commissioners for Foreign Missions. Internal Macedonian Revolutionary Organization. Kidnapping. Macedonia. Missions and Missionaries. Roosevelt, Theodore. Stone, Ellen M. USA. 1901-02. *275*
American Friends Service Committee. Arab-Israeli conflict. Foreign Policy. Friends, Society of. Palestine Liberation Organization. USA. 1970's. *334*
Americas (North and South). Organization of American States. 1970-71. *19*
Amin, Hafizullah. Afghanistan. Karmal, Babrak. Revolution. USSR. 1979-81. *358*
Amin, Idi. Obote, Milton. Political violence. Uganda. 1962-72. *585*
—. Political instability. Uganda. 1962-80. *597*
Anarchism. Communist Parties and Movements. Germany, West. Italy. Socialism. 1960-79. *202*
—. Marxism. 1872-1972. *249*
—. Revolutionary Movements. Russia. 19c. 1977. *448*
Anti-Communist Movements. Death squads. Latin America. 1950's-83. *522*
—. Doriot, Jacques. France. Political Parties. Rightist groups. Rocque, François de la. 1936-37. *208*
Anti-Semitism. 1980-83. *91*
—. Argentina. Catholic Church. Subversion. 1975. *556*
—. Blumberg, Janice Rothschild. Bombing. Personal Narratives. Public Opinion. Trials. USA (Georgia; Atlanta). 1958-59. *558*
—. France. 1930's. 1960's-83. *211*
Apartheid. Guerrilla warfare. Public Policy. South Africa. 1976-84. *594*
Aquino, Benigno, Jr. Assassination. Diokno, José. Foreign Relations. Interviews. Marcos, Ferdinand. Philippines. 1972-83. *433*
Arab states. Becker, Jillian. Israel. Palestine Liberation Organization (review article). Political Change. 1967-83. *366*
—. Boundaries. Israel. Joint Chiefs of Staff. USA. War. 1967. *400*
—. Boundaries. Israel. Military Occupation. 1970. *322*
—. Civil war. Lebanon. Models. Palestine Liberation Organization. 1975-76. *304*

Arab states

—. Civil War. Lebanon. Palestine Liberation Organization. 1982-83. *345*
—. Europe, Western. Foreign Relations. Palestine Liberation Organization. 1973-78. *288*
—. Foreign Relations. Israel. Palestine Liberation Organization. 1960's-79. *348*
—. Foreign Relations. Palestine Liberation Organization. 1964-81. *402*
—. Israel. USSR. 1967-74. *309*
—. Israel. War. 1947-74. *351*
—. Palestine Liberation Organization. Political Factions. 1974-83. *286*
—. Palestine Liberation Organization. Rabat Conference (1974). 1974. *353*
Arab-Israeli conflict. American Friends Service Committee. Foreign Policy. Friends, Society of. Palestine Liberation Organization. USA. 1970's. *334*
—. Blacks. Foreign Policy. Palestine Liberation Organization. Southern Christian Leadership Conference. USA. 1979. *411*
—. Diaries. Israel. Sharett, Moshe. 1953-57. *370*
—. Foreign policy. Hostages. Iran. Television. USA. 1975-81. *294*
—. Israel. Palestine Liberation Organization. Political Factions. 1973-76. *359*
—. Israel. Palestinians. UN. 1950's-70's. *297*
—. Lebanon. War. 1947-82. *407*
—. Palestine Liberation Organization. 1947-75. *349*
Arabs. Great Britain. Israel. Trials. 1982. *184*
—. Guerrilla Warfare. Israel. 1940's-60's. *356*
—. Israel. Land Tenure. Plan Dalet. 1930's-67. *398*
—. Israel. Middle East. Palestinians. Peace. 1948-72. *327*
—. Israel. Palestine Liberation Organization. 1973-79. *335*
—. Israel. Palestine Liberation Organization. Political parties. 1970-79. *386*
—. Israel. Palestine Liberation Organization. USA. USSR. 1942-75. *409*
—. Jews. Nationalist Movements. Palestine (review article). Porath, Yehoshua. 1918-39. *361*
Arafat, Yasser. Geneva conference. Middle East. Militants. Palestine Liberation Organization. 1974. *371*
—. Imperialism. Interviews. Palestine Liberation Organization. Zionism. 1960's-70's. *292*
—. Interviews. Palestine Liberation Organization. 1964-81. *422*
Araña, Carlos Manuel. Guatemala. Political instability. 1971. *512*
Archives Nationales. Documents. France (Paris). Political Protest. Revolutionary Movements. Russia. 1882-1910. *459*
Argentina. Anti-Semitism. Catholic Church. Subversion. 1975. *556*
—. Catholic Church. Clergy. Movement of Priests for the Third World. Radicals and Radicalism. Violence. 1969-70's. *506*
—. Charities. Multinational corporations. 1955-80. *496*
—. Foreign Relations. Military Government. USA. 1940-81. *525*
—. Guerrilla Warfare. Political repression. 1973-77. *542*
—. Jews. Peronism. 1940-77. *547*
—. People's Revolutionary Army (ERP). 1968-74. *514*
Armaments. Costa Rica. Foreign Relations. Nicaragua. Rudd, Eldon. USA. Vance, Cyrus. 1978-79. *554*
Armenia. Turkey. 1914-82. *323*
Armenian Revolutionary Federation. Independence Movements. Ottoman Empire. 1830-1921. *28*
Asencio, Diego C.. Colombia (Bogotá). Diplomacy. Interviews. M-19. USA. 1980. *523*
—. Diplomacy. Interviews. USA. 1980-83. *495*

Asia. Diplomacy. Europe. Guerrilla warfare. Latin America. 1960-72. *88*
—. Revolutionary Movements. 1970's. *434*
Assassination. 1968-80. *104*
—. Adler, Friedrich. Austria. Socialism. 1900-17. *126*
—. Agca, Mehmet Ali. Bulgaria. Italy (Rome). John Paul II, Pope. Secret service. 1979-81. *220*
—. Agca, Mehmet Ali. Bulgaria. Italy (Rome). John Paul II, Pope. USSR. 1979-81. *174*
—. Albania. Demi, Ahmet. Revolution. Rustem, Avni. Zog I. 1924. *155*
—. Amendola, Giovanni. Fascism. Italy. 1920-25. *237*
—. Aquino, Benigno, Jr. Diokno, José. Foreign Relations. Interviews. Marcos, Ferdinand. Philippines. 1972-83. *433*
—. Bangladesh. Coups d'etat. Foreign policy. Rahman, Mujibur. ca 1945-76. *461*
—. Bishop, Maurice. Cuba. Documents. Grenada. 1983. *555*
—. Bishop, Maurice. Grenada. Intervention. Military operations. Politics. USA. 1980-83. *526*
—. Bogotazo. Colombia. Gaitán, Jorge Eliécer. Rural Areas. 1928-48. *545*
—. Bolsheviks. Brest-Litovsk, Treaty of. Mirbach, Wilhelm von. Political Factions. Socialist Revolutionaries. USSR. 1918. *475*
—. Botswana. Nationalism. Political ideology. Ratshosa, Simon. 1916-32. *592*
—. Boutros Pasha. Egypt. Great Britain. Ibrahim Nasif al-Wardani. 1875-1911. *379*
—. Bulgaria. Catholics. John Paul II, Pope. Poland. USSR. 1979-83. *127*
—. Bulgaria. Communist Countries. John Paul II, Pope. Secret service. Trotsky, Leon. USSR. 1940-82. *107*
—. Catholic Church. El Salvador. Human rights. Romero, Oscar. Social change. 1977-80. *501*
—. Cavendish, Frederick Charles. Ireland (Dublin). Spencer, John Poyntz, 5th Earl. 1889-1910. *154*
—. Chile. Parliaments. Social Classes. 1920-70. *497*
—. China. Political theory. Revolutionary Movements. 1903-12. *457*
—. Colonial Government. Ethiopia. Graziani, Rodolfo. Italy. Political repression. 1936-37. *595*
—. Committee of State Security (KGB). Foreign Policy. Kidnapping. USSR. 1920's-60's. *489*
—. Coups d'Etat. Generals. Indonesia. 1965. *443*
—. Democracy. Guyana. Rodney, Walter. Violence. 1800-1980. *538*
—. Egypt. 1910-54. *368*
—. Egypt (Cairo). Moyne, 1st Baron. Palestine. 1939-45. *412*
—. El Salvador. Revolution. Romero, Oscar. 1970's-80. *527*
—. Foreign Policy. John Paul II, Pope. NATO. Poland. Turkey. USSR. 1980-83. *175*
—. Foreign Relations. Iorga, Nicolae. Romania. 1900-40. *148*
—. Foreign Relations. Korea, South. Park Chung-hee. Politics. USA. 1979-82. *425*
—. France (Paris). Jews. Petliura, Simon. Schwartzbard, Shalom. Ukraine. 1926. *466*
—. Francis Ferdinand. Habsburg Empire. Stürgkh, Karl. World War I. 1914-18. *125*
—. Germany. Haase, Hugo. Revolution. Social Democratic Party. 1894-1919. *188*
—. Germany. Montalègre, Commandant. Plebiscites. Poland. Silesia (Bytom). 1921. *205*
—. Germany. Right. Seeckt, Hans von. 1919-33. *149*
—. Great Britain. Irish Republican Army. Police. Special Branch. 1972-74. *204*
—. Great Britain. Moyne, 1st Baron. Palestine. 1944-45. *307*

—. Greece. Papadopoulos, George. ca 1956-76. *186*
—. Guatemala. Politics. 1954-81. *539*
—. Gun control. National Characteristics. Presidents. USA. 20c. *568*
—. Guyana. People's National Congress. Revolution. Rodney, Walter. 1966-81. *505*
—. Iorga, Nicolae. Iron Guard. Madgearu, Virgil. Police. Romania. 1940. *279*
—. Italy. Matteotti, Giacomo. Mussolini, Benito. Socialists. 1924-26. *210*
—. Italy. Moro, Aldo. Political Leadership. 1947-78. *192*
—. Japan. Politics. 1868-1941. *476*
—. Mexico. Spain (Barcelona). Trotsky, Leon. 1940. *502*
—. Northern Ireland (Belfast). 1969-78. *199*
—. Poland. Steiger, Stanislaw. Trials. Wojciechowski, Stanislaw. 1924-25. *193*
—. Russia. Trepov, Fëdor. Trials. Zasulich, Vera. 1878-81. *428*
Assimilation. Muslims. Thailand. 1972-74. *424*
Association of Southeast Asian Nations. Communist Party. Revolutionary Movements. Violence. 1965-83. *485*
Atomic Energy Commission (US). Hijacking. Nuclear Arms. 1970-74. *57*
Attitudes. Canadians. Irish Republican Army. Northern Ireland. 1969-82. *266*
—. Government. Kataeb party. Lebanon. Militia. 1936-73. *392*
—. Russia. 1500-1917. *442*
Austria. Adler, Friedrich. Assassination. Socialism. 1900-17. *126*
—. Foreign Relations. Italy. South Tyrol. Treaties. 1946-69. *226*
—. Neo-Nazism. Political parties. 1938-82. *283*
Austria (Vorarlberg). Nazism. 1933-34. *265*
Authority. Iran. Khomeini, Ruhollah. Religion. Revolution. 1970-82. *299*
Autonomia Operaia. Italy (Padua). Red Brigades. Trials. 1970's. *255*
Autonomy. Diplomacy. Egypt. Israel. Palestinians. USA. 1978-81. *355*
Awakening Hungarians. Hungary. Party of National Unity. Secret societies. Social Democrats. 1922-26. *248*

B

Baader-Meinhof Gang. Germany, West. Meinhof, Ulrike. Radicals and Radicalism. Trials. 1975. *197*
—. Germany, West. Politics. 1970's. *238*
Balance of power. Foreign policy. Reagan, Ronald. USA. 1980-81. *84*
Bangladesh. Assassination. Coups d'etat. Foreign policy. Rahman, Mujibur. ca 1945-76. *461*
Bangladesh (Chittagong Hill Tracts). Political Protest. Shanti Bahini. Social integration. 1951-80. *447*
Basques. Economic Conditions. Politics. Spain. 1976-81. *247*
—. Euzkadi Ta Askatatuna (ETA). Fascism. Nationalism. Spain (Burgos). Trials. 1970. *244*
—. Government. Political Factions. Spain. Suárez, Adolfo. 1977-79. *177*
—. Regionalism. Separatist Movements. Spain. 19c-20c. *147*
Becker, Jillian. Arab states. Israel. Palestine Liberation Organization (review article). Political Change. 1967-83. *366*
Begin, Menachem. Fascism. Israel. Jabotinsky, Vladimir. Palestinians. Zionism (Revisionism). 1923-82. *302*
Behavior. Hijacking. 1970's. *100*
Bell, Daniel. Intellectuals. Leftism. Personal narratives. Violence. 1919-80. *11*

Bengali. Burma. Revolutionary Movements. 1920-38. *430*
Bibliographies. 1960-81. *54*
—. Committee of State Security (KGB). Intelligence gathering. USSR. 1946-70. *452*
—. International Red Aid. Ryle, J. Martin. USSR. 1922-28. *460*
Bishop, Maurice. Assassination. Cuba. Documents. Grenada. 1983. *555*
—. Assassination. Grenada. Intervention. Military operations. Politics. USA. 1980-83. *526*
Black Liberation Army. Boudin, Kathy. Kidnapping. Leftism. USA. Weathermen. 1967-81. *563*
Black September. Middle East. Palestinians. Refugees. 1967-73. *415*
—. Palestinians. Political strategy. 1967-73. *374*
Blacks. Arab-Israeli conflict. Foreign Policy. Palestine Liberation Organization. Southern Christian Leadership Conference. USA. 1979. *411*
—. Political repression. Racism. 1712-1981. *571*
Blumberg, Janice Rothschild. Anti-Semitism. Bombing. Personal Narratives. Public Opinion. Trials. USA (Georgia; Atlanta). 1958-59. *558*
Boats. Foreign Relations. France (Cherbourg). Israel. 1967-74. *163*
Bogotazo. *See also* Violencia.
—. Assassination. Colombia. Gaitán, Jorge Eliécer. Rural Areas. 1928-48. *545*
Bolivia. Government. Nationalist Popular Front. 1971-73. *492*
Bolsheviks. Assassination. Brest-Litovsk, Treaty of. Mirbach, Wilhelm von. Political Factions. Socialist Revolutionaries. USSR. 1918. *475*
—. Lenin, V. I. Revolutionaries. Russia. Zagorski, Vladimir M. 1902-19. *426*
Bolshevism. Russian Revolution. Social Revolutionary Party. 1917. *441*
Bombing. Anti-Semitism. Blumberg, Janice Rothschild. Personal Narratives. Public Opinion. Trials. USA (Georgia; Atlanta). 1958-59. *558*
—. Cities. Violence. 1969-71. *64*
—. Conspiracy. Government. Italy (Milan; Piazza Fontana). 1969-77. *130*
—. Embassies. Lebanon (Beirut). Marines. USA. 22d Marine Amphibious Unit, US. 1983. *354*
—. Foreign Ministry Sales Act (US). Iraq (Tammuz). Israel. Nuclear Power Plants. USA. 1974-82. *300*
Bonapartism. Fascism. Nazism. 1848-1939. *161*
Botswana. Assassination. Nationalism. Political ideology. Ratshosa, Simon. 1916-32. *592*
Boudin, Kathy. Black Liberation Army. Kidnapping. Leftism. USA. Weathermen. 1967-81. *563*
Boundaries. Arab States. Israel. Joint Chiefs of Staff. USA. War. 1967. *400*
—. Arab states. Israel. Military Occupation. 1970. *322*
Boutros Pasha. Assassination. Egypt. Great Britain. Ibrahim Nasif al-Wardani. 1875-1911. *379*
Boycotts. Jews. Olympic Games. 1930's-70's. *63*
Brest-Litovsk, Treaty of. Assassination. Bolsheviks. Mirbach, Wilhelm von. Political Factions. Socialist Revolutionaries. USSR. 1918. *475*
British Columbia. Doukhobors. Sons of Freedom. 1870's-1981. *579*
Bulgaria. Agca, Mehmet Ali. Assassination. Italy (Rome). John Paul II, Pope. Secret service. 1979-81. *220*
—. Agca, Mehmet Ali. Assassination. Italy (Rome). John Paul II, Pope. USSR. 1979-81. *174*
—. Assassination. Catholics. John Paul II, Pope. Poland. USSR. 1979-83. *127*

118 Bulgaria

—. Assassination. Communist Countries. John Paul II, Pope. Secret service. Trotsky, Leon. USSR. 1940-82. *107*
—. Communist Party. Czechoslovakia. 1925. *128*
—. Communist Party. Political repression. 1923-44. *182*
—. Documents. International Red Aid. 1927. *170*
—. Stamboliski, Aleksandr. 1879-1979. *278*
Bulgarians. Exarchate Church. Greeks. Letters. Macedonia (Megarovo, Turnovo). 1870-1904. *129*
Buraku Liberation League. Coalitions. Communist Party. Japan. Minobe, Ryokichi. Yoka High School. 1974. *472*
Burials. Cyprus. Hydrochloric acid. Independence Movements. Prisoners. 1955-59. *395*
Burma. Bengali. Revolutionary Movements. 1920-38. *430*
—. Independence Movements. India. Ottama, Bhikhu U. 1905-39. *431*
Burma (Rangoon). Korea, North. Korea, South. 1983. *490*

C

Cambodia. Government. Political Leadership. 1970-79. *488*
Camp David agreement. Egypt. Israel. Palestinians. UN. USA. 1978-79. *376*
Camus, Albert. Lukács, Georg. Russia. 1880-1980. *432*
Canada. Ethnic Groups. Regionalism. 1970's. *577*
—. Foreign Relations. Hijacking. International Civil Aviation Organization. International Law. 1959-72. *560*
—. Great Britain. Ideology. Reporters and Reporting. 1980. *337*
Canada (Quebec). French Canadians. Separatist Movements. 1763-1971. *581*
Canadians. Attitudes. Irish Republican Army. Northern Ireland. 1969-82. *266*
Carlists. Fascism. Political Culture. Sindicalismo Libre. Spain. 1830-1980. *273*
Carranza, Venustiano. Mexicans. Mexico. Rebellions. USA (Texas). 1848-1920. *575*
Carter, Jimmy. Hostages. Iran. Presidents. Public opinion. USA. USA (Kentucky; Lexington). 1979. *310*
Cartoons and Caricatures (political). Great Britain. Northern Ireland. Prejudice. 1968-80. *190*
Castro, Raul. Cuba. Kidnapping. USA. 1958. *552*
Catholic Church. Anti-Semitism. Argentina. Subversion. 1975. *556*
—. Argentina. Clergy. Movement of Priests for the Third World. Radicals and Radicalism. Violence. 1969-70's. *506*
—. Assassination. El Salvador. Human rights. Romero, Oscar. Social change. 1977-80. *501*
Catholicism. Ireland. Revolutionary Movements. 1848-1923. *219*
Catholics. Assassination. Bulgaria. John Paul II, Pope. Poland. USSR. 1979-83. *127*
—. Coalitions. Northern Ireland Executive. Provincial government. Social Democratic Labour Party. 1974. *212*
—. Latin America. Marxism. Politics. Religion (review article). 20c. *521*
—. Northern ireland. Politics. Protestants. Violence. 1912-72. *246*
Cavendish, Frederick Charles. Assassination. Ireland (Dublin). Spencer, John Poyntz, 5th Earl. 1889-1910. *154*
Central America. 1970's. *493*
Chalo movement. India (Mysore). Political Protest. Satyagraha. 1947. *483*
Charities. Argentina. Multinational corporations. 1955-80. *496*
Childers, Erskine. Childers, Molly Osborn. Ireland. Irish Republican Army. USA (Massachusetts; Boston). 1903-22. *272*
Childers, Molly Osborn. Childers, Erskine. Ireland. Irish Republican Army. USA (Massachusetts; Boston). 1903-22. *272*
Children. Civil disturbances. Genocide. Northern Ireland. Personality testing. 1971-75. *164*
Chile. Assassination. Parliaments. Social Classes. 1920-70. *497*
—. Cuba. Elections. Foreign Relations. Military aid. USA. Venezuela. 1963-64. *517*
—. Militarism. Violence. 1970-74. *494*
China. Assassination. Political theory. Revolutionary Movements. 1903-12. *457*
—. Foreign relations. Palestine Liberation Organization. 1955-76. *326*
—. Middle East. USSR. 1965-80. *462*
—. Quantitative Methods. Violence. 1966-78. *455*
Christian Democratic Party. Italy. Kidnapping. Moro, Aldo. Red Brigades. 1978. *264*
—. Italy. Moro, Aldo. Murder. Red Brigades. 1975-83. *150*
Churchill, Winston. Foreign policy. Great Britain. Palestine. World War II. 1937-47. *306*
Cities. Bombing. Violence. 1969-71. *64*
—. International politics. Mass media. 1970's. *103*
Civil aviation, international. Hijacking. USA. 1960-76. *557*
Civil disobedience. India (Bengal). Political Participation. Strikes. Women. 1928-35. *474*
Civil disturbances. Children. Genocide. Northern Ireland. Personality testing. 1971-75. *164*
—. Ireland. Northern Ireland. 13c-20c. *171*
—. Northern Ireland. Politics. 1945-72. *224*
Civil Rights. Federal Bureau of Investigation. Federal Government (US). USA. 1977-82. *81*
—. International Law. 1944-77. *61*
—. Martial Law. Nuclear Power Plants. Plutonium. 1970's. *47*
Civil service. Germany (Prussia). Grzesinski, Albert C. Social Democratic Party. 1926-30. *169*
Civil war. Arab states. Lebanon. Models. Palestine Liberation Organization. 1975-76. *304*
—. Arab states. Lebanon. Palestine Liberation Organization. 1982-83. *345*
—. Economic conditions. Finland. Revolutionary movements. Violence. 1905-18. *189*
—. El Salvador. Leadership. 1972-81. *553*
—. El Salvador. Military Government. 1961-79. *500*
—. Ethnicity. Nigeria. 1966-67. *596*
—. Intervention. Lebanon. Palestine Liberation Organization. Syria. 1968-76. *311*
—. Ireland. Irish Republican Brotherhood. 1921-24. *222*
—. Lebanon. 1943-75. *391*
—. Lebanon. 1975-76. *316*
—. Lebanon. Palestine Liberation Organization. 1950's-70's. *284*
—. Lebanon. Political Factions. Religion. Violence. 1975-82. *421*
—. Lebanon. Sects, Religious. Social Organization. 1975-77. *404*
—. Lebanon, southern. 1970-79. *403*
Class struggle. Commission on Industrial Relations. Plug uglies. Progressive era. Violence. 1890-1920. *570*
—. Communist Party. Elections. Fascism. Italy (Liguria). 1922-26. *230*
Clergy. Argentina. Catholic Church. Movement of Priests for the Third World. Radicals and Radicalism. Violence. 1969-70's. *506*
Coalitions. Buraku Liberation League. Communist Party. Japan. Minobe, Ryokichi. Yoka High School. 1974. *472*

—. Catholics. Northern Ireland Executive. Provincial government. Social Democratic Labour Party. 1974. *212*
Collins, Michael. Guerrilla warfare. Independence Movements. Ireland. Irish Republican Army. 1919-21. *144*
Colombia. Assassination. Bogotazo. Gaitán, Jorge Eliécer. Rural Areas. 1928-48. *545*
—. Modernization. Violencia. 1945-53. *536*
—. Political Parties. Socioeconomic Change. Violence. 1948-63. *18*
—. Political Parties. Socioeconomic change. Violence. 1948-63. *499*
—. *Violencia.* 1946-64. *511*
Colombia (Bogotá). Asencio, Diego C.. Diplomacy. Interviews. M-19. USA. 1980. *523*
—. Diplomats. Dominican Republic. Embassies. 1980. *546*
Colonial Government. Assassination. Ethiopia. Graziani, Rodolfo. Italy. Political repression. 1936-37. *595*
Colonialism. Great Britain. Northern Ireland. 1850-1980. *110*
Columbians, Inc. Patriotism. Racism. USA (Georgia; Atlanta). Violence. 1946-47. *564*
Comintern. Fascism. Ideology. 1921-39. *216*
Commission on Industrial Relations. Class conflict. Plug uglies. Progressive era. Violence. 1890-1920. *570*
Committee of State Security (KGB). Assassination. Foreign Policy. Kidnapping. USSR. 1920's-60's. *489*
—. Bibliographies. Intelligence gathering. USSR. 1946-70. *452*
—. Foreign Policy. USSR. 1926-65. *118*
—. Political repression. USSR. 1977. *438*
Communism. Mao Tse-tung. Political Theory. Revolution. Violence. ca 1850-1970's. *487*
—. USA. Vietnam War. 1957-71. *77*
Communist Countries. Assassination. Bulgaria. John Paul II, Pope. Secret service. Trotsky, Leon. USSR. 1940-82. *107*
Communist Parties and Movements. Anarchism. Germany, West. Italy. Socialism. 1960-79. *202*
—. Germany. Holz, Max. Revolutionary Movements. 1889-1933. *228*
—. Lenin, V. I. Political Theory. Revolutionary movements. Violence. 1890's-1970's. *160*
—. Middle East. Palestine Liberation Organization. 1967-70. *295*
Communist Party. Association of Southeast Asian Nations. Revolutionary Movements. Violence. 1965-83. *485*
—. Bulgaria. Czechoslovakia. 1925. *128*
—. Bulgaria. Political repression. 1923-44. *182*
—. Buraku Liberation League. Coalitions. Japan. Minobe, Ryokichi. Yoka High School. 1974. *472*
—. Class struggle. Elections. Fascism. Italy (Liguria). 1922-26. *230*
—. Coups d'Etat. Military Government. Political Leadership. Thailand. 1950-78. *464*
—. France. Violence. 1929-31. *134*
—. Government. Revolutionary movements. Uruguay. 1974. *535*
—. Ireland. 1950-76. *225*
—. Iron Guard. Romania. 1930's-40's. *252*
—. Political collaboration. Romania. Workers' and Peasants' Bloc. 1922-33. *159*
—. Political Factions. Turkey. 1920-70's. *456*
—. Tupamaros. Uruguay. 1952-73. *549*
—. Turkey. 1920-80. *340*
Communists. Malaysia. 1974-76. *446*
Concentration camps. Resistance. Socialists. World War II. 1939-45. *162*
Conflict and Conflict Resolution. UN. War. 1946-64. *8*
—. Violence. 1968-81. *24*

Conspiracy. Bombing. Government. Italy (Milan; Piazza Fontana). 1969-77. *130*
Convention on Terrorism (US draft, 1972). 1945-73. *31*
Convention on the Physical Protection of Nuclear Materials. Nuclear materials. Treaties. UN. 1966-82. *59*
Convention on the Prevention and Punishment of Crimes against Internationally Protected Persons. Diplomats. Treaties. UN. 1977. *101*
—. Diplomats. UN General Assembly. 1970-73. *73*
Costa Rica. Armaments. Foreign Relations. Nicaragua. Rudd, Eldon. USA. Vance, Cyrus. 1978-79. *554*
Coups d'Etat. Africa. Violence. 19c-20c. *598*
—. Assassination. Bangladesh. Foreign policy. Rahman, Mujibur. ca 1945-76. *461*
—. Assassination. Generals. Indonesia. 1965. *443*
—. Communist Party. Military Government. Political Leadership. Thailand. 1950-78. *464*
—. Uganda. Violence. 1971-73. *590*
Courts. Extradition. Foreign Relations. USA. 1970-81. *576*
Croatian Liberation Movement. Separatist Movements. Ustaše. Yugoslavia. 1929-72. *271*
Cuba. Airplanes. Deportation. Hijacking. International law. Refugees. USA. 1983. *520*
—. Assassination. Bishop, Maurice. Documents. Grenada. 1983. *555*
—. Castro, Raul. Kidnapping. USA. 1958. *552*
—. Chile. Elections. Foreign Relations. Military aid. USA. Venezuela. 1963-64. *517*
Culture. Literature. Russia. USSR. 17c-20c. *435*
Cyprus. Burials. Hydrochloric acid. Independence Movements. Prisoners. 1955-59. *395*
—. Makarios, Archbishop. 1946-74. *227*
—. Trials. 1956. *394*
Cyprus (Leukosia). EOKA (organization). Murder. 1956. *393*
Cyprus (Liopetrios). EOKA (organization). Great Britain. 1958. *396*
Czechoslovakia. Bulgaria. Communist Party. 1925. *128*

D

Death squads. Anti-Communist Movements. Latin America. 1950's-83. *522*
Decolonization. Immigration. Netherlands. 1945-79. *269*
Defense Department. Government investigations. Lebanon (Beirut). Military Strategy. 1983. *416*
Defense policy. International law. Oil Industry and Trade. Western Nations. 1980-81. *62*
Degaev, Sergei (Alexander Pell, pseud.). Exile. Russia. South Dakota, University of. USA. 1854-1910. *436*
Demi, Ahmet. Albania. Assassination. Revolution. Rustem, Avni. Zog I. 1924. *155*
Democracy. 1917-75. *29*
—. Assassination. Guyana. Rodney, Walter. Violence. 1800-1980. *538*
—. Ethics. Liberalism. Political Theory. Violence. 1960's-83. *80*
—. Great Britain. Irish Republican Army. 1969-78. *142*
—. Marxism. -1973. *55*
—. Mass media. 1960's-70's. *112*
—. Spain. 1974-79. *214*
Democracy (review article). 1950's-70's. *10*
Demonstrations. Israel. Police. Religion. Violence. 1950-79. *346*
Deportation. Airplanes. Cuba. Hijacking. International law. Refugees. USA. 1983. *520*
—. Israel. Palestinians. Statistics. 1967-78. *347*
Developing nations. Industrialized countries. 20c. *41*

Development. Economic Policy. Politics. Social Change. Turkey. 1960-80. *418*
Diaries. Arab-Israeli Conflict. Israel. Sharett, Moshe. 1953-57. *370*
Dictatorship. Alexander I. Fascism. Yugoslavia. 1918-39. *277*
—. Foreign Policy. Latin America. Revolutionary Movements. USA. 1958-79. *516*
Dimitrov, Georgi. Fascism. Historiography. Marxism. 1930's-70's. *82*
Diokno, José. Aquino, Benigno, Jr. Assassination. Foreign Relations. Interviews. Marcos, Ferdinand. Philippines. 1972-83. *433*
Diplock Report. Northern Ireland. Political Imprisonment. Trials. 1971-74. *151*
Diplomacy. 1968-76. *39*
—. Asencio, Diego C.. Colombia (Bogotá). Interviews. M-19. USA. 1980. *523*
—. Asencio, Diego C. Interviews. USA. 1980-83. *495*
—. Asia. Europe. Guerrilla warfare. Latin America. 1960-72. *88*
—. Autonomy. Egypt. Israel. Palestinians. USA. 1978-81. *355*
—. Hostages. Iran. USA. 1979-80. *414*
—. Israel. Palestine Liberation Organization. 1973-. *314*
—. Missions and Missionaries. Navies. Ottoman Empire. Roosevelt, Theodore. USA. 1903-04. *329*
Diplomatic and Consular Conventions. Vienna Conventions (1961, 1963). 1960-74. *30*
Diplomats. Colombia (Bogotá). Dominican Republic. Embassies. 1980. *546*
—. Convention on the Prevention and Punishment of Crimes against Internationally Protected Persons. Treaties. UN. 1977. *101*
—. Convention on the Prevention and Punishment of Crimes Against Internationally Protected Persons. UN General Assembly. 1970-73. *73*
—. Europe, Western. International Law. USA. 1955-73. *58*
Disarmament. Middle East. UN. USSR. 1972. *97*
Dissent. Hijacking. Sosnovski, Vasili. USSR. 1958-77. *427*
Documents. Archives Nationales. France (Paris). Political Protest. Revolutionary Movements. Russia. 1882-1910. *459*
—. Assassination. Bishop, Maurice. Cuba. Grenada. 1983. *555*
—. Bulgaria. International Red Aid. 1927. *170*
—. UN General Assembly. 1981. *124*
Dominican Republic. Colombia (Bogotá). Diplomats. Embassies. 1980. *546*
Doriot, Jacques. Anti-Communist Movements. France. Political Parties. Rightist groups. Rocque, François de la. 1936-37. *208*
Doukhobors. British Columbia. Sons of Freedom. 1870's-1981. *579*
Duca, Ion. Romania. Titulescu, Nicolae. 1919-39. *276*
Duvalier family. Government, resistance to. Haiti. Political repression. USA. 1957-74. *508*

E

Economic Conditions. Airplanes. Hijacking. USA. 1961-76. *572*
—. Basques. Politics. Spain. 1976-81. *247*
—. Civil war. Finland. Revolutionary movements. Violence. 1905-18. *189*
—. Elections. Political change. Tupamaros. Uruguay. 1962-71. *528*
—. Fascism. Germany. Nazism. Social Conditions. 1926-36. *173*
—. Foreign policy. Intelligence gathering. USA. 1970's. *559*
—. Foreign Relations. Turkey. 1974-78. *360*
—. Social Conditions. Turkey. 1950-80. *389*
Economic development. Political development. Spain. 1975-79. *229*
Economic Policy. Development. Politics. Social Change. Turkey. 1960-80. *418*
Egypt. Assassination. 1910-54. *368*
—. Assassination. Boutros Pasha. Great Britain. Ibrahim Nasif al-Wardani. 1875-1911. *379*
—. Autonomy. Diplomacy. Israel. Palestinians. USA. 1978-81. *355*
—. Camp David agreement. Israel. Palestinians. UN. USA. 1978-79. *376*
—. Great Britain. Nationalism. Secret societies. 1870-1924. *339*
Egypt (Cairo). Assassination. Moyne, 1st Baron. Palestine. 1939-45. *412*
Ejército Revolucionario Popular. See People's Revolutionary Army (ERP).
El Salvador. 1970's. *550*
—. Assassination. Catholic Church. Human rights. Romero, Oscar. Social change. 1977-80. *501*
—. Assassination. Revolution. Romero, Oscar. 1970's-80. *527*
—. Civil war. Leadership. 1972-81. *553*
—. Civil war. Military Government. 1961-79. *500*
—. Foreign Policy. Immigration. Refugees. USA. Violence. 1979-82. *548*
—. Government. Violence. 1900-76. *524*
—. Guatemala. Violence. 1970-79. *531*
—. Human rights. Statistics. USA. 1980-82. *504*
—. Political crisis. USA. 1972-81. *537*
—. Political Repression. USA. 1970-81. *533*
—. Social Conditions. Violence. 1980. *510*
Elections. Chile. Cuba. Foreign Relations. Military aid. USA. Venezuela. 1963-64. *517*
—. Class struggle. Communist Party. Fascism. Italy (Liguria). 1922-26. *230*
—. Economic conditions. Political change. Tupamaros. Uruguay. 1962-71. *528*
Elites. Israel. Jordan. Palestine Liberation Organization. Politics. West Bank. 1946-77. *357*
Embassies. Bombing. Lebanon (Beirut). Marines. USA. 22d Marine Amphibious Unit, US. 1983. *354*
—. Colombia (Bogotá). Diplomats. Dominican Republic. 1980. *546*
Entebbe raid. Hijacking. International law. Israel. Popular Front for the Liberation of Palestine. Uganda. 1976. *4*
—. Hijacking. International law. Israel. Uganda. 1961-76. *3*
—. Israel. Uganda. 1968-77. *589*
EOKA (organization). Cyprus (Leukosia). Murder. 1956. *393*
—. Cyprus (Liopetrios). Great Britain. 1958. *396*
Ethics. Democracy. Liberalism. Political Theory. Violence. 1960's-83. *80*
Ethiopia. Assassination. Colonial Government. Graziani, Rodolfo. Italy. Political repression. 1936-37. *595*
Ethnic conflict. Irish Republican Army. Northern Ireland. 1920's-70's. *256*
Ethnic Groups. Canada. Regionalism. 1970's. *577*
Ethnicity. Civil war. Nigeria. 1966-67. *596*
Europe. 1968-82. *179*
—. 1970's. *243*
—. Asia. Diplomacy. Guerrilla warfare. Latin America. 1960-72. *88*
—. Government. Revolution. ca 10c-20c. *66*
—. Middle East. Palestine Liberation Organization. Peace. 1980. *65*
—. Neofascism. 1977-81. *53*
—. Right. 1980-84. *178*
Europe, Western. Arab States. Foreign Relations. Palestine Liberation Organization. 1973-78. *288*
—. Diplomats. International Law. USA. 1955-73. *58*

—. Latin America. 1968-74. *121*
—. Police. 1970-81. *152*
Euzkadi Ta Askatatuna (ETA). Basques. Fascism. Nationalism. Spain (Burgos). Trials. 1970. *244*
Exarchate Church. Bulgarians. Greeks. Letters. Macedonia (Megarovo, Turnovo). 1870-1904. *129*
Executive Power. Foreign Relations. Hostages. Iran. USA. 1981. *373*
Exile. Degaev, Sergei (Alexander Pell, pseud.). Russia. South Dakota, University of. USA. 1854-1910. *436*
Extradition. Courts. Foreign Relations. USA. 1970-81. *576*

F

Fanon, Franz. Gandhi, Mahatma. Political Theory. Revolution. Violence. 1918-70. *51*
Fascism. Action Française. France. Italy. 1919-26. *143*
—. Alexander I. Dictatorship. Yugoslavia. 1918-39. *277*
—. Amendola, Giovanni. Assassination. Italy. 1920-25. *237*
—. Basques. Euzkadi Ta Askatatuna (ETA). Nationalism. Spain (Burgos). Trials. 1970. *244*
—. Begin, Menachem. Israel. Jabotinsky, Vladimir. Palestinians. Zionism (Revisionism). 1923-82. *302*
—. Bonapartism. Nazism. 1848-1939. *161*
—. Carlists. Political Culture. Sindicalismo Libre. Spain. 1830-1980. *273*
—. Class struggle. Communist Party. Elections. Italy (Liguria). 1922-26. *230*
—. Comintern. Ideology. 1921-39. *216*
—. Dimitrov, Georgi. Historiography. Marxism. 1930's-70's. *82*
—. Economic Conditions. Germany. Nazism. Social Conditions. 1926-36. *173*
—. Futurism. Intellectuals. Italy. 1896-1929. *223*
—. Ideology. Portugal. 1920's-60's. *195*
—. Italian Social Republic. 1943-45. *139*
—. Italy. Matteotti, Giacomo. 1922-24. *209*
—. Italy. Political Participation. 1930's. *6*
—. Italy. Violence. 1919-22. *218*
—. Italy. Violence. 1919-23. *207*
—. Italy. Violence. 1919-29. *231*
—. Italy (Brescia). Trials. 1974-78. *132*
—. Leftism. 1970-80. *119*
—. Political Systems. 1914-40's. *35*
Federal Bureau of Investigation. Civil Rights. Federal Government (US). USA. 1977-82. *81*
Federal Government (US). Civil Rights. Federal Bureau of Investigation. USA. 1977-82. *81*
—. Legislation. State Government. 1970's-80's. *580*
Films. Germany, West. Nazism. Public Opinion. 1933-45. 1970's. *270*
Finland. Civil war. Economic conditions. Revolutionary movements. Violence. 1905-18. *189*
—. Kidnapping. Lapua movement. 1930. *251*
—. Revolutionary movements. Socialists. 1906-08. *194*
Foreign Legion. Africa. France. Intervention. 1961-78. *582*
Foreign Ministry Sales Act (US). Bombing. Iraq (Tammuz). Israel. Nuclear Power Plants. USA. 1974-82. *300*
Foreign Policy. Africa, southern. South Africa. 1970's-82. *584*
—. American Friends Service Committee. Arab-Israeli conflict. Friends, Society of. Palestine Liberation Organization. USA. 1970's. *334*
—. Arab-Israeli conflict. Blacks. Palestine Liberation Organization. Southern Christian Leadership Conference. USA. 1979. *411*

—. Arab-Israeli conflict. Hostages. Iran. Television. USA. 1975-81. *294*
—. Assassination. Bangladesh. Coups d'etat. Rahman, Mujibur. ca 1945-76. *461*
—. Assassination. Committee of State Security (KGB). Kidnapping. USSR. 1920's-60's. *489*
—. Assassination. John Paul II, Pope. NATO. Poland. Turkey. USSR. 1980-83. *175*
—. Balance of power. Reagan, Ronald. USA. 1980-81. *84*
—. Churchill, Winston. Great Britain. Palestine. World War II. 1937-47. *306*
—. Committee of State Security (KGB). USSR. 1926-65. *118*
—. Dictatorship. Latin America. Revolutionary Movements. USA. 1958-79. *516*
—. Economics (international). Intelligence gathering. USA. 1970's. *559*
—. El Salvador. Immigration. Refugees. USA. Violence. 1979-82. *548*
—. Government. USA. Vietnam War. 1960-75. *450*
—. Hostages. Iran. Public Opinion. USA (Kentucky; Lexington). 1979. *569*
—. Human rights. USA. 1975-81. *86*
—. Intelligence gathering. Military Strategy. 1984. *574*
—. Israel. Palestine Liberation Organization. Reagan, Ronald. UN. USA. 1975-81. *383*
—. Israel. Palestine Liberation Organization. Syria. UN Security Council. 1975-76. *321*
—. Middle East. Palestine Liberation Organization. 1974-80. *410*
—. Middle East. Palestine Liberation Organization. Rabat Conference (1974). USA. 1967-75. *408*
—. North America. Palestine Congress of North America. 1979. *406*
—. Palestine Liberation Organization. USSR. 1947-80. *319*
—. Reagan, Ronald. USA. USSR. 1981-82. *578*
Foreign Relations. Aquino, Benigno, Jr. Assassination. Diokno, José. Interviews. Marcos, Ferdinand. Philippines. 1972-83. *433*
—. Arab States. Europe, Western. Palestine Liberation Organization. 1973-78. *288*
—. Arab states. Israel. Palestine Liberation Organization. 1960's-79. *348*
—. Arab states. Palestine Liberation Organization. 1964-81. *402*
—. Argentina. Military Government. USA. 1940-81. *525*
—. Armaments. Costa Rica. Nicaragua. Rudd, Eldon. USA. Vance, Cyrus. 1978-79. *554*
—. Assassination. Iorga, Nicolae. Romania. 1900-40. *148*
—. Assassination. Korea, South. Park Chung-hee. Politics. USA. 1979-82. *425*
—. Austria. Italy. South Tyrol. Treaties. 1946-69. *226*
—. Boats. France (Cherbourg). Israel. 1967-74. *163*
—. Canada. Hijacking. International Civil Aviation Organization. International Law. 1959-72. *560*
—. Chile. Cuba. Elections. Military aid. USA. Venezuela. 1963-64. *517*
—. China. Palestine Liberation Organization. 1955-76. *326*
—. Courts. Extradition. USA. 1970-81. *576*
—. Economic Conditions. Turkey. 1974-78. *360*
—. Executive Power. Hostages. Iran. USA. 1981. *373*
—. Gaza Strip. Jordan. Palestine Liberation Organization. West Bank. 1967-77. *369*
—. Great Britain. Ireland. Political Attitudes. 1921. *198*
—. Hostages. Iran. Navies. USA. 1979-80. *328*
—. Hostages. Iran. Rescues. USA. 1979-80. *423*
—. Hostages. Iran. USA. 1979-80. *344*
—. Hungary. Revolution. 1919. *262*
—. Middle East. 1982. *385*

—. Middle East. Reagan, Ronald. USA. USSR. 1981. *331*
—. Palestine Liberation Organization. 1964-79. *318*
—. Palestine Liberation Organization. 1964-80. *296*
—. Palestine Liberation Organization. 1973-77. *291*
—. Palestine Liberation Organization. Political Factions. 1964-75. *285*
—. Palestine Liberation Organization. Revolutionary movements. 1964-75. *352*
France. 1980-83. *166*
—. Action Française. Fascism. Italy. 1919-26. *143*
—. Affiche Rouge. Psychological Warfare. Resistance. Trials. World War II. 1944. *203*
—. Africa. Foreign Legion. Intervention. 1961-78. *582*
—. Algeria. Secret Army (OAS). 1961-62. *583*
—. Anti-Communist Movements. Doriot, Jacques. Political Parties. Rightist groups. Rocque, François de la. 1936-37. *208*
—. Anti-Semitism. 1930's. 1960's-83. *211*
—. Communist Party. Violence. 1929-31. *134*
—. Germany. Law and society. Lawyers. Literature. Military Occupation. Nazism. World War II. 1850-1945. *282*
—. Resistance. Women. World War II. 1940-44. *191*
France (Brittany). Nationalism. 1880-1978. *165*
France (Cherbourg). Boats. Foreign Relations. Israel. 1967-74. *163*
France (Paris). Archives Nationales. Documents. Political Protest. Revolutionary Movements. Russia. 1882-1910. *459*
—. Assassination. Jews. Petliura, Simon. Schwartzbard, Shalom. Ukraine. 1926. *466*
Francis Ferdinand. Assassination. Habsburg Empire. Stürgkh, Karl. World War I. 1914-18. *125*
Freedom of the Press. Law Enforcement. Mass Media. 1968-78. *9*
French. Algeria. Independence Movements. Secret Army (OAS). 1954-61. *588*
French Canadians. Canada (Quebec). Separatist Movements. 1763-1971. *581*
Friends, Society of. American Friends Service Committee. Arab-Israeli conflict. Foreign Policy. Palestine Liberation Organization. USA. 1970's. *334*
Front de la Libération Nationale (FLN). Algeria. Strategy. 1950's-72. *56*
Front for the Liberation of Zimbabwe (FROLIZI). Guerrilla Warfare. Rhodesia. 1963-72. *586*
Fuerzas Armadas de Liberación. Irish Republican Army. *New York Times.* Red Brigades. Reporters and Reporting. 1977-79. *83*
Futurism. Fascism. Intellectuals. Italy. 1896-1929. *223*

G

Gaitán, Jorge Eliécer. Assassination. Bogotazo. Colombia. Rural Areas. 1928-48. *545*
Gandhi, Mahatma. Fanon, Franz. Political Theory. Revolution. Violence. 1918-70. *51*
—. Indian National Congress. National revolutionaries. 1919-35. *470*
Gaza Strip. Foreign Relations. Jordan. Palestine Liberation Organization. West Bank. 1967-77. *369*
—. Israel. Jordan. Palestine Liberation Organization. Political Leadership. West Bank. 1970's. *350*
—. National Front. Palestine Liberation Organization. Political activism. West Bank. 1967-73. *380*
Generals. Assassination. Coups d'Etat. Indonesia. 1965. *443*

Geneva conference. Arafat, Yasser. Middle East. Militants. Palestine Liberation Organization. 1974. *371*
Genocide. Children. Civil disturbances. Northern Ireland. Personality testing. 1971-75. *164*
Germany. Assassination. Haase, Hugo. Revolution. Social Democratic Party. 1894-1919. *188*
—. Assassination. Montalègre, Commandant. Plebiscites. Poland. Silesia (Bytom). 1921. *205*
—. Assassination. Right. Seeckt, Hans von. 1919-33. *149*
—. Communist Parties and Movements. Holz, Max. Revolutionary Movements. 1889-1933. *228*
—. Economic Conditions. Fascism. Nazism. Social Conditions. 1926-36. *173*
—. France. Law and society. Lawyers. Literature. Military Occupation. Nazism. World War II. 1850-1945. *282*
—. Hitler, Adolf. Political protest. 1943. *250*
—. Militia. Paramilitary forces. Political Parties. Violence. 1920-32. *136*
Germany (Nuremberg). Judicial system. Police. Political Repression. SA (Sturmabteilung). 1933-34. *240*
Germany (Prussia). Civil service. Grzesinski, Albert C. Social Democratic Party. 1926-30. *169*
Germany, West. Anarchism. Communist Parties and Movements. Italy. Socialism. 1960-79. *202*
—. Baader-Meinhof Gang. Meinhof, Ulrike. Radicals and Radicalism. Trials. 1975. *197*
—. Baader-Meinhof gang. Politics. 1970's. *238*
—. Films. Nazism. Public Opinion. 1933-45. 1970's. *270*
—. Government. 1970's. *180*
—. Lawyers. Political repression. 1971-76. *268*
—. Political socialization. 1968-80. *267*
Golan Heights. Middle East. Military. Palestine Liberation Organization. Sinai Peninsula. 1973-75. *336*
Government. Attitudes. Kataeb party. Lebanon. Militia. 1936-73. *392*
—. Basques. Political Factions. Spain. Suárez, Adolfo. 1977-79. *177*
—. Bolivia. Nationalist Popular Front. 1971-73. *492*
—. Bombing. Conspiracy. Italy (Milan; Piazza Fontana). 1969-77. *130*
—. Cambodia. Political Leadership. 1970-79. *488*
—. Communist Party. Revolutionary movements. Uruguay. 1974. *535*
—. El Salvador. Violence. 1900-76. *524*
—. Europe. Revolution. ca 10c-20c. *16*
—. Foreign Policy. USA. Vietnam War. 1960-75. *450*
—. Germany, West. 1970's. *180*
—. Guatemala. Violence. 1966-80. *491*
—. Iran. Liberia. Libya. Nicaragua. USA. 1979-80. *27*
—. Italy. Press. 1978-82. *206*
—. Northern Ireland. 1968-80. *200*
Government investigations. Defense Department. Lebanon (Beirut). Military Strategy. 1983. *416*
Government, resistance to. Duvalier family. Haiti. Political repression. USA. 1957-74. *508*
Graziani, Rodolfo. Assassination. Colonial Government. Ethiopia. Italy. Political repression. 1936-37. *595*
Great Britain. Arabs. Israel. Trials. 1982. *184*
—. Assassination. Boutros Pasha. Egypt. Ibrahim Nasif al-Wardani. 1875-1911. *379*
—. Assassination. Irish Republican Army. Police. Special Branch. 1972-74. *204*
—. Assassination. Moyne, 1st Baron. Palestine. 1944-45. *307*
—. Canada. Ideology. Reporters and Reporting. 1980. *337*
—. Cartoons and Caricatures (political). Northern Ireland. Prejudice. 1968-80. *190*

Hostages 123

—. Churchill, Winston. Foreign policy. Palestine. World War II. 1937-47. *306*
—. Colonialism. Northern Ireland. 1850-1980. *110*
—. Cyprus (Liopetrios). EOKA (organization). 1958. *396*
—. Democracy. Irish Republican Army. 1969-78. *142*
—. Egypt. Nationalism. Secret societies. 1870-1924. *339*
—. Foreign Relations. Ireland. Political Attitudes. 1921. *198*
—. Guerrilla Warfare. Irish Republican Army. Northern Ireland. 1970's. *153*
—. Ireland. Northern Ireland. Sunningdale Conference. 1973. *196*
—. Irish Republican Army. Military training. Northern Ireland. 1969-70's. *157*
—. Irish Republican Army. Northern Ireland. Novels. Stereotypes. 1975-79. *257*
—. National Front. Racism. 1970's. *141*
—. National Front. Voting and Voting Behavior. 1979. *181*
—. Northern Ireland. Politics. Violence. 1690-1972. *239*
—. Northern Ireland. Social Problems (review article). Violence. 1918-78. *183*
—. Palestine. Zionism. 1939-48. *308*
—. Police. 1970-79. *172*
—. Political Systems. Reporters and Reporting. 1970's. *245*
Greece. Assassination. Papadopoulos, George. ca 1956-76. *186*
Greeks. Bulgarians. Exarchate Church. Letters. Macedonia (Megarovo, Turnovo). 1870-1904. *129*
Grenada. Assassination. Bishop, Maurice. Cuba. Documents. 1983. *555*
—. Assassination. Bishop, Maurice. Intervention. Military operations. Politics. USA. 1980-83. *526*
Grzesinski, Albert C. Civil service. Germany (Prussia). Social Democratic Party. 1926-30. *169*
Guatemala. Araña, Carlos Manuel. Political instability. 1971. *512*
—. Assassination. Politics. 1954-81. *539*
—. El Salvador. Violence. 1970-79. *531*
—. Government. Violence. 1966-80. *491*
—. Labor Unions and Organizations. Politics. Violence. 1973-82. *518*
—. Land tenure. Violence. 1940's-70's. *515*
—. Violence. 1966-72. *498*
Guerrilla movements. Latin America. Middle East. 1970-75. *94*
Guerrilla warfare. 1945-74. *21*
—. 19c-20c. *70*
—. Apartheid. Public Policy. South Africa. 1976-84. *594*
—. Arabs. Israel. 1940's-60's. *356*
—. Argentina. Political repression. 1973-77. *542*
—. Asia. Diplomacy. Europe. Latin America. 1960-72. *88*
—. Collins, Michael. Independence Movements. Ireland. Irish Republican Army. 1919-21. *144*
—. Front for the Liberation of Zimbabwe (FROLIZI). Rhodesia. 1963-72. *586*
—. Great Britain. Irish Republican Army. Northern Ireland. 1970's. *153*
—. International Politics. Models, structural. 1965-74. *13*
—. Irish Republican Army. 1916-21. *259*
—. Irish Republican Army. Northern Ireland. 1921-72. *281*
—. Latin America. 1970-84. *540*
—. Military Strategy. Revolutionary war. 1688-1973. *40*
—. Tupamaros. Uruguay. 1962-73. *532*
Gun control. Assassination. National Characteristics. Presidents. USA. 20c. *568*

Gurakuqi, Luigj. Albania. Nationalism. Politics. 1911-25. *232*
Guyana. Assassination. Democracy. Rodney, Walter. Violence. 1800-1980. *538*
—. Assassination. People's National Congress. Revolution. Rodney, Walter. 1966-81. *505*
—. Intellectuals. Political Leadership. Rodney, Walter. 1960's-80. *503*
—. Rodney, Walter. Working People's Alliance. 1953-79. *543*

H

Haase, Hugo. Assassination. Germany. Revolution. Social Democratic Party. 1894-1919. *188*
Habsburg Empire. Assassination. Francis Ferdinand. Stürgkh, Karl. World War I. 1914-18. *125*
Haganah. Irgun. Israel. Labor movement. Political Factions. Stern Gang. Zionism (Revisionism). 1930's-82. *320*
Haiti. Duvalier family. Government, resistance to. Political repression. USA. 1957-74. *508*
Hijacking. Airplanes. Cuba. Deportation. International law. Refugees. USA. 1983. *520*
—. Airplanes. Economic Conditions. USA. 1961-76. *572*
—. Airplanes. International Civil Aviation Organization. 1963-80. *37*
—. Airplanes. International law. 1930-73. *1*
—. Airplanes. International Law. 1950-70. *32*
—. Airplanes. International law. 1970-73. *109*
—. Airplanes. International Law. USA. 1971-74. *561*
—. Airplanes. Montreal Agreement. Victims. Warsaw Convention. 1929-73. *89*
—. Atomic Energy Commission (US). Nuclear Arms. 1970-74. *57*
—. Behavior. 1970's. *100*
—. Canada. Foreign Relations. International Civil Aviation Organization. International Law. 1959-72. *560*
—. Civil aviation, international. USA. 1960-76. *557*
—. Dissent. Sosnovski, Vasili. USSR. 1958-77. *427*
—. Entebbe raid. International law. Israel. Popular Front for the Liberation of Palestine. Uganda. 1976. *4*
—. Entebbe (raid). International law. Israel. Uganda. 1961-76. *3*
—. International Civil Aviation Organization. International Law. 1947-71. *2*
—. International Civil Aviation Organization. International Law. 1948-71. *38*
—. International law. 1944-70. *120*
—. International Law. 1961-73. *36*
—. International law. 1970's. *105*
—. Prevention programs. USA. 1968-71. *565*
Historiography. Dimitrov, Georgi. Fascism. Marxism. 1930's-70's. *82*
Hitler, Adolf. Germany. Political protest. 1943. *250*
Holz, Max. Communist Parties and Movements. Germany. Revolutionary Movements. 1889-1933. *228*
Hostages. Arab-Israeli conflict. Foreign policy. Iran. Television. USA. 1975-81. *294*
—. Carter, Jimmy. Iran. Presidents. Public opinion. USA. USA (Kentucky; Lexington). 1979. *310*
—. Diplomacy. Iran. USA. 1979-80. *414*
—. Executive Power. Foreign Relations. Iran. USA. 1981. *373*
—. Foreign policy. Iran. Public Opinion. USA (Kentucky; Lexington). 1979. *569*
—. Foreign Relations. Iran. Navies. USA. 1979-80. *328*
—. Foreign Relations. Iran. Rescues. USA. 1979-80. *423*
—. Foreign Relations. Iran. USA. 1979-80. *344*

124   Hostages

—. Inaugurals. Iran. Reagan, Ronald. Reporters and Reporting. Television. USA. 1980-81. *301*
—. International law. Iran. USA. 1979-80. *378*
—. Iran. Military Strategy. Rescues. USA. 1980. *313*
—. Iran. Public Opinion Polls. Students. USA. 1976-81. *401*
—. Iran. Rescues. USA. World Court. 1979-80. *390*
—. Treaties. UN. 1975-79. *7*
—. Treaties. UN General Assembly. USSR. 1976-79. *79*
Human rights. Assassination. Catholic Church. El Salvador. Romero, Oscar. Social change. 1977-80. *501*
—. El Salvador. Statistics. USA. 1980-82. *504*
—. Foreign Policy. USA. 1975-81. *86*
—. International Law. 1970-80. *95*
—. Northern Ireland. 1967-78. *158*
Humanism (review article). Merleau-Ponty, Maurice. Political Theory. Violence. 1946-47. *458*
Hungary. Awakening Hungarians. Party of National Unity. Secret societies. Social Democrats. 1922-26. *248*
—. Foreign Relations. Revolution. 1919. *262*
Hussein, King. Jordan. Palestine Liberation Organization. 1967-79. *397*
—. Jordan (Jerusalem). Political status. 1948-67. *387*
Hydrochloric acid. Burials. Cyprus. Independence Movements. Prisoners. 1955-59. *395*

I

Ibrahim Nasif al-Wardani. Assassination. Boutros Pasha. Egypt. Great Britain. 1875-1911. *379*
ICBM's. Nuclear Science and Technology. 1960's-70's. *14*
Ideology. Canada. Great Britain. Reporters and Reporting. 1980. *337*
—. Comintern. Fascism. 1921-39. *216*
—. Fascism. Portugal. 1920's-60's. *195*
—. Italy. Red Brigades. Violence. 1968-80. *201*
—. Tactics. 1970's. *74*
Immigration. Decolonization. Netherlands. 1945-79. *269*
—. El Salvador. Foreign Policy. Refugees. USA. Violence. 1979-82. *548*
Imperialism. Arafat, Yasser. Interviews. Palestine Liberation Organization. Zionism. 1960's-70's. *292*
—. USA. USSR. 1981. *34*
Inaugurals. Hostages. Iran. Reagan, Ronald. Reporters and Reporting. Television. USA. 1980-81. *301*
Independence Movements. Algeria. French. Secret Army (OAS). 1954-61. *588*
—. Armenian Revolutionary Federation. Ottoman Empire. 1830-1921. *28*
—. Burials. Cyprus. Hydrochloric acid. Prisoners. 1955-59. *395*
—. Burma. India. Ottama, Bhikhu U. 1905-39. *431*
—. Collins, Michael. Guerrilla warfare. Ireland. Irish Republican Army. 1919-21. *144*
—. India. Secret Societies (*Samiti*). 1927-29. *439*
—. Kidnapping. Macedonia. Missions and Missionaries. Stone, Ellen M. USA. 1901-03. *274*
India. Akali Dal Party. Nehru, Jawaharlal. Separatist Movements. Sikhs. Singh, Tara. 1960-61. *478*
—. Burma. Independence Movements. Ottama, Bhikhu U. 1905-39. *431*
—. Independence Movements. Secret Societies (*Samiti*). 1927-29. *439*

—. Marxism-Leninism. Political Theory. Singh, Bhagat. 1930-31. *463*
—. Naxalite movement. 1975. *486*
—. Nehru, Jawaharlal. Socialism. 1920-64. *440*
India (Bengal). Civil disobedience. Political Participation. Strikes. Women. 1928-35. *474*
India (Bihar; Bhojpur). Naxalite movement. Peasants. Political repression. Rebellions. 1967-79. *465*
India (Mysore). Chalo movement. Political Protest. Satyagraha. 1947. *483*
India (Srikakulam District). Naxalite movement. Rebellions. Social Conditions. 1968-70. *471*
Indian National Congress. Gandhi, Mahatma. National revolutionaries. 1919-35. *470*
Indonesia. Assassination. Coups d'Etat. Generals. 1965. *443*
—. Political Imprisonment. Suharto, T. N. J. 1965-76. *481*
Industrialization. 1945-78. *52*
Industrialized countries. Developing nations. 20c. *41*
Intellectuals. Bell, Daniel. Leftism. Personal narratives. Violence. 1919-80. *11*
—. Fascism. Futurism. Italy. 1896-1929. *223*
—. Guyana. Political Leadership. Rodney, Walter. 1960's-80. *503*
Intelligence gathering. Bibliographies. Committee of State Security (KGB). USSR. 1946-70. *452*
—. Economics (international). Foreign policy. USA. 1970's. *559*
—. Foreign Policy. Military Strategy. 1984. *574*
—. International Law. 1967-78. *111*
—. Violence. 1967-81. *96*
Internal Macedonian Revolutionary Organization. American Board Commissioners for Foreign Missions. Kidnapping. Macedonia. Missions and Missionaries. Roosevelt, Theodore. Stone, Ellen M. USA. 1901-02. *275*
International Civil Aviation Organization. Airplanes. Hijacking. 1963-80. *37*
—. Canada. Foreign Relations. Hijacking. International Law. 1959-72. *560*
—. Hijacking. International Law. 1947-71. *2*
—. Hijacking. International Law. 1948-71. *38*
International Convention against the Taking of Hostages. International law. Treaties. 1949-79. *117*
International Law. -1973. *106*
—. 1972. *72*
—. 1980-81. *16*
—. Airplanes. Cuba. Deportation. Hijacking. Refugees. USA. 1983. *520*
—. Airplanes. Hijacking. 1930-73. *1*
—. Airplanes. Hijacking. 1950-76. *32*
—. Airplanes. Hijacking. 1970-73. *109*
—. Airplanes. Hijacking. USA. 1971-74. *561*
—. Canada. Foreign Relations. Hijacking. International Civil Aviation Organization. 1959-72. *560*
—. Civil Rights. 1944-77. *61*
—. Defense policy. Oil Industry and Trade. Western Nations. 1980-81. *62*
—. Diplomats. Europe, Western. USA. 1955-73. *58*
—. Entebbe raid. Hijacking. Israel. Popular Front for the Liberation of Palestine. Uganda. 1976. *4*
—. Entebbe (raid). Hijacking. Israel. Uganda. 1961-76. *3*
—. Hijacking. 1944-70. *120*
—. Hijacking. 1961-73. *36*
—. Hijacking. 1970's. *105*
—. Hijacking. International Civil Aviation Organization. 1947-71. *2*
—. Hijacking. International Civil Aviation Organization. 1948-71. *38*
—. Hostages. Iran. USA. 1979-80. *378*
—. Human rights. 1970-80. *95*

Israel 125

—. Intelligence gathering. 1967-78. *111*
—. International Convention against the Taking of Hostages. Treaties. 1949-79. *117*
—. UN. 1963-83. *115*
—. UN. 1970's. *43*
—. UN. 1972-. *122*
—. UN. 20c. *45*
International politics. Cities. Mass media. 1970's. *103*
—. Guerrilla Warfare. Models, structural. 1965-74. *13*
International Red Aid. Bibliographies. Ryle, J. Martin. USSR. 1922-28. *460*
—. Bulgaria. Documents. 1927. *170*
—. Poland. 1922-24. *135*
Intervention. Africa. Foreign Legion. France. 1961-78. *582*
—. Assassination. Bishop, Maurice. Grenada. Military operations. Politics. USA. 1980-83. *526*
—. Civil war. Lebanon. Palestine Liberation Organization. Syria. 1968-76. *311*
—. Lebanon. Military Strategy. Palestine Liberation Organization. Syria. 1976. *419*
—. Religion. War. 1960's-70's. *25*
Interviews. Aquino, Benigno, Jr. Assassination. Diokno, José. Foreign Relations. Marcos, Ferdinand. Philippines. 1972-83. *433*
—. Arafat, Yasser. Imperialism. Palestine Liberation Organization. Zionism. 1960's-70's. *292*
—. Arafat, Yasser. Palestine Liberation Organization. 1964-81. *422*
—. Asencio, Diego C.. Colombia (Bogotá). Diplomacy. M-19. USA. 1980. *523*
—. Asencio, Diego C. Diplomacy. USA. 1980-83. *495*
Iorga, Nicolae. Assassination. Foreign Relations. Romania. 1900-40. *148*
—. Assassination. Iron Guard. Madgearu, Virgil. Police. Romania. 1940. *279*
Iran. 1900's-82. *420*
—. Arab-Israeli conflict. Foreign policy. Hostages. Television. USA. 1975-81. *294*
—. Authority. Khomeini, Ruhollah. Religion. Revolution. 1970-82. *299*
—. Carter, Jimmy. Hostages. Presidents. Public opinion. USA. USA (Kentucky; Lexington). 1979. *310*
—. Diplomacy. Hostages. USA. 1979-80. *414*
—. Executive Power. Foreign Relations. Hostages. USA. 1981. *373*
—. Foreign policy. Hostages. Public Opinion. USA (Kentucky; Lexington). 1979. *569*
—. Foreign Relations. Hostages. Navies. USA. 1979-80. *328*
—. Foreign Relations. Hostages. Rescues. USA. 1979-80. *423*
—. Foreign Relations. Hostages. USA. 1979-80. *344*
—. Government. Liberia. Libya. Nicaragua. USA. 1979-80. *27*
—. Hostages. Inaugurals. Reagan, Ronald. Reporters and Reporting. Television. USA. 1980-81. *301*
—. Hostages. International law. USA. 1979-80. *378*
—. Hostages. Military Strategy. Rescues. USA. 1980. *313*
—. Hostages. Public Opinion Polls. Students. USA. 1976-81. *401*
—. Hostages. Rescues. USA. World Court. 1979-80. *390*
—. Legitimacy. Political Systems. Revolution. 1979-81. *287*
Iraq (Tammuz). Bombing. Foreign Ministry Sales Act (US). Israel. Nuclear Power Plants. USA. 1974-82. *300*
Ireland. Catholicism. Revolutionary Movements. 1848-1923. *219*

—. Childers, Erskine. Childers, Molly Osborn. Irish Republican Army. USA (Massachusetts; Boston). 1903-22. *272*
—. Civil Disturbances. Northern Ireland. 13c-20c. *171*
—. Civil war. Irish Republican Brotherhood. 1921-24. *222*
—. Collins, Michael. Guerrilla warfare. Independence Movements. Irish Republican Army. 1919-21. *144*
—. Communist Party. 1950-76. *225*
—. Foreign Relations. Great Britain. Political Attitudes. 1921. *198*
—. Great Britain. Northern Ireland. Sunningdale Conference. 1973. *196*
—. Irish Republican Army. Railroads. Strikes. 1921. *258*
Ireland (Dublin). Assassination. Cavendish, Frederick Charles. Spencer, John Poyntz, 5th Earl. 1889-1910. *154*
Irgun. Haganah. Israel. Labor movement. Political Factions. Stern Gang. Zionism (Revisionism). 1930's-82. *320*
Irish Republican Army. Assassination. Great Britain. Police. Special Branch. 1972-74. *204*
—. Attitudes. Canadians. Northern Ireland. 1969-82. *266*
—. Childers, Erskine. Childers, Molly Osborn. Ireland. USA (Massachusetts; Boston). 1903-22. *272*
—. Collins, Michael. Guerrilla warfare. Independence Movements. Ireland. 1919-21. *144*
—. Democracy. Great Britain. 1969-78. *142*
—. Ethnic conflict. Northern Ireland. 1920's-70's. *256*
—. Fuerzas Armadas de Liberación. New York Times. Red Brigades. Reporters and Reporting. 1977-79. *83*
—. Great Britain. Guerrilla Warfare. Northern Ireland. 1970's. *153*
—. Great Britain. Military training. Northern Ireland. 1969-70's. *157*
—. Great Britain. Northern Ireland. Novels. Stereotypes. 1975-79. *257*
—. Guerrilla warfare. 1916-21. *259*
—. Guerrilla Warfare. Northern Ireland. 1921-72. *281*
—. Ireland. Railroads. Strikes. 1921. *258*
—. Nationalism. Newspapers. 1896-1922. *168*
—. Northern Ireland. Political Theory. Violence. 1924-75. *233*
—. Northern Ireland. Politics. Propaganda. 1969-79. *260*
—. Political Factions. Political Leadership. 1920-80. *221*
Irish Republican Army (Provisional). 1969-75. *261*
—. Northern Ireland. Public opinion. 1916-80. *215*
—. Northern Ireland. Rebellions. 1973. *138*
Irish Republican Brotherhood. Civil war. Ireland. 1921-24. *222*
Iron Guard. Assassination. Iorga, Nicolae. Madgearu, Virgil. Police. Romania. 1940. *279*
—. Communist Party. Romania. 1930's-40's. *252*
Israel. Arab states. Becker, Jillian. Palestine Liberation Organization (review article). Political Change. 1967-83. *366*
—. Arab States. Boundaries. Joint Chiefs of Staff. USA. War. 1967. *400*
—. Arab states. Boundaries. Military Occupation. 1970. *322*
—. Arab states. Foreign Relations. Palestine Liberation Organization. 1960's-79. *348*
—. Arab States. USSR. 1967-74. *309*
—. Arab States. War. 1947-74. *351*
—. Arab-Israeli Conflict. Diaries. Sharett, Moshe. 1953-57. *374*
—. Arab-Israeli conflict. Palestine Liberation Organization. Political Factions. 1973-76. *359*

Israel

—. Arab-Israeli conflict. Palestinians. UN. 1950's-70's. *297*
—. Arabs. Great Britain. Trials. 1982. *184*
—. Arabs. Guerrilla Warfare. 1940's-60's. *356*
—. Arabs. Land Tenure. Plan Dalet. 1930's-67. *398*
—. Arabs. Middle East. Palestinians. Peace. 1948-72. *327*
—. Arabs. Palestine Liberation Organization. 1973-79. *335*
—. Arabs. Palestine Liberation Organization. Political parties. 1970-79. *386*
—. Arabs. Palestine Liberation Organization. USA. USSR. 1942-75. *409*
—. Autonomy. Diplomacy. Egypt. Palestinians. USA. 1978-81. *355*
—. Begin, Menachem. Fascism. Jabotinsky, Vladimir. Palestinians. Zionism (Revisionism). 1923-82. *302*
—. Boats. Foreign Relations. France (Cherbourg). 1967-74. *163*
—. Bombing. Foreign Ministry Sales Act (US). Iraq (Tammuz). Nuclear Power Plants. USA. 1974-82. *300*
—. Camp David agreement. Egypt. Palestinians. UN. USA. 1978-79. *376*
—. Demonstrations. Police. Religion. Violence. 1950-79. *346*
—. Deportation. Palestinians. Statistics. 1967-78. *347*
—. Diplomacy. Palestine Liberation Organization. 1973-. *314*
—. Elites. Jordan. Palestine Liberation Organization. Politics. West Bank. 1946-77. *357*
—. Entebbe raid. Hijacking. International law. Popular Front for the Liberation of Palestine. Uganda. 1976. *4*
—. Entebbe (raid). Hijacking. International law. Uganda. 1961-76. *3*
—. Entebbe raid. Uganda. 1968-77. *589*
—. Foreign Policy. Palestine Liberation Organization. Reagan, Ronald. UN. USA. 1975-81. *383*
—. Foreign Policy. Palestine Liberation Organization. Syria. UN Security Council. 1975-76. *321*
—. Gaza Strip. Jordan. Palestine Liberation Organization. Political Leadership. West Bank. 1970's. *350*
—. Haganah. Irgun. Labor movement. Political Factions. Stern Gang. Zionism (Revisionism). 1930's-82. *320*
—. Lebanon. Palestine Liberation Organization. Palestinians. War. 1967-82. *375*
—. Lebanon (Bekaa Valley). Mutinies. Palestine Liberation Organization. Political Factions. 1983. *317*
—. National Council of Churches. Palestine Liberation Organization. Protestantism. USA. 1974-81. *333*
—. National liberation movement. Palestinians. 1948-67. *342*
—. Nationalism. Palestinians. 1956-82. *372*
—. Palestine Liberation Organization. Political Attitudes. 1973-82. *388*
—. Palestinians. 1920's-73. *290*
—. Palestinians. Politics. 1967-78. *312*
Israel (Tel Aviv, Lod Airport). Japan. Popular Front for the Liberation of Palestine. United Red Army. 1960-73. *341*
Italian Social Republic. Fascism. 1943-45. *139*
Italy. 1965-81. *133*
—. 1970's. *242*
—. 1971-81. *253*
—. 19c. *217*
—. 20c. *137*
—. 20c. *263*

—. Action Française. Fascism. France. 1919-26. *143*
—. Amendola, Giovanni. Assassination. Fascism. 1920-25. *237*
—. Anarchism. Communist Parties and Movements. Germany, West. Socialism. 1960-79. *202*
—. Assassination. Colonial Government. Ethiopia. Graziani, Rodolfo. Political repression. 1936-37. *595*
—. Assassination. Matteotti, Giacomo. Mussolini, Benito. Socialists. 1924-26. *210*
—. Assassination. Moro, Aldo. Political Leadership. 1947-78. *192*
—. Austria. Foreign Relations. South Tyrol. Treaties. 1946-69. *226*
—. Christian Democratic Party. Kidnapping. Moro, Aldo. Red Brigades. 1978. *264*
—. Christian Democratic Party. Moro, Aldo. Murder. Red Brigades. 1975-83. *150*
—. Fascism. Futurism. Intellectuals. 1896-1929. *223*
—. Fascism. Matteotti, Giacomo. 1922-24. *209*
—. Fascism. Political Participation. 1930's. *6*
—. Fascism. Violence. 1919-22. *218*
—. Fascism. Violence. 1919-23. *207*
—. Fascism. Violence. 1919-29. *231*
—. Government. Press. 1978-82. *206*
—. Ideology. Red Brigades. Violence. 1968-80. *201*
—. Left. Political Factions. Violence. 1970's. *167*
—. Left. Right. 1960's-77. *241*
—. Leftism. Potere Operaio. Trials. 1979-82. *280*
—. Moro, Aldo. Murder. Politics. Red Brigades. 1970-78. *214*
—. Moro, Aldo. Politics. 1978-81. *236*
—. Political Culture. 1960-81. *140*
—. Political Theory. 1970's. *131*
—. Social Organization. 1960's-82. *146*
Italy (Brescia). Fascism. Trials. 1974-78. *132*
Italy (Liguria). Class struggle. Communist Party. Elections. Fascism. 1922-26. *230*
Italy (Milan; Piazza Fontana). Bombing. Conspiracy. Government. 1969-77. *130*
Italy (Padua). Autonomia Operaia. Red Brigades. Trials. 1970's. *255*
Italy (Rome). Agca, Mehmet Ali. Assassination. Bulgaria. John Paul II, Pope. Secret service. 1979-81. *220*
—. Agca, Mehmet Ali. Assassination. Bulgaria. John Paul II, Pope. USSR. 1979-81. *174*

J

Jabotinsky, Vladimir. Begin, Menachem. Fascism. Israel. Palestinians. Zionism (Revisionism). 1923-82. *302*
Jamaica. Political Protest. Ras-Tafarians. 1970's. *551*
Japan. Assassination. Politics. 1868-1941. *476*
—. Buraku Liberation League. Coalitions. Communist Party. Minobe, Ryokichi. Yoka High School. 1974. *472*
—. Israel (Tel Aviv, Lod Airport). Popular Front for the Liberation of Palestine. United Red Army. 1960-73. *341*
—. Okamoto, Kozo. Red Army Faction. 1972. *479*
—. Right. 1970's. *480*
Jews. See also Anti-Semitism.
—. Arabs. Nationalist Movements. Palestine (review article). Porath, Yehoshua. 1918-39. *361*
—. Argentina. Peronism. 1940-77. *547*
—. Assassination. France (Paris). Petliura, Simon. Schwartzbard, Shalom. Ukraine. 1926. *466*
—. Boycotts. Olympic Games. 1930's-70's. *63*
John Paul II, Pope. Agca, Mehmet Ali. Assassination. Bulgaria. Italy (Rome). Secret service. 1979-81. *220*

—. Agca, Mehmet Ali. Assassination. Bulgaria. Italy (Rome). USSR. 1979-81. *174*
—. Assassination. Bulgaria. Catholics. Poland. USSR. 1979-83. *127*
—. Assassination. Bulgaria. Communist Countries. Secret service. Trotsky, Leon. USSR. 1940-82. *107*
—. Assassination. Foreign Policy. NATO. Poland. Turkey. USSR. 1980-83. *175*
Joint Chiefs of Staff. Arab States. Boundaries. Israel. USA. War. 1967. *400*
Jordan. Elites. Israel. Palestine Liberation Organization. Politics. West Bank. 1946-77. *357*
—. Foreign Relations. Gaza Strip. Palestine Liberation Organization. West Bank. 1967-77. *369*
—. Gaza Strip. Israel. Palestine Liberation Organization. Political Leadership. West Bank. 1970's. *350*
—. Hussein, King. Palestine Liberation Organization. 1967-79. *397*
Jordan (Jerusalem). Hussein, King. Political status. 1948-67. *387*
Judicial system. Germany (Nuremberg). Police. Political Repression. SA (Sturmabteilung). 1933-34. *240*

K

Karmal, Babrak. Afghanistan. Amin, Hafizullah. Revolution. USSR. 1979-81. *358*
Kataeb party. Attitudes. Government. Lebanon. Militia. 1936-73. *392*
Khomeini, Ruhollah. Authority. Iran. Religion. Revolution. 1970-82. *299*
Kidnapping. American Board Commissioners for Foreign Missions. Internal Macedonian Revolutionary Organization. Macedonia. Missions and Missionaries. Roosevelt, Theodore. Stone, Ellen M. USA. 1901-02. *275*
—. Assassination. Committee of State Security (KGB). Foreign Policy. USSR. 1920's-60's. *489*
—. Black Liberation Army. Boudin, Kathy. Leftism. USA. Weathermen. 1967-81. *563*
—. Castro, Raul. Cuba. USA. 1958. *552*
—. Christian Democratic Party. Italy. Moro, Aldo. Red Brigades. 1978. *264*
—. Finland. Lapua movement. 1930. *251*
—. Independence Movements. Macedonia. Missions and Missionaries. Stone, Ellen M. USA. 1901-03. *274*
Korea, North. Burma (Rangoon). Korea, South. 1983. *490*
Korea, South. Assassination. Foreign Relations. Park Chung-hee. Politics. USA. 1979-82. *425*
—. Burma (Rangoon). Korea, North. 1983. *490*
Kroecher, Norbert. Operation Leo. Sweden (Stockholm). 1970-79. *254*

L

Labor movement. Haganah. Irgun. Israel. Political Factions. Stern Gang. Zionism (Revisionism). 1930's-82. *320*
—. Mapai. Palestine. Political Factions. Violence. 1932-35. *381*
Labor Unions and Organizations. Guatemala. Politics. Violence. 1973-82. *518*
Land Tenure. Arabs. Israel. Plan Dalet. 1930's-67. *398*
—. Guatemala. Violence. 1940's-70's. *515*
Lapua movement. Finland. Kidnapping. 1930. *251*
Latin America. 1970-78. *544*
—. Anti-Communist Movements. Death squads. 1950's-83. *522*
—. Asia. Diplomacy. Europe. Guerrilla warfare. 1960-72. *88*
—. Catholics. Marxism. Politics. Religion (review article). 20c. *521*
—. Dictatorship. Foreign Policy. Revolutionary Movements. USA. 1958-79. *516*
—. Europe, Western. 1968-74. *121*
—. Guerrilla movements. Middle East. 1970-75. *94*
—. Guerrilla Warfare. 1970-84. *540*
—. Political conditions. Populism (review article). 1960-80. *541*
—. Riots. Social Psychology. 1949-63. *513*
Law and society. France. Germany. Lawyers. Literature. Military Occupation. Nazism. World War II. 1850-1945. *282*
Law Enforcement. Freedom of the Press. Mass Media. 1968-78. *9*
—. Northern Ireland. Special Powers Act. 1922-79. *145*
Lawyers. France. Germany. Law and society. Literature. Military Occupation. Nazism. World War II. 1850-1945. *282*
—. Germany, West. Political repression. 1971-76. *268*
—. Northern Ireland. 1973-81. *185*
Leadership. Civil war. El Salvador. 1972-81. *553*
League of Nations. UN. 1934-82. *48*
Lebanon. Arab states. Civil war. Models. Palestine Liberation Organization. 1975-76. *304*
—. Arab states. Civil War. Palestine Liberation Organization. 1982-83. *345*
—. Arab-Israeli conflict. War. 1947-82. *407*
—. Attitudes. Government. Kataeb party. Militia. 1936-73. *392*
—. Civil war. 1943-75. *391*
—. Civil war. 1975-76. *316*
—. Civil war. Intervention. Palestine Liberation Organization. Syria. 1968-76. *311*
—. Civil War. Palestine Liberation Organization. 1950's-70's. *284*
—. Civil War. Political Factions. Religion. Violence. 1975-82. *421*
—. Civil war. Sects, Religious. Social Organization. 1975-77. *404*
—. Intervention. Military Strategy. Palestine Liberation Organization. Syria. 1976. *419*
—. Israel. Palestine Liberation Organization. Palestinians. War. 1967-82. *375*
—. Naji, Talal. Palestine Liberation Organization. 1948-78. *289*
Lebanon (Beirut). Bombing. Embassies. Marines. USA. 22d Marine Amphibious Unit, US. 1983. *354*
—. Defense Department. Government investigations. Military Strategy. 1983. *416*
Lebanon (Bekaa Valley). Israel. Mutinies. Palestine Liberation Organization. Political Factions. 1983. *317*
Lebanon, southern. Civil War. 1970-79. *403*
Left. Italy. Political Factions. Violence. 1970's. *167*
—. Italy. Right. 1960's-77. *241*
—. Moderates. Political parties. Venezuela. 1958-69. *507*
—. Turkey. 1960-79. *325*
Leftism. Bell, Daniel. Intellectuals. Personal narratives. Violence. 1919-80. *11*
—. Black Liberation Army. Boudin, Kathy. Kidnapping. USA. Weathermen. 1967-81. *563*
—. Fascism. 1970-80. *119*
—. Italy. Potere Operaio. Trials. 1979-82. *280*
Legislation. Federal Government (US). State Government. 1970's-80's. *580*
—. Taiwan. 1949-81. *437*
Legitimacy. Iran. Political Systems. Revolution. 1979-81. *287*
Lehi (Lohamei Herut Israel). Haganah. Irgun. Israel. Labor movement. Political Factions. Zionism (Revisionism). 1930's-82. *320*
Lenin, V. I. Bolsheviks. Revolutionaries. Russia. Zagorski, Vladimir M. 1902-19. *426*

—. Communist parties and Movements. Political Theory. Revolutionary movements. Violence. 1890's-1970's. *160*
—. Nechaev, Sergei. Political Leadership. Psychohistory. Stalin, Joseph. USSR. 1869-72. 20c. *469*
Letters. Bulgarians. Exarchate Church. Greeks. Macedonia (Megarovo, Turnovo). 1870-1904. *129*
Liberalism. Democracy. Ethics. Political Theory. Violence. 1960's-83. *80*
Liberia. Government. Iran. Libya. Nicaragua. USA. 1979-80. *27*
Libya. Government. Iran. Liberia. Nicaragua. USA. 1979-80. *27*
Literature. Culture. Russia. USSR. 17c-20c. *435*
—. France. Germany. Law and society. Lawyers. Military Occupation. Nazism. World War II. 1850-1945. *282*
—. Politics. 1960's-70's. *71*
Lukács, Georg. Camus, Albert. Russia. 1880-1980. *432*

M

Macedonia. American Board Commissioners for Foreign Missions. Internal Macedonian Revolutionary Organization. Kidnapping. sions and Missionaries. Roosevelt, Theodore. Stone, Ellen M. USA. 1901-02. *275*
—. Independence Movements. Kidnapping. Missions and Missionaries. Stone, Ellen M. USA. 1901-03. *274*
Macedonia (Megarovo, Turnovo). Bulgarians. Exarchate Church. Greeks. Letters. 1870-1904. *129*
Madgearu, Virgil. Assassination. Iorga, Nicolae. Iron Guard. Police. Romania. 1940. *279*
Makarios, Archbishop. Cyprus. 1946-74. *227*
Malaysia. Communists. 1974-76. *446*
Mao Tse-tung. Communism. Political Theory. Revolution. Violence. ca 1850-1970's. *487*
Mapai. Labor movement. Palestine. Political Factions. Violence. 1932-35. *381*
Marcos, Ferdinand. Aquino, Benigno, Jr. Assassination. Diokno, José. Foreign Relations. Interviews. Philippines. 1972-83. *433*
Marines. Bombing. Embassies. Lebanon (Beirut). USA. 22d Marine Amphibious Unit, US. 1983. *354*
Martial Law. Civil Rights. Nuclear Power Plants. Plutonium. 1970's. *47*
Marxism. Anarchism. 1872-1972. *249*
—. Catholics. Latin America. Politics. Religion (review article). 20c. *521*
—. Democracy. -1973. *55*
—. Dimitrov, Georgi. Fascism. Historiography. 1930's-70's. *82*
—. People's Liberation Front. Political Parties. Rebellions. Sri Lanka. 1932-71. *429*
Marxism-Leninism. India. Political Theory. Singh, Bhagat. 1930-31. *463*
—. Political Theory. 1870's-1972. *85*
Mass media. Cities. International politics. 1970's. *103*
—. Democracy. 1960's-70's. *112*
—. Freedom of the Press. Law Enforcement. 1968-78. *9*
—. Police. 1970's. *5*
Matteotti, Giacomo. Assassination. Italy. Mussolini, Benito. Socialists. 1924-26. *210*
—. Fascism. Italy. 1922-24. *209*
Meinhof, Ulrike. Baader-Meinhof Gang. Germany, West. Radicals and Radicalism. Trials. 1975. *197*

Merleau-Ponty, Maurice. Humanism (review article). Political Theory. Violence. 1946-47. *458*
Mexicans. Carranza, Venustiano. Mexico. Rebellions. USA (Texas). 1848-1920. *575*
Mexico. Assassination. Spain (Barcelona). Trotsky, Leon. 1940. *502*
—. Carranza, Venustiano. Mexicans. Rebellions. USA (Texas). 1848-1920. *575*
Middle East. Arabs. Israel. Palestinians. Peace. 1948-72. *327*
—. Arafat, Yasser. Geneva conference. Militants. Palestine Liberation Organization. 1974. *371*
—. Black September. Palestinians. Refugees. 1967-73. *415*
—. China. USSR. 1965-80. *462*
—. Communist parties and Movements. Palestine Liberation Organization. 1967-70. *295*
—. Disarmament. UN. USSR. 1972. *97*
—. Europe. Palestine Liberation Organization. Peace. 1980. *65*
—. Foreign Policy. Palestine Liberation Organization. 1974-80. *410*
—. Foreign Policy. Palestine Liberation Organization. Rabat Conference (1974). USA. 1967-75. *408*
—. Foreign Relations. 1982. *385*
—. Foreign Relations. Reagan, Ronald. USA. USSR. 1981. *331*
—. Golan Heights. Military. Palestine Liberation Organization. Sinai Peninsula. 1973-75. *336*
—. Guerrilla movements. Latin America. 1970-75. *94*
—. Nuclear arms. Palestine Liberation Organization. 1970-75. *298*
Militants. Arafat, Yasser. Geneva conference. Middle East. Palestine Liberation Organization. 1974. *371*
Militarism. Chile. Violence. 1970-74. *494*
Military. Golan Heights. Middle East. Palestine Liberation Organization. Sinai Peninsula. 1973-75. *336*
—. Oklahoma, University of. Police. Simulation and Games. 1970's. *102*
Military aid. Chile. Cuba. Elections. Foreign Relations. USA. Venezuela. 1963-64. *517*
Military Government. Argentina. Foreign Relations. USA. 1940-81. *525*
—. Civil war. El Salvador. 1961-79. *500*
—. Communist Party. Coups d'Etat. Political Leadership. Thailand. 1950-78. *464*
—. Nigeria. 1966-79. *593*
Military Occupation. Arab states. Boundaries. Israel. 1970. *322*
—. France. Germany. Law and society. Lawyers. Literature. Nazism. World War II. 1850-1945. *282*
Military operations. Assassination. Bishop, Maurice. Grenada. Intervention. Politics. USA. 1980-83. *526*
—. Palestine Liberation Organization. Politics. 1967-71. *293*
Military Strategy. Defense Department. Government investigations. Lebanon (Beirut). 1983. *416*
—. Foreign Policy. Intelligence gathering. 1984. *574*
—. Guerrilla Warfare. Revolutionary war. 1688-1973. *40*
—. Hostages. Iran. Rescues. USA. 1980. *313*
—. Intervention. Lebanon. Palestine Liberation Organization. Syria. 1976. *419*
—. Viet Cong. Vietnam War. 1960's-70's. *477*
Military training. Great Britain. Irish Republican Army. Northern Ireland. 1969-70's. *157*
Militia. Attitudes. Government. Kataeb party. Lebanon. 1936-73. *392*
—. Germany. Paramilitary forces. Political Parties. Violence. 1920-32. *136*

Minobe, Ryokichi. Buraku Liberation League. Coalitions. Communist Party. Japan. Yoka High School. 1974. *472*
Mirbach, Wilhelm von. Assassination. Bolsheviks. Brest-Litovsk, Treaty of. Political Factions. Socialist Revolutionaries. USSR. 1918. *475*
Missions and Missionaries. American Board Commissioners for Foreign Missions. Internal Macedonian Revolutionary Organization. Kidnapping. Macedonia. Roosevelt, Theodore. Stone, Ellen M. USA. 1901-02. *275*
—. Diplomacy. Navies. Ottoman Empire. Roosevelt, Theodore. USA. 1903-04. *329*
—. Independence Movements. Kidnapping. Macedonia. Stone, Ellen M. USA. 1901-03. *274*
Mitrione, Dan A. Agency for International Development. Tupamaros. Uruguay. USA. 1969-73. *519*
Models. Arab states. Civil war. Lebanon. Palestine Liberation Organization. 1975-76. *304*
Models (Poisson). Quantitative Methods. USA. 1968-74. *567*
Models, structural. Guerrilla Warfare. International Politics. 1965-74. *13*
Moderates. Left. Political parties. Venezuela. 1958-69. *507*
Modernization. Colombia. *Violencia*. 1945-53. *536*
—. Turkey. Violence. 1946-80. *363*
Montalègre, Commandant. Assassination. Germany. Plebiscites. Poland. Silesia (Bytom). 1921. *205*
Montreal Agreement. Airplanes. Hijacking. Victims. Warsaw Convention. 1929-73. *89*
Moro, Aldo. Assassination. Italy. Political Leadership. 1947-78. *192*
—. Christian Democratic Party. Italy. Kidnapping. Red Brigades. 1978. *264*
—. Christian Democratic Party. Italy. Murder. Red Brigades. 1975-83. *150*
—. Italy. Murder. Politics. Red Brigades. 1970-78. *214*
—. Italy. Politics. 1978-81. *236*
Movement of Priests for the Third World. Argentina. Catholic Church. Clergy. Radicals and Radicalism. Violence. 1969-70's. *506*
Moyne, 1st Baron. Assassination. Egypt (Cairo). Palestine. 1939-45. *412*
—. Assassination. Great Britain. Palestine. 1944-45. *307*
Multinational corporations. Argentina. Charities. 1955-80. *496*
Murder. Christian Democratic Party. Italy. Moro, Aldo. Red Brigades. 1975-83. *150*
—. Cyprus (Leukosia). EOKA (organization). 1956. *393*
—. Italy. Moro, Aldo. Politics. Red Brigades. 1970-78. *214*
Muslims. Assimilation. Thailand. 1972-74. *424*
Mussolini, Benito. Assassination. Italy. Matteotti, Giacomo. Socialists. 1924-26. *210*
Mutinies. Israel. Lebanon (Bekaa Valley). Palestine Liberation Organization. Political Factions. 1983. *317*
M-19. Asencio, Diego C.. Colombia (Bogotá). Diplomacy. Interviews. USA. 1980. *523*

N

Naji, Talal. Lebanon. Palestine Liberation Organization. 1948-78. *289*
National Characteristics. Assassination. Gun control. Presidents. USA. 20c. *568*
National Council of Churches. Israel. Palestine Liberation Organization. Protestantism. USA. 1974-81. *333*
National Front. Gaza Strip. Palestine Liberation Organization. Political activism. West Bank. 1967-73. *380*

—. Great Britain. Racism. 1970's. *141*
—. Great Britain. Voting and Voting Behavior. 1979. *181*
National liberation movement. Israel. Palestinians. 1948-67. *342*
—. Palestinians. 1967-76. *343*
National revolutionaries. Gandhi, Mahatma. Indian National Congress. 1919-35. *470*
National Self-image. Palestine Liberation Organization. 1964-76. *384*
Nationalism. Albania. Gurakuqi, Luigj. Politics. 1911-25. *232*
—. Algeria. World War II. 1942-45. *587*
—. Assassination. Botswana. Political ideology. Ratshosa, Simon. 1916-32. *592*
—. Basques. Euzkadi Ta Askatatuna (ETA). Fascism. Spain (Burgos). Trials. 1970. *244*
—. Egypt. Great Britain. Secret societies. 1870-1924. *339*
—. France (Brittany). 1880-1978. *165*
—. Irish Republican Army. Newspapers. 1896-1922. *168*
—. Israel. Palestinians. 1956-82. *372*
—. Palestine Liberation Organization. 20c. *330*
—. Palestine Liberation Organization. Political leadership. 1930-76. *367*
—. Ukraine. 1950's-70's. *444*
—. Arabs. Jews. Palestine (review article). Porath, Yehoshua. 1918-39. *361*
Nationalist Popular Front. Bolivia. Government. 1971-73. *492*
NATO. Assassination. Foreign Policy. John Paul II, Pope. Poland. Turkey. USSR. 1980-83. *175*
Navies. Diplomacy. Missions and Missionaries. Ottoman Empire. Roosevelt, Theodore. USA. 1903-04. *329*
—. Foreign Relations. Hostages. Iran. USA. 1979-80. *328*
Naxalite movement. India. 1975. *486*
—. India (Bihar; Bhojpur). Peasants. Political repression. Rebellions. 1967-79. *465*
—. India (Srikakulam District). Rebellions. Social Conditions. 1968-70. *471*
Nazism. Austria (Vorarlberg). 1933-34. *265*
—. Bonapartism. Fascism. 1848-1939. *161*
—. Economic Conditions. Fascism. Germany. Social Conditions. 1926-36. *173*
—. Films. Germany, West. Public Opinion. 1933-45. 1970's. *270*
—. France. Germany. Law and society. Lawyers. Literature. Military Occupation. World War II. 1850-1945. *282*
Nechaev, Sergei. Lenin, V. I. Political Leadership. Psychohistory. Stalin, Joseph. USSR. 1869-72. 20c. *469*
Nehru, Jawaharlal. Akali Dal Party. India. Separatist Movements. Sikhs. Singh, Tara. 1960-61. *478*
—. India. Socialism. 1920-64. *440*
Neofascism. Europe. 1977-81. *53*
Neo-Nazism. Austria. Political parties. 1938-82. *283*
Netherlands. Decolonization. Immigration. 1945-79. *269*
—. South Moluccans. 1950's-70's. *176*
New York Times. Fuerzas Armadas de Liberación. Irish Republican Army. Red Brigades. Reporters and Reporting. 1977-79. *83*
Newspapers. Irish Republican Army. Nationalism. 1896-1922. *168*
Nicaragua. Armaments. Costa Rica. Foreign Relations. Rudd, Eldon. USA. Vance, Cyrus. 1978-79. *554*
—. Government. Iran. Liberia. Libya. USA. 1979-80. *7*
—. Political Leadership. Somoza, Anastasio. 1933-36. *509*
—. Somoza family. 1956-70's. *530*
Nigeria. Civil war. Ethnicity. 1966-67. *596*

130 Nigeria

—. Military government. 1966-79. *593*
North America. Foreign Policy. Palestine Congress of North America. 1979. *406*
Northern Ireland. Attitudes. Canadians. Irish Republican Army. 1969-82. *266*
—. Cartoons and Caricatures (political). Great Britain. Prejudice. 1968-80. *190*
—. Catholics. Politics. Protestants. Violence. 1912-72. *246*
—. Children. Civil disturbances. Genocide. Personality testing. 1971-75. *164*
—. Civil Disturbances. Ireland. 13c-20c. *171*
—. Civil Disturbances. Politics. 1945-72. *224*
—. Colonialism. Great Britain. 1850-1980. *110*
—. Diplock Report. Political Imprisonment. Trials. 1971-74. *151*
—. Ethnic conflict. Irish Republican Army. 1920's-70's. *256*
—. Government. 1968-80. *200*
—. Great Britain. Guerrilla Warfare. Irish Republican Army. 1970's. *153*
—. Great Britain. Ireland. Sunningdale Conference. 1973. *196*
—. Great Britain. Irish Republican Army. Military training. 1969-70's. *157*
—. Great Britain. Irish Republican Army. Novels. Stereotypes. 1975-79. *257*
—. Great Britain. Politics. Violence. 1690-1972. *239*
—. Great Britain. Social Problems (review article). Violence. 1918-78. *183*
—. Guerrilla Warfare. Irish Republican Army. 1921-72. *281*
—. Human rights. 1967-78. *158*
—. Irish Republican Army. Political Theory. Violence. 1924-75. *233*
—. Irish Republican Army. Politics. Propaganda. 1969-79. *260*
—. Irish Republican Army (Provisional). Public opinion. 1916-80. *215*
—. Irish Republican Army, Provisional. Rebellions. 1973. *138*
—. Law Enforcement. Special Powers Act. 1922-79. *145*
—. Lawyers. 1973-81. *185*
—. Pacifism. Political Factions. 1969-79. *187*
—. Palestine. Political theory. Tactics. Uruguay. ca 1960's-70's. *90*
—. Violence. 1969-77. *213*
Northern Ireland (Belfast). Assassination. 1969-78. *199*
Northern Ireland Executive. Catholics. Coalitions. Provincial government. Social Democratic Labour Party. 1974. *212*
Novels. Great Britain. Irish Republican Army. Northern Ireland. Stereotypes. 1975-79. *257*
Nuclear Arms. Atomic Energy Commission (US). Hijacking. 1970-74. *57*
—. Middle East. Palestine Liberation Organization. 1970-75. *298*
Nuclear materials. Convention on the Physical Protection of Nuclear Materials. Treaties. UN. 1966-82. *59*
Nuclear Power Plants. 1974. *98*
—. Bombing. Foreign Ministry Sales Act (US). Iraq (Tammuz). Israel. USA. 1974-82. *300*
—. Civil Rights. Martial Law. Plutonium. 1970's. *47*
Nuclear Science and Technology. ca 1972-74. *68*
—. ICBM's. 1960's-70's. *14*

O

Obote, Milton. Amin, Idi. Political violence. Uganda. 1962-72. *585*
Oil Industry and Trade. Defense policy. International law. Western Nations. 1980-81. *62*
Okamoto, Kozo. Japan. Red Army Faction. 1972. *479*
Okhrana. Plehve, Vyacheslav. Russia. Secret police. 1880's-1900's. *449*
Oklahoma, University of. Military. Police. Simulation and Games. 1970's. *102*
Olympic Games. Boycotts. Jews. 1930's-70's. *63*
Operation Leo. Kroecher, Norbert. Sweden (Stockholm). 1970-79. *254*
Organization of American States. Americas (North and South). 1970-71. *19*
Ottama, Bhikhu U. Burma. Independence Movements. India. 1905-39. *431*
Ottoman Empire. Armenian Revolutionary Federation. Independence Movements. 1830-1921. *28*
—. Diplomacy. Missions and Missionaries. Navies. Roosevelt, Theodore. USA. 1903-04. *329*

P

Pacifism. Northern Ireland. Political Factions. 1969-79. *187*
Palestine. Assassination. Egypt (Cairo). Moyne, 1st Baron. 1939-45. *412*
—. Assassination. Great Britain. Moyne, 1st Baron. 1944-45. *307*
—. Churchill, Winston. Foreign policy. Great Britain. World War II. 1937-47. *306*
—. Great Britain. Zionism. 1939-48. *308*
—. Labor movement. Mapai. Political Factions. Violence. 1932-35. *381*
—. Northern Ireland. Political theory. Tactics. Uruguay. ca 1960's-70's. *90*
—. Palestine Liberation Organization. Refugees. Revolutionary Movements. Sayeh, Mai. Union of Palestinian Women. Women. 1956-82. *377*
Palestine Congress of North America. Foreign Policy. North America. 1979. *406*
Palestine Liberation Organization. 1948-75. *405*
—. 1970's. *365*
—. 1970-82. *364*
—. American Friends Service Committee. Arab-Israeli conflict. Foreign Policy. Friends, Society of. USA. 1970's. *334*
—. Arab states. Civil War. Lebanon. 1982-83. *345*
—. Arab states. Civil war. Lebanon. Models. 1975-76. *304*
—. Arab States. Europe, Western. Foreign Relations. 1973-78. *288*
—. Arab states. Foreign Relations. 1964-81. *402*
—. Arab states. Foreign Relations. Israel. 1960's-79. *348*
—. Arab states. Political Factions. 1974-83. *286*
—. Arab States. Rabat Conference (1974). 1974. *353*
—. Arab-Israeli conflict. 1947-75. *349*
—. Arab-Israeli conflict. Blacks. Foreign Policy. Southern Christian Leadership Conference. USA. 1979. *411*
—. Arab-Israeli conflict. Israel. Political Factions. 1973-76. *359*
—. Arabs. Israel. 1973-79. *335*
—. Arabs. Israel. Political parties. 1970-79. *386*
—. Arabs. Israel. USA. USSR. 1942-75. *409*
—. Arafat, Yasser. Geneva conference. Middle East. Militants. 1974. *371*
—. Arafat, Yasser. Imperialism. Interviews. Zionism. 1960's-70's. *292*
—. Arafat, Yasser. Interviews. 1964-81. *422*
—. China. Foreign relations. 1955-76. *326*

Police   131

—. Civil war. Intervention. Lebanon. Syria. 1968-76. *311*
—. Civil War. Lebanon. 1950's-70's. *284*
—. Communist parties and Movements. Middle East. 1967-70. *295*
—. Diplomacy. Israel. 1973-. *314*
—. Elites. Israel. Jordan. Politics. West Bank. 1946-77. *357*
—. Europe. Middle East. Peace. 1980. *65*
—. Foreign Policy. Israel. Reagan, Ronald. UN. USA. 1975-81. *383*
—. Foreign Policy. Israel. Syria. UN Security Council. 1975-76. *321*
—. Foreign Policy. Middle East. 1974-80. *410*
—. Foreign Policy. Middle East. Rabat Conference (1974). USA. 1967-75. *408*
—. Foreign Policy. USSR. 1947-80. *319*
—. Foreign Relations. 1964-79. *318*
—. Foreign Relations. 1964-80. *296*
—. Foreign Relations. 1973-77. *291*
—. Foreign Relations. Gaza Strip. Jordan. West Bank. 1967-77. *369*
—. Foreign Relations. Political Factions. 1964-75. *285*
—. Foreign Relations. Revolutionary movements. 1964-75. *352*
—. Gaza Strip. Israel. Jordan. Political Leadership. West Bank. 1970's. *350*
—. Gaza Strip. National Front. Political activism. West Bank. 1967-73. *380*
—. Golan Heights. Middle East. Military. Sinai Peninsula. 1973-75. *336*
—. Hussein, King. Jordan. 1967-79. *397*
—. Institutional development. 1964-75. *324*
—. Intervention. Lebanon. Military Strategy. Syria. 1976. *419*
—. Israel. Lebanon. Palestinians. War. 1967-82. *375*
—. Israel. Lebanon (Bekaa Valley). Mutinies. Political Factions. 1983. *317*
—. Israel. National Council of Churches. Protestantism. USA. 1974-81. *333*
—. Israel. Political Attitudes. 1973-82. *388*
—. Lebanon. Naji, Talal. 1948-78. *289*
—. Middle East. Nuclear arms. 1970-75. *298*
—. Military operations. Politics. 1967-71. *293*
—. National Self-image. 1964-76. *384*
—. Nationalism. 20c. *330*
—. Nationalism. Political leadership. 1930-76. *367*
—. Palestine. Refugees. Revolutionary Movements. Sayeh, Mai. Union of Palestinian Women. Women. 1956-82. *377*
—. Political Development. 1948-83. *305*
—. Radio. 1954-75. *303*
—. UN. 1964-79. *338*
—. USSR. 1964-74. *417*
Palestine Liberation Organization (review article). Arab states. Becker, Jillian. Israel. Political Change. 1967-83. *366*
Palestine (review article). Arabs. Jews. Nationalist Movements. Porath, Yehoshua. 1918-39. *361*
Palestinians. 1896-1978. *362*
—. Arab-Israeli conflict. Israel. UN. 1950's-70's. *297*
—. Arabs. Israel. Middle East. Peace. 1948-72. *327*
—. Autonomy. Diplomacy. Egypt. Israel. USA. 1978-81. *355*
—. Begin, Menachem. Fascism. Israel. Jabotinsky, Vladimir. Zionism (Revisionism). 1923-82. *302*
—. Black September. Middle East. Refugees. 1967-73. *415*
—. Black September. Political strategy. 1967-73. *374*
—. Camp David agreement. Egypt. Israel. UN. USA. 1978-79. *376*
—. Deportation. Israel. Statistics. 1967-78. *347*
—. Israel. 1920's-73. *290*
—. Israel. Lebanon. Palestine Liberation Organization. War. 1967-82. *375*
—. Israel. National liberation movement. 1948-67. *342*
—. Israel. Nationalism. 1956-82. *372*
—. Israel. Politics. 1967-78. *312*
—. National liberation movement. 1967-76. *343*
—. Refugees. UN. 1948-82. *399*
—. UN. 1974-79. *382*
Papadopoulos, George. Assassination. Greece. ca 1956-76. *186*
Paramilitary forces. Germany. Militia. Political Parties. Violence. 1920-32. *136*
Park Chung-hee. Assassination. Foreign Relations. Korea, South. Politics. USA. 1979-82. *425*
Parliaments. Assassination. Chile. Social Classes. 1920-70. *497*
Party of National Unity. Awakening Hungarians. Hungary. Secret societies. Social Democrats. 1922-26. *248*
Patriotism. Columbians, Inc. Racism. USA (Georgia; Atlanta). Violence. 1946-47. *564*
Peace. Arabs. Israel. Middle East. Palestinians. 1948-72. *327*
—. Europe. Middle East. Palestine Liberation Organization. 1980. *65*
Peasants. India (Bihar; Bhojpur). Naxalite movement. Political repression. Rebellions. 1967-79. *465*
—. Political attitudes. Russia. Socialist Revolutionaries. 1907-08. *467*
—. Rebellions. Russia. 1905-18. *451*
People's Liberation Front. Marxism. Political parties. Rebellions. Sri Lanka. 1932-71. *429*
People's National Congress. Assassination. Guyana. Revolution. Rodney, Walter. 1966-81. *505*
People's Revolutionary Army (ERP). Argentina. 1968-74. *514*
People's Will. Revolutionary Movements. Russia. 19c-20c. *468*
Peronism. Argentina. Jews. 1940-77. *547*
Personal Narratives. Anti-Semitism. Blumberg, Janice Rothschild. Bombing. Public Opinion. Trials. USA (Georgia; Atlanta). 1958-59. *558*
—. Bell, Daniel. Intellectuals. Leftism. Violence. 1919-80. *11*
Personality testing. Children. Civil disturbances. Genocide. Northern Ireland. 1971-75. *164*
Petliura, Simon. Assassination. France (Paris). Jews. Schwartzbard, Shalom. Ukraine. 1926. *466*
Philippines. Aquino, Benigno, Jr. Assassination. Diokno, José. Foreign Relations. Interviews. Marcos, Ferdinand. 1972-83. *433*
Plan Dalet. Arabs. Israel. Land Tenure. 1930's-67. *398*
Plebiscites. Assassination. Germany. Montalègre, Commandant. Poland. Silesia (Bytom). 1921. *205*
Plehve, Vyacheslav. Okhrana. Russia. Secret police. 1880's-1900's. *449*
Plug uglies. Class conflict. Commission on Industrial Relations. Progressive era. Violence. 1890-1920. *570*
Plutonium. Civil Rights. Martial Law. Nuclear Power Plants. 1970's. *47*
Poland. Assassination. Bulgaria. Catholics. John Paul II, Pope. USSR. 1979-83. *177*
—. Assassination. Foreign Policy. John Paul II, Pope. NATO. Turkey. USSR. 1980-83. *175*
—. Assassination. Germany. Montalègre, Commandant. Plebiscites. Silesia (Bytom). 1921. *205*
—. Assassination. Steiger, Stanislaw. Trials. Wojciechowski, Stanislaw. 1924-25. *193*
—. International Red Aid. 1922-24. *135*
Police. Assassination. Great Britain. Irish Republican Army. Special Branch. 1972-74. *204*

132 Police

—. Assassination. Iorga, Nicolae. Iron Guard. Madgearu, Virgil. Romania. 1940. *279*
—. Demonstrations. Israel. Religion. Violence. 1950-79. *346*
—. Europe, Western. 1970-81. *152*
—. Germany (Nuremberg). Judicial system. Political Repression. SA (Sturmabteilung). 1933-34. *240*
—. Great Britain. 1970-79. *172*
—. Mass Media. 1970's. *5*
—. Military. Oklahoma, University of. Simulation and Games. 1970's. *102*
Political activism. Gaza Strip. National Front. Palestine Liberation Organization. West Bank. 1967-73. *380*
Political Attitudes. Foreign Relations. Great Britain. Ireland. 1921. *198*
—. Israel. Palestine Liberation Organization. 1973-82. *388*
—. Peasants. Russia. Socialist Revolutionaries. 1907-08. *467*
Political Change. 1982-83. *76*
—. Arab states. Becker, Jillian. Israel. Palestine Liberation Organization (review article). 1967-83. *366*
—. Economic conditions. Elections. Tupamaros. Uruguay. 1962-71. *528*
—. Spain. 1970's. *235*
Political collaboration. Communist Party. Romania. Workers' and Peasants' Bloc. 1922-33. *159*
Political conditions. Latin America. Populism (review article). 1960-80. *541*
Political crisis. El Salvador. USA. 1972-81. *537*
Political Culture. Carlists. Fascism. Sindicalismo Libre. Spain. 1830-1980. *273*
—. Italy. 1960-81. *140*
Political development. Economic development. Spain. 1975-79. *229*
—. Palestine Liberation Organization. 1948-83. *305*
—. Palestine Liberation Organization. 1964-75. *324*
Political Factions. Arab states. Palestine Liberation Organization. 1974-83. *286*
—. Arab-Israeli conflict. Israel. Palestine Liberation Organization. 1973-76. *359*
—. Assassination. Bolsheviks. Brest-Litovsk, Treaty of. Mirbach, Wilhelm von. Socialist Revolutionaries. USSR. 1918. *475*
—. Basques. Government. Spain. Suárez, Adolfo. 1977-79. *177*
—. Civil War. Lebanon. Religion. Violence. 1975-82. *421*
—. Communist Party. Turkey. 1920-70's. *456*
—. Foreign Relations. Palestine Liberation Organization. 1964-75. *285*
—. Haganah. Irgun. Israel. Labor movement. Stern Gang. Zionism (Revisionism). 1930's-82. *320*
—. Irish Republican Army. Political Leadership. 1920-80. *221*
—. Israel. Lebanon (Bekaa Valley). Mutinies. Palestine Liberation Organization. 1983. *317*
—. Italy. Left. Violence. 1970's. *167*
—. Labor movement. Mapai. Palestine. Violence. 1932-35. *381*
—. Northern Ireland. Pacifism. 1969-79. *187*
Political history. Afghanistan. 1947-72. *413*
Political ideology. Assassination. Botswana. Nationalism. Ratshosa, Simon. 1916-32. *592*
Political Imprisonment. Diplock Report. Northern Ireland. Trials. 1971-74. *151*
—. Indonesia. Suharto, T. N. J. 1965-76. *481*
Political instability. Amin, Idi. Uganda. 1962-80. *597*
—. Araña, Carlos Manuel. Guatemala. 1971. *512*
Political Leadership. Assassination. Italy. Moro, Aldo. 1947-78. *192*
—. Cambodia. Government. 1970-79. *488*
—. Communist Party. Coups d'Etat. Military Government. Thailand. 1950-78. *464*

—. Gaza Strip. Israel. Jordan. Palestine Liberation Organization. West Bank. 1970's. *350*
—. Guyana. Intellectuals. Rodney, Walter. 1960's-80. *503*
—. Irish Republican Army. Political Factions. 1920-80. *221*
—. Lenin, V. I. Nechaev, Sergei. Psychohistory. Stalin, Joseph. USSR. 1869-72. 20c. *469*
—. Nationalism. Palestine Liberation Organization. 1930-76. *367*
—. Nicaragua. Somoza, Anastasio. 1933-36. *509*
Political movements. 1793-1973. *17*
Political Participation. Civil disobedience. India (Bengal). Strikes. Women. 1928-35. *474*
—. Fascism. Italy. 1930's. *6*
Political Parties. Anti-Communist Movements. Doriot, Jacques. France. Rightist groups. Rocque, François de la. 1936-37. *208*
—. Arabs. Israel. Palestine Liberation Organization. 1970-79. *386*
—. Austria. Neo-Nazism. 1938-82. *283*
—. Colombia. Socioeconomic Change. Violence. 1948-63. *18*
—. Colombia. Socioeconomic change. Violence. 1948-63. *499*
—. Germany. Militia. Paramilitary forces. Violence. 1920-32. *136*
—. Left. Moderates. Venezuela. 1958-69. *507*
—. Marxism. People's Liberation Front. Rebellions. Sri Lanka. 1932-71. *429*
Political Protest. Archives Nationales. Documents. France (Paris). Revolutionary Movements. Russia. 1882-1910. *459*
—. Bangladesh (Chittagong Hill Tracts). Shanti Bahini. Social integration. 1951-80. *447*
—. Chalo movement. India (Mysore). Satyagraha. 1947. *483*
—. Germany. Hitler, Adolf. 1943. *250*
—. Jamaica. Ras-Tafarians. 1970's. *551*
Political repression. Argentina. Guerrilla Warfare. 1973-77. *542*
—. Assassination. Colonial Government. Ethiopia. Graziani, Rodolfo. Italy. 1936-37. *595*
—. Blacks. Racism. 1712-1981. *571*
—. Bulgaria. Communist Party. 1923-44. *182*
—. Committee of State Security (KGB). USSR. 1977. *438*
—. Duvalier family. Government, resistance to. Haiti. USA. 1957-74. *508*
—. El Salvador. USA. 1970-81. *533*
—. Germany (Nuremberg). Judicial system. Police. SA (Sturmabteilung). 1933-34. *240*
—. Germany, West. Lawyers. 1971-76. *268*
—. India (Bihar; Bhojpur). Naxalite movement. Peasants. Rebellions. 1967-79. *465*
—. Revolution. War. 20c. *113*
Political socialization. Germany, West. 1968-80. *267*
Political status. Hussein, King. Jordan (Jerusalem). 1948-77. *387*
Political strategy. Black September. Palestinians. 1967-73. *374*
Political Systems. Fascism. 1914-40's. *35*
—. Great Britain. Reporters and Reporting. 1970's. *245*
—. Iran. Legitimacy. Revolution. 1979-81. *287*
Political theory. Assassination. China. Revolutionary Movements. 1903-12. *457*
—. Communism. Mao Tse-tung. Revolution. Violence. ca 1850-1970's. *487*
—. Communist parties and Movements. Lenin, V. I. Revolutionary movements. Violence. 1890's-1970's. *160*
—. Democracy. Ethics. Liberalism. Violence. 1960's-83. *80*
—. Fanon, Franz. Gandhi, Mahatma. Revolution. Violence. 1918-70. *51*
—. Humanism (review article). Merleau-Ponty, Maurice. Violence. 1946-47. *458*

—. India. Marxism-Leninism. Singh, Bhagat. 1930-31. *463*
—. Irish Republican Army. Northern Ireland. Violence. 1924-75. *233*
—. Italy. 1970's. *131*
—. Marxism-Leninism. 1870's-1972. *85*
—. Northern Ireland. Palestine. Tactics. Uruguay. ca 1960's-70's. *90*
Political violence. Amin, Idi. Obote, Milton. Uganda. 1962-72. *585*
Politics. 1969-76. *87*
—. Albania. Gurakuqi, Luigj. Nationalism. 1911-25. *232*
—. Assassination. Bishop, Maurice. Grenada. Intervention. Military operations. USA. 1980-83. *526*
—. Assassination. Foreign Relations. Korea, South. Park Chung-hee. USA. 1979-82. *425*
—. Assassination. Guatemala. 1954-81. *539*
—. Assassination. Japan. 1868-1941. *476*
—. Baader-Meinhof gang. Germany, West. 1970's. *238*
—. Basques. Economic Conditions. Spain. 1976-81. *247*
—. Catholics. Latin America. Marxism. Religion (review article). 20c. *521*
—. Catholics. Northern ireland. Protestants. Violence. 1912-72. *246*
—. Civil Disturbances. Northern Ireland. 1945-72. *224*
—. Development. Economic Policy. Social Change. Turkey. 1960-80. *418*
—. Elites. Israel. Jordan. Palestine Liberation Organization. West Bank. 1946-77. *357*
—. Great Britain. Northern Ireland. Violence. 1690-1972. *239*
—. Guatemala. Labor Unions and Organizations. Violence. 1973-82. *518*
—. Irish Republican Army. Northern Ireland. Propaganda. 1969-79. *260*
—. Israel. Palestinians. 1967-78. *312*
—. Italy. Moro, Aldo. 1978-81. *236*
—. Italy. Moro, Aldo. Murder. Red Brigades. 1970-78. *214*
—. Literature. 1960's-70's. *71*
—. Military operations. Palestine Liberation Organization. 1967-71. *293*
Politics and the Military. Tupamaros. Uruguay. 1964-74. *529*
Popular Front for the Liberation of Palestine. Entebbe raid. Hijacking. International law. Israel. Uganda. 1976. *4*
—. Israel (Tel Aviv, Lod Airport). Japan. United Red Army. 1960-73. *341*
Populism (review article). Latin America. Political conditions. 1960-80. *541*
Porath, Yehoshua. Arabs. Jews. Nationalist Movements. Palestine (review article). 1918-39. *361*
Portugal. Fascism. Ideology. 1920's-60's. *195*
Potere Operaio. Italy. Leftism. Trials. 1979-82. *280*
Prejudice. Cartoons and Caricatures (political). Great Britain. Northern Ireland. 1968-80. *190*
Presidents. Assassination. Gun control. National Characteristics. USA. 20c. *568*
—. Carter, Jimmy. Hostages. Iran. Public opinion. USA. USA (Kentucky; Lexington). 1979. *310*
Press. Government. Italy. 1978-82. *206*
Prevention programs. Hijacking. USA. 1968-71. *565*
Prisoners. Burials. Cyprus. Hydrochloric acid. Independence Movements. 1955-59. *395*
Progressive era. Class conflict. Commission on Industrial Relations. Plug uglies. Violence. 1890-1920. *570*
Propaganda. Irish Republican Army. Northern Ireland. Politics. 1969-79. *260*

Protestantism. Israel. National Council of Churches. Palestine Liberation Organization. USA. 1974-81. *333*
Protestants. Catholics. Northern ireland. Politics. Violence. 1912-72. *246*
Provincial government. Catholics. Coalitions. Northern Ireland Executive. Social Democratic Labour Party. 1974. *212*
Psychohistory. Lenin, V. I. Nechaev, Sergei. Political Leadership. Stalin, Joseph. USSR. 1869-72. 20c. *469*
Psychological Warfare. *Affiche Rouge.* France. Resistance. Trials. World War II. 1944. *203*
—. Public Opinion. 20c. *50*
Public Opinion. Anti-Semitism. Blumberg, Janice Rothschild. Bombing. Personal Narratives. Trials. USA (Georgia; Atlanta). 1958-59. *558*
—. Carter, Jimmy. Hostages. Iran. Presidents. USA. USA (Kentucky; Lexington). 1979. *310*
—. Films. Germany, West. Nazism. 1933-45. 1970's. *270*
—. Foreign policy. Hostages. Iran. USA (Kentucky; Lexington). 1979. *569*
—. Irish Republican Army (Provisional). Northern Ireland. 1916-80. *215*
—. Psychological Warfare. 20c. *50*
Public Opinion Polls. Hostages. Iran. Students. USA. 1976-81. *401*
Public Policy. Apartheid. Guerrilla warfare. South Africa. 1976-84. *594*

Q

Quantitative Methods. 1968-72. *26*
—. China. Violence. 1966-78. *455*
—. Models (Poisson). USA. 1968-74. *567*
—. Violence. 1972. *23*

R

Rabat Conference (1974). Arab States. Palestine Liberation Organization. 1974. *353*
—. Foreign Policy. Middle East. Palestine Liberation Organization. USA. 1967-75. *408*
Racism. Blacks. Political repression. 1712-1981. *571*
—. Columbians, Inc. Patriotism. USA (Georgia; Atlanta). Violence. 1946-47. *564*
—. Great Britain. National Front. 1970's. *141*
—. USA (Florida; Miami; Colored Town). 1896-1930. *566*
Radicals and Radicalism. 20c. *78*
—. Argentina. Catholic Church. Clergy. Movement of Priests for the Third World. Violence. 1969-70's. *506*
—. Baader-Meinhof Gang. Germany, West. Meinhof, Ulrike. Trials. 1975. *197*
Radio. Palestine Liberation Organization. 1954-75. *303*
Rahman, Mujibur. Assassination. Bangladesh. Coups d'etat. Foreign policy. ca 1945-76. *461*
Railroads. Ireland. Irish Republican Army. Strikes. 1921. *258*
Ras-Tafarians. Jamaica. Political Protest. 1970's. *551*
Ratshosa, Simon. Assassination. Botswana. Nationalism. Political ideology. 1916-32. *592*
Reagan, Ronald. Balance of power. Foreign policy. USA. 1980-81. *84*
—. Foreign Policy. Israel. Palestine Liberation Organization. UN. USA. 1975-81. *383*
—. Foreign policy. USA. USSR. 1981-82. *578*
—. Foreign Relations. Middle East. USA. USSR. 1981. *331*
—. Hostages. Inaugurals. Iran. Reporters and Reporting. Television. USA. 1980-81. *301*
Rebellions. Carranza, Venustiano. Mexicans. Mexico. USA (Texas). 1848-1920. *575*

134 Rebellions

—. India (Bihar; Bhojpur). Naxalite movement. Peasants. Political repression. 1967-79. *465*
—. India (Srikakulam District). Naxalite movement. Social Conditions. 1968-70. *471*
—. Irish Republican Army, Provisional. Northern Ireland. 1973. *138*
—. Marxism. People's Liberation Front. Political Parties. Sri Lanka. 1932-71. *429*
—. Peasants. Russia. 1905-18. *451*
Red Army Faction. Japan. Okamoto, Kozo. 1972. *479*
Red Brigades. Autonomia Operaia. Italy (Padua). Trials. 1970's. *255*
—. Christian Democratic Party. Italy. Kidnapping. Moro, Aldo. 1978. *264*
—. Christian Democratic Party. Italy. Moro, Aldo. Murder. 1975-83. *150*
—. Fuerzas Armadas de Liberación. Irish Republican Army. New York Times. Reporters and Reporting. 1977-79. *83*
—. Ideology. Italy. Violence. 1968-80. *201*
—. Italy. Moro, Aldo. Murder. Politics. 1970-78. *214*
Refugees. Airplanes. Cuba. Deportation. Hijacking. International law. USA. 1983. *520*
—. Black September. Middle East. Palestinians. 1967-73. *415*
—. El Salvador. Foreign Policy. Immigration. USA. Violence. 1979-82. *548*
—. Palestine. Palestine Liberation Organization. Revolutionary Movements. Sayeh, Mai. Union of Palestinian Women. Women. 1956-82. *377*
—. Palestinians. UN. 1948-82. *399*
Regionalism. Basques. Separatist Movements. Spain. 19c-20c. *147*
—. Canada. Ethnic Groups. 1970's. *577*
Religion. Authority. Iran. Khomeini, Ruhollah. Revolution. 1970-82. *299*
—. Civil War. Lebanon. Political Factions. Violence. 1975-82. *421*
—. Demonstrations. Israel. Police. Violence. 1950-79. *346*
—. Intervention. War. 1960's-70's. *25*
Religion (review article). Catholics. Latin America. Marxism. Politics. 20c. *521*
Reporters and Reporting. Canada. Great Britain. Ideology. 1980. *337*
—. Fuerzas Armadas de Liberación. Irish Republican Army. New York Times. Red Brigades. 1977-79. *83*
—. Great Britain. Political Systems. 1970's. *245*
—. Hostages. Inaugurals. Iran. Reagan, Ronald. Television. USA. 1980-81. *301*
—. Television. USA. 1968-71. *114*
Rescues. Foreign Relations. Hostages. Iran. USA. 1979-80. *423*
—. Hostages. Iran. Military Strategy. USA. 1980. *313*
—. Hostages. Iran. USA. World Court. 1979-80. *390*
Resistance. Affiche Rouge. France. Psychological Warfare. Trials. World War II. 1944. *203*
—. Concentration camps. Socialists. World War II. 1939-45. *162*
—. France. Women. World War II. 1940-44. *191*
Revolution. Afghanistan. Amin, Hafizullah. Karmal, Babrak. USSR. 1979-81. *358*
—. Albania. Assassination. Demi, Ahmet Rustem, Avni. Zog I. 1924. *155*
—. Assassination. El Salvador. Romero, Oscar. 1970's-80. *527*
—. Assassination. Germany. Haase, Hugo. Social Democratic Party. 1894-1919. *188*
—. Assassination. Guyana. People's National Congress. Rodney, Walter. 1966-81. *505*
—. Authority. Iran. Khomeini, Ruhollah. Religion. 1970-82. *299*

—. Communism. Mao Tse-tung. Political Theory. Violence. ca 1850-1970's. *487*
—. Europe. Government. ca 10c-20c. *66*
—. Fanon, Franz. Gandhi, Mahatma. Political Theory. Violence. 1918-70. *51*
—. Foreign Relations. Hungary. 1919. *262*
—. Iran. Legitimacy. Political Systems. 1979-81. *287*
—. Political Repression. War. 20c. *113*
—. Social change. Yugoslavia. 1945-70's. *156*
—. USA. Weathermen. 1962-71. *562*
—. USSR. 1906-73. 1960's-70's. *473*
Revolutionaries. Bolsheviks. Lenin, V. I. Russia. Zagorski, Vladimir M. 1902-19. *426*
Revolutionary Movements. Anarchism. Russia. 19c. 1977. *448*
—. Archives Nationales. Documents. France (Paris). Political Protest. Russia. 1882-1910. *459*
—. Asia. 1970's. *434*
—. Assassination. China. Political theory. 1903-12. *457*
—. Association of Southeast Asian Nations. Communist Party. Violence. 1965-83. *485*
—. Bengali. Burma. 1920-38. *430*
—. Catholicism. Ireland. 1848-1923. *219*
—. Civil war. Economic conditions. Finland. Violence. 1905-18. *189*
—. Communist Parties and Movements. Germany. Holz, Max. 1889-1933. *228*
—. Communist parties and Movements. Lenin, V. I. Political Theory. Violence. 1890's-1970's. *160*
—. Communist Party. Government. Uruguay. 1974. *535*
—. Dictatorship. Foreign Policy. Latin America. USA. 1958-79. *516*
—. Finland. Socialists. 1906-08. *194*
—. Foreign Relations. Palestine Liberation Organization. 1964-75. *352*
—. Palestine. Palestine Liberation Organization. Refugees. Sayeh, Mai. Union of Palestinian Women. Women. 1956-82. *377*
—. People's Will. Russia. 19c-20c. *468*
—. Western nations. 1972-80. *108*
Revolutionary war. Guerrilla Warfare. Military Strategy. 1688-1973. *40*
Rhodesia. Front for the Liberation of Zimbabwe (FROLIZI). Guerrilla Warfare. 1963-72. *586*
Right. Assassination. Germany. Seeckt, Hans von. 1919-33. *149*
—. Europe. 1980-84. *178*
—. Italy. Left. 1960's-77. *241*
—. Japan. 1970's. *480*
Rightist groups. Anti-Communist Movements. Doriot, Jacques. France. Political Parties. Rocque, François de la. 1936-37. *208*
Riots. Latin America. Social Psychology. 1949-63. *513*
—. USA (New York City). 1690-1980. *573*
Rocque, François de la. Anti-Communist Movements. Doriot, Jacques. France. Political Parties. Rightist groups. 1936-37. *208*
Rodney, Walter. Assassination. Democracy. Guyana. Violence. 1800-1980. *538*
—. Assassination. Guyana. People's National Congress. Revolution. 1966-81. *505*
—. Guyana. Intellectuals. Political Leadership. 1960's-80. *503*
—. Guyana. Working People's Alliance. 1953-79. *543*
Romania. Assassination. Foreign Relations. Iorga, Nicolae. 1900-40. *148*
—. Assassination. Iorga, Nicolae. Iron Guard. Madgearu, Virgil. Police. 1940. *279*
—. Communist Party. Iron Guard. 1930's-40's. *252*
—. Communist Party. Political collaboration. Workers' and Peasants' Bloc. 1922-33. *159*
—. Duca, Ion. Titulescu, Nicolae. 1919-39. *276*

Romero, Oscar. Assassination. Catholic Church. El Salvador. Human rights. Social change. 1977-80. *501*
—. Assassination. El Salvador. Revolution. 1970's-80. *527*
Roosevelt, Theodore. American Board Commissioners for Foreign Missions. Internal Macedonian Revolutionary Organization. Kidnapping. Macedonia. Missions and Missionaries. Stone, Ellen M. USA. 1901-02. *275*
—. Diplomacy. Missions and Missionaries. Navies. Ottoman Empire. USA. 1903-04. *329*
Rudd, Eldon. Armaments. Costa Rica. Foreign Relations. Nicaragua. USA. Vance, Cyrus. 1978-79. *554*
Rural Areas. Assassination. Bogotazo. Colombia. Gaitán, Jorge Eliécer. 1928-48. *545*
Russia. Adolescence. Stalin, Joseph. 1879-1917. *482*
—. Anarchism. Revolutionary Movements. 19c. 1977. *448*
—. Archives Nationales. Documents. France (Paris). Political Protest. Revolutionary Movements. 1882-1910. *459*
—. Assassination. Trepov, Fëdor. Trials. Zasulich, Vera. 1878-81. *428*
—. Attitudes. 1500-1917. *442*
—. Bolsheviks. Lenin, V. I. Revolutionaries. Zagorski, Vladimir M. 1902-19. *426*
—. Camus, Albert. Lukács, Georg. 1880-1980. *432*
—. Culture. Literature. USSR. 17c-20c. *435*
—. Degaev, Sergei (Alexander Pell, pseud.). Exile. South Dakota, University of. USA. 1854-1910. *436*
—. Okhrana. Plehve, Vyacheslav. Secret police. 1880's-1900's. *449*
—. Peasants. Political attitudes. Socialist Revolutionaries. 1907-08. *467*
—. Peasants. Rebellions. 1905-18. *451*
—. People's Will. Revolutionary Movements. 19c-20c. *468*
—. Socialist Revolutionaries. Women. 1905-08. *453*
Russian Revolution. Bolshevism. Social Revolutionary Party. 1917. *441*
Rustem, Avni. Albania. Assassination. Demi, Ahmet. Revolution. Zog I. 1924. *155*
Ryle, J. Martin. Bibliographies. International Red Aid. USSR. 1922-28. *460*

S

SA (Sturmabteilung). Germany (Nuremberg). Judicial system. Police. Political Repression. 1933-34. *240*
Satyagraha. Chalo movement. India (Mysore). Political Protest. 1947. *483*
Sayeh, Mai. Palestine. Palestine Liberation Organization. Refugees. Revolutionary Movements. Union of Palestinian Women. Women. 1956-82. *377*
Schwartzbard, Shalom. Assassination. France (Paris). Jews. Petliura, Simon. Ukraine. 1926. *466*
Secret Army (OAS). Algeria. France. 1961-62. *583*
—. Algeria. French. Independence Movements. 1954-61. *588*
Secret police. Okhrana. Plehve, Vyacheslav. Russia. 1880's-1900's. *449*
Secret service. Agca, Mehmet Ali. Assassination. Bulgaria. John Paul II, Pope (Rome). Italy. 1979-81. *220*
—. Assassination. Bulgaria. Communist Countries. John Paul II, Pope. Trotsky, Leon. USSR. 1940-82. *107*
Secret societies. Awakening Hungarians. Hungary. Party of National Unity. Social Democrats. 1922-26. *248*

—. Egypt. Great Britain. Nationalism. 1870-1924. *339*
Secret Societies (Samiti). Independence Movements. India. 1927-29. *439*
Sects, Religious. Civil war. Lebanon. Social Organization. 1975-77. *404*
Seeckt, Hans von. Assassination. Germany. Right. 1919-33. *149*
Separatist Movements. Akali Dal Party. India. Nehru, Jawaharlal. Sikhs. Singh, Tara. 1960-61. *478*
—. Basques. Regionalism. Spain. 19c-20c. *147*
—. Canada (Quebec). French Canadians. 1763-1971. *581*
—. Croatian Liberation Movement. Ustaše. Yugoslavia. 1929-72. *271*
—. Sri Lanka. Tamils. 1956-80. *454*
Shanti Bahini. Bangladesh (Chittagong Hill Tracts). Political Protest. Social integration. 1951-80. *447*
Sharett, Moshe. Arab-Israeli Conflict. Diaries. Israel. 1953-57. *370*
Sikhs. Akali Dal Party. India. Nehru, Jawaharlal. Separatist Movements. Singh, Tara. 1960-61. *478*
Silesia (Bytom). Assassination. Germany. Montalègre, Commandant. Plebiscites. Poland. 1921. *205*
Simulation and Games. Military. Oklahoma, University of. Police. 1970's. *102*
Sinai Peninsula. Golan Heights. Middle East. Military. Palestine Liberation Organization. 1973-75. *336*
Sindicalismo Libre. Carlists. Fascism. Political Culture. Spain. 1830-1980. *273*
Singh, Bhagat. India. Marxism-Leninism. Political Theory. 1930-31. *463*
Singh, Tara. Akali Dal Party. India. Nehru, Jawaharlal. Separatist Movements. Sikhs. 1960-61. *478*
Social change. Assassination. Catholic Church. El Salvador. Human rights. Romero, Oscar. 1977-80. *501*
—. Development. Economic Policy. Politics. Turkey. 1960-80. *418*
—. Revolution. Yugoslavia. 1945-70's. *156*
Social Classes. Assassination. Chile. Parliaments. 1920-70. *497*
Social Conditions. Economic Conditions. Fascism. Germany. Nazism. 1926-36. *173*
—. Economic Conditions. Turkey. 1950-80. *389*
—. El Salvador. Violence. 1980. *510*
—. India (Srikakulam District). Naxalite movement. Rebellions. 1968-70. *471*
Social Democratic Labour Party. Catholics. Coalitions. Northern Ireland Executive. Provincial government. 1974. *212*
Social Democratic Party. Assassination. Germany. Haase, Hugo. Revolution. 1894-1919. *188*
—. Civil service. Germany (Prussia). Grzesinski, Albert C. 1926-30. *169*
Social Democrats. Awakening Hungarians. Hungary. Party of National Unity. Secret societies. 1922-26. *248*
Social integration. Bangladesh (Chittagong Hill Tracts). Political Protest. Shanti Bahini. 1951-80. *447*
Social Organization. Civil war. Lebanon. Sects, Religious. 1975-77. *404*
—. Italy. 1960's-82. *146*
Social Problems (review article). Great Britain. Northern Ireland. Violence. 1918-78. *183*
Social Psychology. Latin America. Riots. 1949-63. *513*
Social Surveys. 1966-76. *93*
Socialism. Adler, Friedrich. Assassination. Austria. 1900-17. *126*

136 Socialism

—. Anarchism. Communist Parties and Movements. Germany, West. Italy. 1960-79. *202*
—. India. Nehru, Jawaharlal. 1920-64. *440*
Socialist Revolutionaries. Assassination. Bolsheviks. Brest-Litovsk, Treaty of. Mirbach, Wilhelm von. Political Factions. USSR. 1918. *475*
—. Bolshevism. Russian Revolution. 1917. *441*
—. Peasants. Political attitudes. Russia. 1907-08. *467*
—. Russia. Women. 1905-08. *453*
Socialists. Assassination. Italy. Matteotti, Giacomo. Mussolini, Benito. 1924-26. *210*
—. Concentration camps. Resistance. World War II. 1939-45. *162*
—. Finland. Revolutionary movements. 1906-08. *194*
Socioeconomic Change. Colombia. Political Parties. Violence. 1948-63. *18*
—. Colombia. Political Parties. Violence. 1948-63. *499*
Somoza, Anastasio. Nicaragua. Political Leadership. 1933-36. *509*
Somoza family. Nicaragua. 1956-70's. *530*
Sons of Freedom. British Columbia. Doukhobors. 1870's-1981. *579*
Sosnovski, Vasili. Dissent. Hijacking. USSR. 1958-77. *427*
South Africa. Africa, southern. Foreign Policy. 1970's-82. *584*
—. Apartheid. Guerrilla warfare. Public Policy. 1976-84. *594*
South Dakota, University of. Degaev, Sergei (Alexander Pell, pseud.). Exile. Russia. USA. 1854-1910. *436*
South Moluccans. Netherlands. 1950's-70's. *176*
South Tyrol. Austria. Foreign Relations. Italy. Treaties. 1946-69. *226*
Southern Christian Leadership Conference. Arab-Israeli conflict. Blacks. Foreign Policy. Palestine Liberation Organization. USA. 1979. *411*
Spain. Basques. Economic Conditions. Politics. 1976-81. *247*
—. Basques. Government. Political Factions. Suárez, Adolfo. 1977-79. *177*
—. Basques. Regionalism. Separatist Movements. 19c-20c. *147*
—. Carlists. Fascism. Political Culture. Sindicalismo Libre. 1830-1980. *273*
—. Democracy. 1974-79. *234*
—. Economic development. Political development. 1975-79. *229*
—. Political change. 1970's. *235*
Spain (Barcelona). Assassination. Mexico. Trotsky, Leon. 1940. *502*
Spain (Burgos). Basques. Euzkadi Ta Askatatuna (ETA). Fascism. Nationalism. Trials. 1970. *244*
Special Branch. Assassination. Great Britain. Irish Republican Army. Police. 1972-74. *204*
Special Powers Act. Law Enforcement. Northern Ireland. 1922-79. *145*
Spencer, John Poyntz, 5th Earl. Assassination. Cavendish, Frederick Charles. Ireland (Dublin). 1889-1910. *154*
Sri Lanka. Marxism. People's Liberation Front. Political Parties. Rebellions. 1932-71. *429*
—. Separatist Movements. Tamils. 1956-80. *454*
Stalin, Joseph. Adolescence. Russia. 1879-1917. *482*
—. Lenin, V. I. Nechaev, Sergei. Political Leadership. Psychohistory. USSR. 1869-72. 20c. *469*
Stalinism. USSR. 1917-40. *484*
Stamboliski, Aleksandr. Bulgaria. 1879-1979. *278*
State Government. Federal Government (US). Legislation. 1970's-80's. *580*
Statistics. Deportation. Israel. Palestinians. 1967-78. *347*

—. El Salvador. Human rights. USA. 1980-82. *504*
Steiger, Stanislaw. Assassination. Poland. Trials. Wojciechowski, Stanislaw. 1924-25. *193*
Stereotypes. Great Britain. Irish Republican Army. Northern Ireland. Novels. 1975-79. *257*
Sterling, Claire (review article). USSR. 1968-80. *92*
Stern Gang. *See* Lehi (Lohamei Herut Israel).
Stone, Ellen M. American Board Commissioners for Foreign Missions. Internal Macedonian Revolutionary Organization. Kidnapping. Macedonia. Missions and Missionaries. Roosevelt, Theodore. USA. 1901-02. *275*
—. Independence Movements. Kidnapping. Macedonia. Missions and Missionaries. USA. 1901-03. *274*
Strategy. 1945-75. *44*
—. Algeria. Front de la Libération Nationale (FLN). 1950's-72. *56*
Strikes. Civil disobedience. India (Bengal). Political Participation. Women. 1928-35. *474*
—. Ireland. Irish Republican Army. Railroads. 1921. *258*
Students. Hostages. Iran. Public Opinion Polls. USA. 1976-81. *401*
Stürgkh, Karl. Assassination. Francis Ferdinand. Habsburg Empire. World War I. 1914-18. *125*
Suárez, Adolfo. Basques. Government. Political Factions. Spain. 1977-79. *177*
Subversion. Anti-Semitism. Argentina. Catholic Church. 1975. *556*
Suharto, T. N. J. Indonesia. Political Imprisonment. 1965-76. *481*
Sunningdale Conference. Great Britain. Ireland. Northern Ireland. 1973. *196*
Sweden (Stockholm). Kroecher, Norbert. Operation Leo. 1970-79. *254*
Syria. Civil war. Intervention. Lebanon. Palestine Liberation Organization. 1968-76. *311*
—. Foreign Policy. Israel. Palestine Liberation Organization. UN Security Council. 1975-76. *321*
—. Intervention. Lebanon. Military Strategy. Palestine Liberation Organization. 1976. *419*

T

Tactics. Ideology. 1970's. *74*
—. Northern Ireland. Palestine. Political theory. Uruguay. ca 1960's-70's. *90*
Taiwan. Legislation. 1949-81. *437*
Tamils. Separatist Movements. Sri Lanka. 1956-80. *454*
Technology. Violence. 1950's-70's. *99*
Television. Arab-Israeli conflict. Foreign policy. Hostages. Iran. USA. 1975-81. *294*
—. Hostages. Inaugurals. Iran. Reagan, Ronald. Reporters and Reporting. USA. 1980-81. *301*
—. Reporters and Reporting. USA. 1968-71. *114*
Thailand. Assimilation. Muslims. 1972-74. *424*
—. Communist Party. Coups d'Etat. Military Government. Political Leadership. 1950-78. *464*
Titulescu, Nicolae. Duca, Ion. Romania. 1919-39. *276*
Treaties. 1934-74. *42*
—. Austria. Foreign Relations. Italy. South Tyrol. 1946-69. *226*
—. Convention on the Physical Protection of Nuclear Materials. Nuclear materials. UN. 1966-82. *59*
—. Convention on the Prevention and Punishment of Crimes against Internationally Protected Persons. Diplomats. UN. 1977. *101*
—. Hostages. UN. 1975-79. *7*
—. Hostages. UN General Assembly. USSR. 1976-79. *79*
—. International Convention against the Taking of Hostages. International law. 1949-79. *117*

Trepov, Fëdor. Assassination. Russia. Trials. Zasulich, Vera. 1878-81. *428*
Trials. *Affiche Rouge*. France. Psychological Warfare. Resistance. World War II. 1944. *203*
—. Anti-Semitism. Blumberg, Janice Rothschild. Bombing. Personal Narratives. Public Opinion. USA (Georgia; Atlanta). 1958-59. *558*
—. Arabs. Great Britain. Israel. 1982. *184*
—. Assassination. Poland. Steiger, Stanislaw. Wojciechowski, Stanislaw. 1924-25. *193*
—. Assassination. Russia. Trepov, Fëdor. Zasulich, Vera. 1878-81. *428*
—. Autonomia Operaia. Italy (Padua). Red Brigades. 1970's. *255*
—. Baader-Meinhof Gang. Germany, West. Meinhof, Ulrike. Radicals and Radicalism. 1975. *197*
—. Basques. Euzkadi Ta Askatatuna (ETA). Fascism. Nationalism. Spain (Burgos). 1970. *244*
—. Cyprus. 1956. *394*
—. Diplock Report. Northern Ireland. Political Imprisonment. 1971-74. *151*
—. Fascism. Italy (Brescia). 1974-78. *132*
—. Italy. Leftism. Potere Operaio. 1979-82. *280*
Trotsky, Leon. Assassination. Bulgaria. Communist Countries. John Paul II, Pope. Secret service. USSR. 1940-82. *107*
—. Assassination. Mexico. Spain (Barcelona). 1940. *502*
Tupamaros. Agency for International Development. Mitrione, Dan A. Uruguay. USA. 1969-73. *519*
—. Communist Party. Uruguay. 1952-73. *549*
—. Economic conditions. Elections. Political change. Uruguay. 1962-71. *528*
—. Guerrilla Warfare. Uruguay. 1962-73. *532*
—. Politics and the Military. Uruguay. 1964-74. *529*
—. Uruguay. 1962-72. *534*
Turkey. 1923-80. *315*
—. Armenia. 1914-82. *323*
—. Assassination. Foreign Policy. John Paul II, Pope. NATO. Poland. USSR. 1980-83. *175*
—. Communist Party. 1920-80. *340*
—. Communist Party. Political Factions. 1920-70's. *456*
—. Development. Economic Policy. Politics. Social Change. 1960-80. *418*
—. Economic Conditions. Foreign Relations. 1974-78. *360*
—. Economic Conditions. Social Conditions. 1950-80. *389*
—. Left. 1960-79. *325*
—. Modernization. Violence. 1946-80. *363*

U

Uganda. Amin, Idi. Obote, Milton. Political violence. 1962-72. *585*
—. Amin, Idi. Political instability. 1962-80. *597*
—. Coups d'Etat. Violence. 1971-73. *590*
—. Entebbe (raid). Hijacking. International law. Israel. 1961-76. *3*
—. Entebbe raid. Hijacking. International law. Israel. Popular Front for the Liberation of Palestine. 1976. *4*
—. Entebbe raid. Israel. 1968-77. *589*
Ukraine. Assassination. France (Paris). Jews. Petliura, Simon. Schwartzbard, Shalom. 1926. *466*
—. Nationalism. 1950's-70's. *444*
UN. 1948-79. *49*
—. 1972. *67*
—. 1981. *116*
—. Arab-Israeli conflict. Israel. Palestinians. 1950's-70's. *297*
—. Camp David agreement. Egypt. Israel. Palestinians. USA. 1978-79. *376*
—. Conflict and Conflict Resolution. War. 1946-64. *8*
—. Convention on the Physical Protection of Nuclear Materials. Nuclear materials. Treaties. 1966-82. *59*
—. Convention on the Prevention and Punishment of Crimes against Internationally Protected Persons. Diplomats. Treaties. 1977. *101*
—. Disarmament. Middle East. USSR. 1972. *97*
—. Foreign Policy. Israel. Palestine Liberation Organization. Reagan, Ronald. USA. 1975-81. *383*
—. Hostages. Treaties. 1975-79. *7*
—. International Law. 1963-83. *115*
—. International Law. 1970's. *43*
—. International law. 1972-. *122*
—. International Law. 20c. *45*
—. League of Nations. 1934-82. *48*
—. Palestine Liberation Organization. 1964-79. *338*
—. Palestinians. 1974-79. *382*
—. Palestinians. Refugees. 1948-82. *399*
UN General Assembly. Convention on the Prevention and Punishment of Crimes Against Internationally Protected Persons. Diplomats. 1970-73. *73*
—. Documents. 1981. *124*
—. Hostages. Treaties. USSR. 1976-79. *79*
UN General Assembly, 29th session. 1974-75. *332*
UN Security Council. Foreign Policy. Israel. Palestine Liberation Organization. Syria. 1975-76. *321*
UN (27th session, review). 1972. *46*
Union of Palestinian Women. Palestine. Palestine Liberation Organization. Refugees. Revolutionary Movements. Sayeh, Mai. Women. 1956-82. *377*
United Red Army. Israel (Tel Aviv, Lod Airport). Japan. Popular Front for the Liberation of Palestine. 1960-73. *341*
Uruguay. Agency for International Development. Mitrione, Dan A. Tupamaros. USA. 1969-73. *519*
—. Communist Party. Government. Revolutionary movements. 1974. *535*
—. Communist Party. Tupamaros. 1952-73. *549*
—. Economic conditions. Elections. Political change. Tupamaros. 1962-71. *528*
—. Guerrilla Warfare. Tupamaros. 1962-73. *532*
—. Northern Ireland. Palestine. Political theory. Tactics. ca 1960's-70's. *90*
—. Politics and the Military. Tupamaros. 1964-74. *529*
—. Tupamaros. 1962-72. *534*
USA (Florida; Miami; Colored Town). Racism. 1896-1930. *566*
USA (Georgia; Atlanta). Anti-Semitism. Blumberg, Janice Rothschild. Bombing. Personal Narratives. Public Opinion. Trials. 1958-59. *558*
—. Columbians, Inc. Patriotism. Racism. Violence. 1946-47. *564*
USA (Kentucky; Lexington). Carter, Jimmy. Hostages. Iran. Presidents. Public opinion. USA. 1979. *310*
—. Foreign policy. Hostages. Iran. Public Opinion. 1979. *569*
USA (Massachusetts; Boston). Childers, Erskine. Childers, Molly Osborn. Ireland. Irish Republican Army. 1903-22. *272*
USA (New York City). Riots. 1690-1980. *573*
USA (Texas). Carranza, Venustiano. Mexicans. Mexico. Rebellions. 1848-1920. *575*
USSR. 1960's-70's. *445*
—. Afghanistan. Amin, Hafizullah. Karmal, Babrak. Revolution. 1979-81. *358*
—. Africa. 20c. *591*

USSR

—. Agca, Mehmet Ali. Assassination. Bulgaria. Italy (Rome). John Paul II, Pope. 1979-81. *174*
—. Arab States. Israel. 1967-74. *309*
—. Arabs. Israel. Palestine Liberation Organization. USA. 1942-75. *409*
—. Assassination. Bolsheviks. Brest-Litovsk, Treaty of. Mirbach, Wilhelm von. Political Factions. Socialist Revolutionaries. 1918. *475*
—. Assassination. Bulgaria. Catholics. John Paul II, Pope. Poland. 1979-83. *127*
—. Assassination. Bulgaria. Communist Countries. John Paul II, Pope. Secret service. Trotsky, Leon. 1940-82. *107*
—. Assassination. Committee of State Security (KGB). Foreign Policy. Kidnapping. 1920's-60's. *489*
—. Assassination. Foreign Policy. John Paul II, Pope. NATO. Poland. Turkey. 1980-83. *175*
—. Bibliographies. Committee of State Security (KGB). Intelligence gathering. 1946-70. *452*
—. Bibliographies. International Red Aid. Ryle, J. Martin. 1922-28. *460*
—. China. Middle East. 1965-80. *462*
—. Committee of State Security (KGB). Foreign Policy. 1926-65. *118*
—. Committee of State Security (KGB). Political repression. 1977. *438*
—. Culture. Literature. Russia. 17c-20c. *435*
—. Disarmament. Middle East. UN. 1972. *97*
—. Dissent. Hijacking. Sosnovski, Vasili. 1958-77. *427*
—. Foreign Policy. Palestine Liberation Organization. 1947-80. *319*
—. Foreign policy. Reagan, Ronald. USA. 1981-82. *578*
—. Foreign Relations. Middle East. Reagan, Ronald. USA. 1981. *331*
—. Hostages. Treaties. UN General Assembly. 1976-79. *79*
—. Imperialism. USA. 1981. *34*
—. Lenin, V. I. Nechaev, Sergei. Political Leadership. Psychohistory. Stalin, Joseph. 1869-72. 20c. *469*
—. Palestine Liberation Organization. 1964-74. *417*
—. Revolution. 1906-73. 1960's-70's. *473*
—. Stalinism. 1917-40. *484*
—. Sterling, Claire (review article). 1968-80. *92*
USSR (review article). 1970's. *15*
Ustaše. Croatian Liberation Movement. Separatist Movements. Yugoslavia. 1929-72. *271*

V

Vance, Cyrus. Armaments. Costa Rica. Foreign Relations. Nicaragua. Rudd, Eldon. USA. 1978-79. *554*
Venezuela. Chile. Cuba. Elections. Foreign Relations. Military aid. USA. 1963-64. *517*
—. Left. Moderates. Political parties. 1958-69. *507*
Victims. Airplanes. Hijacking. Montreal Agreement. Warsaw Convention. 1929-73. *89*
Vienna Conventions (1961, 1963). Diplomatic and Consular Conventions. 1960-74. *30*
Viet Cong. Military strategy. Vietnam War. 1960's-70's. *477*
Vietnam War. Communism. USA. 1957-71. *77*
—. Foreign Policy. Government. USA. 1960-75. *450*
—. Military strategy. Viet Cong. 1960's-70's. *477*
Violence. 1970-71. *22*
—. 20c. *69*
—. 20c. *123*
—. Africa. Coups d'Etat. 19c-20c. *598*
—. Argentina. Catholic Church. Clergy. Movement of Priests for the Third World. Radicals and Radicalism. 1969-70's. *506*
—. Assassination. Democracy. Guyana. Rodney, Walter. 1800-1980. *538*
—. Association of Southeast Asian Nations. Communist Party. Revolutionary Movements. 1965-83. *485*
—. Bell, Daniel. Intellectuals. Leftism. Personal narratives. 1919-80. *11*
—. Bombing. Cities. 1969-71. *64*
—. Catholics. Northern ireland. Politics. Protestants. 1912-72. *246*
—. Chile. Militarism. 1970-74. *494*
—. China. Quantitative Methods. 1966-78. *455*
—. Civil war. Economic conditions. Finland. Revolutionary movements. 1905-18. *189*
—. Civil War. Lebanon. Political Factions. Religion. 1975-82. *421*
—. Class conflict. Commission on Industrial Relations. Plug uglies. Progressive era. 1890-1920. *570*
—. Colombia. Political Parties. Socioeconomic Change. 1948-63. *18*
—. Colombia. Political Parties. Socioeconomic change. 1948-63. *499*
—. Columbians, Inc. Patriotism. Racism. USA (Georgia; Atlanta). 1946-47. *564*
—. Communism. Mao Tse-tung. Political Theory. Revolution. ca 1850-1970's. *487*
—. Communist parties and Movements. Lenin, V. I. Political Theory. Revolutionary movements. 1890's-1970's. *160*
—. Communist Party. France. 1929-31. *134*
—. Conflict and Conflict Resolution. 1968-81. *24*
—. Coups d'Etat. Uganda. 1971-73. *590*
—. Democracy. Ethics. Liberalism. Political Theory. 1960's-83. *80*
—. Demonstrations. Israel. Police. Religion. 1950-79. *346*
—. El Salvador. Foreign Policy. Immigration. Refugees. USA. 1979-82. *548*
—. El Salvador. Government. 1900-76. *524*
—. El Salvador. Guatemala. 1970-79. *531*
—. El Salvador. Social Conditions. 1980. *510*
—. Fanon, Franz. Gandhi, Mahatma. Political Theory. Revolution. 1918-70. *51*
—. Fascism. Italy. 1919-22. *218*
—. Fascism. Italy. 1919-23. *207*
—. Fascism. Italy. 1919-29. *231*
—. Germany. Militia. Paramilitary forces. Political Parties. 1920-32. *136*
—. Government. Guatemala. 1966-80. *491*
—. Great Britain. Northern Ireland. Politics. 1690-1972. *239*
—. Great Britain. Northern Ireland. Social Problems (review article). 1918-78. *183*
—. Guatemala. 1966-72. *498*
—. Guatemala. Labor Unions and Organizations. Politics. 1973-82. *518*
—. Guatemala. Land tenure. 1940's-70's. *515*
—. Humanism (review article). Merleau-Ponty, Maurice. Political Theory. 1946-47. *458*
—. Ideology. Italy. Red Brigades. 1968-80. *201*
—. Intelligence Gathering. 1967-81. *96*
—. Irish Republican Army. Northern Ireland. Political Theory. 1924-75. *233*
—. Italy. Left. Political Factions. 1970's. *167*
—. Labor movement. Mapai. Palestine. Political Factions. 1932-35. *381*
—. Modernization. Turkey. 1946-80. *363*
—. Northern Ireland. 1969-77. *213*
—. Quantitative Methods. 1972. *23*
—. Technology. 1950's-70's. *99*
Violence (review article). 1968-79. *20*
Violencia. Colombia. 1946-64. *511*
—. Colombia. Modernization. 1945-53. *536*
Voting and Voting Behavior. Great Britain. National Front. 1979. *181*

W

War. 1950's-70's. *33*
—. 1964-84. *60*
—. Arab States. Boundaries. Israel. Joint Chiefs of Staff. USA. 1967. *400*
—. Arab States. Israel. 1947-74. *351*
—. Arab-Israeli conflict. Lebanon. 1947-82. *407*
—. Conflict and Conflict Resolution. UN. 1946-64. *8*
—. Intervention. Religion. 1960's-70's. *25*
—. Israel. Lebanon. Palestine Liberation Organization. Palestinians. 1967-82. *375*
—. Political Repression. Revolution. 20c. *113*
Warsaw Convention. Airplanes. Hijacking. Montreal Agreement. Victims. 1929-73. *89*
Weapons. 1970's. *75*
Weathermen. Black Liberation Army. Boudin, Kathy. Kidnapping. Leftism. USA. 1967-81. *563*
—. Revolution. USA. 1962-71. *562*
West Bank. Elites. Israel. Jordan. Palestine Liberation Organization. Politics. 1946-77. *357*
—. Foreign Relations. Gaza Strip. Jordan. Palestine Liberation Organization. 1967-77. *369*
—. Gaza Strip. Israel. Jordan. Palestine Liberation Organization. Political Leadership. 1970's. *350*
—. Gaza Strip. National Front. Palestine Liberation Organization. Political activism. 1967-73. *380*
Western Nations. Defense policy. International law. Oil Industry and Trade. 1980-81. *62*
—. Revolutionary Movements. 1972-80. *108*
Wojciechowski, Stanislaw. Assassination. Poland. Steiger, Stanislaw. Trials. 1924-25. *193*
Women. Civil disobedience. India (Bengal). Political Participation. Strikes. 1928-35. *474*
—. France. Resistance. World War II. 1940-44. *191*
—. Palestine. Palestine Liberation Organization. Refugees. Revolutionary Movements. Sayeh, Mai. Union of Palestinian Women. 1956-82. *377*
—. Russia. Socialist Revolutionaries. 1905-08. *453*
Workers' and Peasants' Bloc. Communist Party. Political collaboration. Romania. 1922-33. *159*
Working People's Alliance. Guyana. Rodney, Walter. 1953-79. *543*
World Court. Hostages. Iran. Rescues. USA. 1979-80. *390*
World order. 1945-75. *12*
World War I. Assassination. Francis Ferdinand. Habsburg Empire. Stürgkh, Karl. 1914-18. *125*
World War II. *Affiche Rouge.* France. Psychological Warfare. Resistance. Trials. 1944. *203*
—. Algeria. Nationalist movements. 1942-45. *587*
—. Churchill, Winston. Foreign policy. Great Britain. Palestine. 1937-47. *306*
—. Concentration camps. Resistance. Socialists. 1939-45. *162*
—. France. Germany. Law and society. Lawyers. Literature. Military Occupation. Nazism. 1850-1945. *282*
—. France. Resistance. Women. 1940-44. *191*

Y

Yoka High School. Buraku Liberation League. Coalitions. Communist Party. Japan. Minobe, Ryokichi. 1974. *472*
Yugoslavia. Alexander I. Dictatorship. Fascism. 1918-39. *277*
—. Croatian Liberation Movement. Separatist Movements. Ustaše. 1929-72. *271*
—. Revolution. Social change. 1945-70's. *156*

Z

Zagorski, Vladimir M. Bolsheviks. Lenin, V. I. Revolutionaries. Russia. 1902-19. *426*
Zasulich, Vera. Assassination. Russia. Trepov, Fëdor. Trials. 1878-81. *428*
Zionism. Arafat, Yasser. Imperialism. Interviews. Palestine Liberation Organization. 1960's-70's. *292*
—. Great Britain. Palestine. 1939-48. *308*
Zionism (Revisionism). Begin, Menachem. Fascism. Israel. Jabotinsky, Vladimir. Palestinians. 1923-82. *302*
—. Haganah. Irgun. Israel. Labor movement. Political Factions. Stern Gang. 1930's-82. *320*
Zog I. Albania. Assassination. Demi, Ahmet. Revolution. Rustem, Avni. 1924. *155*

22d Marine Amphibious Unit. Bombing. Embassies. Lebanon (Beirut). Marines. USA. 1983. *354*

AUTHOR INDEX

A

Abramovsky, Abraham 1
AbuLughod, Ibrahim 122
Adler, J. H. 99 100
Aggarwala, Narinder 2
Aguilera Peralta, Gabriel 491
Ahmad, Naveed 284 285
Akhtar, Shameem 286
Akinsanya, Adeoye A. 3 4
Alaolmolki, Nuzar 287
Alba, Carlos 492
Al-Dajani, Ahmad Sidqi 288
Alder, Douglas D. 125 126
Alekseev, A. 289
Alexander, Yonah 5 290
Alexiev, Alex 127
Alpern, Stephen I. 424
Altman, Israel 291
Amort, Čestmír 128
Anderson, Thomas P. 493
Andreadēs, Chrēstos G. 129
Andreoli, Marcella 130 131 132
Angell, Alan 494
April, Serge 73
Aquarone, Alberto 6
Arafat, Yasser 292
Arbatova, N. K. 133
Asencio, Diego C. 495
Ashhab, Naim 293
Aston, Clive C. 7
Audoin, Stephanie 134
Aulas, Marie-Christine 377
Avidan, Dan 369
Avrus, A. I. 135
Ayanian, John Z. 83
Ayçoberry, Pierre 136

B

Bailey, Sydney D. 8
Baker, Edward J. 425
Ball, George W. 294
Banfi, Arialdo 137
Barkey, David W. 496
Bassiouni, M. Cherif 9
Bator, Angelika 295
Bator, Wolfgang 295
Becker, Jillian 10
Beckert, Siegfried 426
Bell, Daniel 11
Bell, J. Bowyer 12 138
Bell, Robert G. 557
Benjelloun, Nadia 296
Ben-Meir, Alon 297
Beres, Louis René 13 298
Bergeron, Francis 427
Bergman, Jay 428
Bertoldi, Silvio 139
Bibes, Geneviève 140
Bicheno, H. E. 497
Bill, James A. 299
Billig, Michael 141
Bishara, Ghassan 300
Bishop, Joseph W., Jr. 142
Blackton, Charles S. 429
Blair, Bruce G. 14
Blatt, Joel 143
Blaufarb, Douglas S. 15
Blishchenko, I. P. 16
Blumberg, Janice Rothschild 558
Bonante, Luigi 17
Booth, John A. 18 498 499

Bormann, Ernest G. 301
Bouma, Rob van der Laan 176
Bourdillat, Nicole 500
Bowden, Tom 144
Bowman, H. Miller 93
Boyce, D. George 145
Brandt, Niels 19
Braungart, Margaret M. 20
Braungart, Richard G. 20
Brenner, Lenni 302
Brewer, Garry D. 14
Brockman, James R. 501
Brown, MacAlister 488
Browne, Donald R. 303
Butenschøn, Nils A. 304

C

Cabrer i Pallas, R. 502
Campbell, Trevor A. 503
Cappadocia, Ezio 146
Capurso, Armando 21
Carr, Raymond 147
Carrère, René 22 23 24 25 26
Ceauşescu, Ilie 148
Centro Universitario de
  Documentación e
  Información (CUD) 504
Chakravarty, S. R. 430 431
Chamberlin, Brewster S. 149
Chandisingh, Rajendra 505
Chang, Maria Hsia 437
Chapman, Robert D. 27
Cherkasov, P. P. 582 583
Cherne, Leo 559
Chiesa, G. 150
Clark, Lorne S. 560
Clutterbuck, Richard 151 152 153 561
Cobban, Helena 305
Cochrane, Raymond 141
Cohen, Michael J. 306 307 308
Colebrook, Joan 309
Congdon, Lee 432
Conover, Pamela Johnston 310 569
Cooke, A. B. 154
Crenshaw, Martha 121 121
Critchley, Julian 281

D

Daniels, Stuart 562
Dasnabedian, Hratch 28
Dean, Tony 337
Decter, Midge 563
Deiner, John T. 506
Demi, Ahmet 155
Denitch, Bogdan 156
Derriennic, Jean Pierre 29
Diokno, José 433
Dishon, Daniel 311
Diskin, Abraham 312
Dodd, Norman L. 157
Dowling, Kathryn 158
Dragne, Florea 159
Duculescu, V. 30
Dudley, J. Wayne 564
Dugard, John 31 122
Duhamel, Luc 160
Dülffer, Jost 161

Dunin-Wąsowicz, Krzysztof 162
Duperier, B. 32
Durán Ros, Manuel M. 33

E

Earl, Robert L. 313
Efremov, V. 34
Eitzen, D. Stanley 496
El-Ayouty, Yassin 314
Ellner, Steve 507
Eshov, V. D. 35
Evans, Alona E. 36 120 122
Eytan, Walter 163

F

Falk, Richard 433
Fay, James R. 315
Fëdorov, V. 434
Fenello, Michael 565
Fields, Rona M. 164
Finger, Seymour Maxwell 37
Fischer-Galati, Stephen 119
Fitzgerald, Gerald F. 38
Fitzhugh, David 39
Fleurant, Gerdes 508
Fortier, David H. 165
Foster, Charles R. 165
Fox, K. O. 40 41
Fozzard, Peter A. 83
Francis, Samuel T. 166
Franck, Thomas M. 42
Fraser, John 167
Friedland, Elaine A. 584
Friedlander, Robert A. 43
Fromkin, David 44
Furlonge, Geoffrey 316

G

Gadant, Monique 377
Galich, Manuel 509
Garfincle, Adam M. 317
George, Paul S. 566
Gerlach, Allen 510
Gibian, George 435
Giffin, Frederick C. 436
Gilhodès, Pierre 511
Giniewski, Paul 318
Glandon, Virginia E. 168
Glaser, Stefan 45
Gleason, John M. 567
Glees, Anthony 169
Glentworth, Garth 585
Golan, Galia 319
Goldberg, Giora 320 346
Goldberg, Harold J. 475
Goldblatt, Murray 46
Goodsell, James Nelson 512
Gordon, Murray 321
Govea, Rodger M. 513
Grahn, Gerlinde 170
Gravel, Mike 47
Green, L. C. 48 49
Greer, Herb 171
Gregor, A. James 119 437
Gregory, F. E. C. 172
Grigg, John 281
Grigorenko, Petro 438
Guggenheim, Willy 322

Author Index

H
Gunter, Michael M. 323
Gupta, Maya 439
Gutman, David 50

Hacker, Susan 51
Häggman, Bertil 52
Hamid, Rashid 324
Hancock, Ian 585
Harris, George S. 325
Harris, Lillian Craig 326
Hashmi, Tajul Islam 440
Hennig, Eike 173
Henry, Ernst 53
Henze, Paul B. 174 175
Heradstveit, Daniel 327
Herman, Valentine 176
Hermet, Guy 177
Heyman, Edward 121
Hickman, William F. 328
Hildemeier, Manfred 441
Hoffman, Bruce 178
Holler, Lyman E. 442
Holtzappel, Coen 443
Hopple, Gerald W. 54
Horchem, Hans Josef 179 180
Horielov, M. Ie. 444
Horner, Charles 445
Horowitz, Irving Louis 55 119
Hourihan, William J. 329
Howe, Irving 123
Hudson, Michael C. 330 331
Husbands, Christopher T. 181
Hutchinson, Martha Crenshaw 56

I
Iliescu, Crişan 182
Indorf, Hans H. 446
Inglis, Alex I. 332
Ingram, Timothy H. 57
Isaac, Rael Jean 333 334
Islam, Syed Nazmul 447
Ivanian, E. A. 568
Ivansky, Zeev 448 449

J
Jacomy-Millette, Anne-Marie 58
Janke, Peter 514
Jaros, Dean 569
Jeffreys-Jones, Rhodri 570
Jenkins, Brian M. 59
Jenkins, Brian Michael 60
Jiryis, Sabri 335
Joes, Anthony James 119
Johnson, Chalmers 61
Johnson, Kenneth F. 515
Johnson, Michael 336
Johnston, A. 183
Jones, Mervyn 184
Jorgensen, Birthe 185
Joyner, Christopher C. 62

K
Kahin, George McT. 450
Kamins'kyi, Ie. Ie. 444
Kanin, David B. 63
Karber, Phillip A. 64
Katris, John 186
Kearney, Richard 187
Keep, John 451

Keller, Elke 188
Kelley, Don Quinn 571
Kelly, William E. 452
Khoros, V. G. 468
Kimche, Jon 65
Kirby, D. G. 189
Kirichenko, V. 516
Kirk, Tony 586
Kirkaldy, John 190
Kittrie, Nicholas 122
Klette, Immanuel J. 517
Kline, Rayna 191
Knight, Amy 453
Knight, Graham 337
Kodikara, S. V. 454
Koerner, Francis 587
Kogan, Eugen 66
Komolova, N. P. 192
Korey, William 67 338
Korzec, Pawel 193
Koshelev, V. S. 339
Koval'ov, V. V. 444
Kowalewski, David 455
Krahenbuhl, Margaret 456
Krebs, Edward S. 457
Krieger, David M. 68
Kujala, Antti 194
Kukushkin, U. M. 195
Kuranov, I. N. 340
Kuriyama, Yoshihiro 341
Kyle, Keith 196

L
Landa, R. G. 342 343
Landes, William M. 572
LaPierre, Laurier 581
Laqueur, Walter 69 70 71
Larson, David L. 344
Lasky, Melvin J. 197
Lawlor, S. M. 198
Leber, Jeffrey R. 72
LeBot, Yvon 518
Lebow, Richard Ned 199
Lee, Alfred McClung 200
Lee, Edward G. 73
Lee, J. J. 224
Lefever, Ernest W. 519
Lefort, Claude 458
Legault, Albert 201
Legrain, Jean-François 345
Legum, Colin 291 369
Lehman-Wilzig, Sam 346
Leich, Marian Nash 520
Leites, Nathan 74
Lesch, Ann M. 347 348
Leshukov, A. S. 202
Lesure, Michel 459
Lever, Évelyne 588
Levine, Daniel H. 521
Lévy, Claude 203
Lewis, Bernard 349
Lissitzyn, Oliver J. 120
Litani, Yehuda 350
Livingstone, N. C. 75 76
Livingstone, Neil C. 522
Livingstone, Susan Morrisey 495 523
Lockwood, Bert B., Jr. 42
Loney, Martin 204
López Vallecillos, Italo 524
Lorch, Netanel 351
Lowenfeld, Andreas F. 120
Lubau, Robert 205
Lumley, Bob 206

L'vunin, Iu. A. 460
Lyon, Peter 461
Lyttelton, Adrian 207

M
Machefer, Philippe 208
Macintyre, Ronald R. 352
Mack Smith, Denis 209 210
Maechling, Charles, Jr. 525
Maingot, Anthony P. 526
Mallin, Jay 77
Malmborg, K. E., Jr. 120
Mantovani, Giovanni 353
Marchese, Stelio 462
Marrus, Michael R. 211
Marshall, Peter 581
Martín-Baró, Ignacio 527
May, William F. 78
McAllister, Ian 212
McDonald, John W., Jr. 79
McDonald, Ronald H. 528 529
McWhinney, Edward 120
Mead, James M. 354
Menarchik, E. Douglas 589
Mickolus, Edward 121
Midlarsky, Manus I. 121 121
Miller, David 80
Millett, Richard 530 531
Milson, Menahem 355
Mishael, I. 356
Mishal, Shaul 357
Mitchell, James K. 213
Mitrokhin, L. V. 463
Mittelman, James H. 590
Monroe, Charles P. 81
Monti, Daniel J. 573
Moore, John Norton 122
More, Vishwanath 120
Morell, David 464
Moss, David 214
Mosse, George L. 119
Mottet, George J. 532
Moxon-Browne, E. 215
Mukherjee, Kalyan 465
Muradov, G. A. 358
Mushkat, Marion 591
Muslih, Muhammad Y. 359

N
Naimark, Norman M. 435
Natoli, Claudio 216
Navarro, Vicente 533
Neeler, V. E. 217
Nello, Paolo 218
Nemes, Dezső 82
Nesterov, N. 360
Nevada, Yosef 466
Newsinger, John 219
Nimrod, Yoram 361
Nisbet, Robert 119
Nowak, Jan 220

O
O'Ballance, Edgar 221
O'Beirne-Ranelagh, John 222
Obici, Giulio 131
O'Brien, Conor Cruise 123
Oestereicher, Emil 223
Ofri, Aric 574
O'Leary, Cornelius 224
Oliveira, Sergio L. d' 534

Author Index

O'Neill, Bard E. 362
O'Riordan, M. 225
Orlow, Dietrich 282 363

P

Paletz, David L. 83
Palm, Thede 84
Parry, Albert 85
Parsons, Q. N. 592
Pastorelli, Pietro 226
Pastorino, Enrique 535
Patkó, Imre 86
Patsavos, Christos C. 227
Paust, Jordan J. 580
Pavlov, E. A. 228
Payne, Stanley G. 229
Pecaut, Daniel 536
Pells, Richard 119
Perillo, Gaetano 230
Péronne, Louis-P. 537
Perrie, Maureen 467
Perry, Victor 364
Petersen, Jens 231
Petrov, Metodi 278
Pierre, Andrew J. 87
Piotrowski, Jerzy 365
Plimak, E. G. 468
Pollo, Stefanaq 232
Pomper, Philip 469
Poulantzas, Nicholas M. 88
Power, Paul F. 233
Pozefsky, Abby L. 89
Premdas, Ralph R. 538
Premo, Daniel L. 539
Preston, Paul 234 235
Pribytkovski, Lev Naumovich 593
Price, H. Edward, Jr. 90
Pryce-Jones, David 366
Puaux, François 236

Q

Quagliariello, Ernesto 237

R

Raab, Earl 91
Raditsa, Leo 92
Radu, Michael S. 540
Raikov, A. V. 463 470
Ramirez, Bruno 280
Rammelstedt, Otthein 238
Rana, Swadesh 367
Randolph, Virgil P., III 239
Ranis, Peter 541
Reddy, N. Subba 471
Regenstreif, Peter 577
Reiche, Eric G. 240
Reid, Donald M. 368
Rekhess, Elie 369
Rich, Paul 594
Richards, David A. J. 282
Richmond, Douglas W. 575
Robbins, Thomas 119
Rochat, Giorgio 595
Rock, David 542
Rodney, Walter 543
Rohlen, Thomas P. 472
Rokach, Livia 370
Romaniecki, Leon 473
Ronchery, Robert 241
Ronchey, Alberto 242
Rondot, Pierre 371 372
Root, Anthony 373

Rouleau, Eric 374
Rubinstein, C. L. 375
Russell, Charles A. 93 94 243 544

S

Saddy, Fehmy 95
St. John, Peter 96
Salomone, Franck A. 596
Samudavanija, Chai-anan 464
Sanakoyev, Sh. 97
Sánchez Gómez, Gonzalo 545
Sarkar, Tanika 474
Sayegh, Fayez A. 376
Sayeh, Mai 377
Scelsi, Filippo 244
Schachter, Oscar 378
Schlaefer, Cindy Verne 576
Schleimer, Joseph D. 98
Schlesinger, Philip 206 245
Scott, R. D. 246
Segre, D. V. 99 100
Seikaly, Samir 379
Sela, Abraham 380
Senn, Alfred Erich 475
Serfaty, Meir 247
Serfőző, Lajos 248
Settembrini, Domenico 249
Sewell, Alan F. 122
Shaked, Haim 291 369
Shamir, Haim 250
Shamwell, Horace F., Jr. 101
Shannon, Kristin 577
Shapira, Anita 381
Sharif, Regina 382
Shattan, Joseph J. 383
Shillony, Ben-Ami 476
Shuaibi, Issa al- 384
Shultz, Richard 477
Sigelman, Lee 310 569
Siltala, Juha 251
Silva, Geraldo Eulálio do Nascimento e 546
Sinclair, B. 225
Singh, Pakir 478
Sisco, Joseph J. 385
Sloan, Stephen 102
Smart, I. M. H. 103
Smirnov, V. Iu. 386
Smith, Brent L. 580
Snitch, Thomas H. 104
Sofer, Eugene F. 547
Sofer, Naim 387
Solberg, Mary 548
Southall, Aidan 597
Spălățelu, Ion 252
Spiegel, Steven L. 388
Starchenkov, G. 389
Stein, Ted L. 390
Steinhoff, Patricia G. 479
Sterling, Claire 253
Stoakes, Frank 391 392
Stylianou, Petrou 393 394 395 396
Suarez, Alberto 549
Sundberg, Jacob 254
Susser, Asher 397
Suudi, M. 398
Swearingen, Rodger 578
Syrkin, Marie 399 400
Szczepanik, Krzysztof 271

T

Tadayon, K. M. 401
Takagi, Masayuki 480
Talpeş, Ioan 148
Tamburino, Giovanni 255
Tapia Salinas, Luis 105
Taylor, Alan R. 402
Taylor, Edmond 106
Taylor, Robert W. 550
Terchek, Ronald J. 256
Thauby García, Fernando 403
Titley, Alan 257
Toelle, Heïdi 377
Toubi, Jamal 404
Townsend, Charles 258 259
Tugwell, Maurice 260
Turki, Fawaz 405 406
Tzur, Daniel 407

U

Ullman, Richard H. 408
Unger, Leopold 107

V

Valat-Morio, Pierre 22 23 25 26
Vanden, Harry E. 550
VanderKroef, Justus M. 481
VanVoris, W. H. 261
Varon, Benno Weiser 409
Vashitz, Joseph 410
Vass, Henrik 262
Veber, Václav 482
Veerathappa, K. 483
Ventura, Angelo 263
Vincent, J. R. 154
Vitiuk, V. V. 108
VonLaue, Theodore H. 484

W

Wagner-Pacifici, Robin 264
Walser, Harald 265
Walsh, Barbara 266
Walters, Ronald W. 411
Warren, G. I. 109
Wasmund, Klaus 267
Wasserstein, Bernard 412
Watson, G. Llewellyn 551
Weatherbee, Donald E. 485
Weisberg, Richard 282
Weiss, Peter 268
Welch, Claude E. 598
Wesseling, H. L. 269
West, Gerald T. 513
Whitteridge, Gordon 413
Wickbom, Kaj 270
Wickramanayake, D. 486
Wilamowski, Jacek 271
Wilkinson, Burke 272
Wilkinson, Paul 110 111 112 113 414
Winston, Colin M. 273
Wohlstetter, Roberta 552
Wolf, John B. 415
Woods, Randall B. 274 275
Woolf, S. J. 119
Wright, Jeffrey W. 416
Wurth-Hough, Sandra 114

X

Xeni, Constantin 276

Y

Yadav, Rajendra Singh 465
Yerbury, J. C. 579
Yin Ch'ing-yao 487
Yoder, Amos 115 116
Yodfat, Arieh Y. 417 418
Yoshida, Fumihiko 121 121
Younger, Sam 419

Z

Zabih, Sepehr 420
Zaharescu, Vladimir 277
Zaïd, Gabriel 553
Zakharieva, Iordanka 278
Zamir, Meir 421
Zasloff, Joseph J. 488
Zhdanov, N. V. 16
Zincă, Haralamb 279

CHRONOLOGY

The following chronology lists terrorist, and terrorist-related, events reported in the press from January 1975 through December 1985. It includes terrorist acts perpetrated by governments, internal political attacks on established regimes, as well as violence committed by dissident individuals and factions. The list is selective and no attempt was made to define terrorist activities in accordance with any particular point of view. For a chronology of terrorist activities prior to 1975 consult B.M. Jenkins and Janera Johnson, *International Terrorism: A Chronology, 1969-1974* (Santa Monica, California: Rand Corporation, 1975).

1975

January		FALN bombs New York City tavern. Four killed, fifty-three injured.
February	11	Malagasy Republic President Richard Ratsimandrava assassinated.
	26	U.S. Consul John P. Egan kidnapped and murdered by the Montenaros in Cordoba, Argentina.
	27	Chairman of the West Berlin Christian Democratic Union (CDU), Peter Lorenz, kidnapped by terrorists (released on 5 March).
March	5	Eight Al Fatah guerrillas attack Tel Aviv.
April	24	*Rote Armee Fraktion* terrorists blow up West German embassy in Stockholm. Military attaché killed, twelve hostages taken, in reprisal for West German government's refusal to release twenty-six imprisoned anarchists.
May	6	Judge Giuseppe de Gennaro kidnapped in Rome by NAP group.
	21	Ulrike Meinhof, Andreas Baader, Gudrun Ensslin and Jan-Karl Raspe (members of the *Rote Armee Fraktion*) on trial in Stuttgart.

July	4	Terrorists bomb Zion Square in Jerusalem. Forty-three Israelis killed, eighty injured.
	30	Francisco de Sola, industrialist, kidnapped by PRA group in El Salvador. Rafael Aguiñada Carranza, leftist labor leader, shot to death.
August	4	Five members of the *Rengo Sekigun* (Japanese Red Army) attack the U.S. and Swedish embassies in Kuala Lumpur, Malaysia, and take fifty-three hostages.
	6	Red Army terrorists and four hostages flown to Libya. Japanese granted sanctuary by Libyan government.
	22	Anti-terrorist law imposing mandatory death sentences for terrorist activity approved by Spanish cabinet.
September		Five Basque terrorists, convicted of killing Spanish policemen, are executed on order of General Franco.
October		IRA terrorists bomb home of MP Hugh Fraser in London. One killed.
November		Ross McWhirter, British sportswriter, murdered by IRA members in reprisal for his attempt to establish a reward fund for information leading to the arrest of terrorists.
December	2	South Moluccan terrorists seize train near Beilin, the Netherlands. Two killed, fifty hostages taken.
	4	South Moluccan terrorists seize the Indonesian consulate in Amsterdam. Twenty-five hostages taken.
	14	South Moluccan train terrorists surrender to police.
	19	Seven South Moluccan terrorists release twenty-five hostages taken at the Indonesian embassy on 4 December.
	21	Pro-Palestinian terrorists take sixty hostages at a meeting of OPEC ministers in Vienna. Two killed.
	22	Algerian government grants asylum to pro-Palestine terrorists flown from Vienna to Algiers. Ten hostages freed.
	23	U.S. CIA station chief Richard S. Welch murdered by terrorists in Athens.
	29	Bombing at La Guardia airport, New York City, kills eleven, injures seventy-five.

1976

January	4	Outbreak of violence in Belfast. Five Catholics killed.
	5	Ten Protestant workmen shot and killed in Belfast. British order troop reinforcements to Ireland.

February		FCLS terrorists hijack school bus near Djibouti. French and Somali troops engage in firefight. Six terrorists, one child killed, several children wounded.
	13	General Murtala Ramat Mohammed, Nigeria's head of state, shot and killed by revolutionaries.
March	11	Former defense minister and twenty-nine others executed in Nigeria for complicity in attempted coup and murder of General Mohammed on 13 February.
June	16	U.S. Ambassador Francis E. Meloy, his advisor Robert O. Waring, and their chauffeur shot and killed in Beirut. Palestinian hijackers seize French airliner carrying Israeli passengers from Paris to Tel Aviv and divert it to Entebbe, Uganda.
July	3–4	Israeli commandoes rescue Israeli hostages in Entebbe. Seven hijackers, twenty Ugandan soldiers, one Israeli soldier killed. Ninety-one passengers and twelve aircrew members returned to Israel.
	15	Ulster Freedom Fighters bomb the Special Criminal Court in Dublin.
	21	British Ambassador Christopher T. E. Ewart-Briggs and his secretary killed by a land mine at his residence in Dublin.
September		Air India airliner hijacked and diverted to Lahore, Pakistan. Crew and passengers released 11 September.
	10–12	New York to Chicago jetliner hijacked by Croatian terrorists and diverted to Paris. Propaganda leaflets dropped over several U.S. cities.
	26	Palestinian guerrillas seize hotel in Damascus and hold ninety hostages. Syrian troops kill one terrorist and four hostages. Three guerrillas hanged 27 September.
November		Maire Drumm, officer of the Provisional IRA, shot and killed by Protestant gunmen in a Belfast hospital.

1977

January	11	Abn Doud, member of the Palestinian Revolutionary Council, suspected leader of the terrorists who murdered Israeli athletes during the 1972 Olympic Games in Munich, released by French authorities.
February	6	Black Rhodesian guerrillas kill seven Catholic missionaries near Salisbury.

March	4	Four *Totenokai* terrorists occupy the Tokyo office of the Federation of Economic Organizations.
	11	Twelve Hanafi Muslim gunmen surrender in Washington, D.C. after seizing three buildings and holding 134 hostages since 9 March.
	18	Marien Ngouabi, Congolese head of state, murdered in abortive coup.
April		Siegried Buback, Chief Federal Prosecutor, West Germany, ambushed, shot, and killed. Andreas Baader, Jan-Karl Raspe, and Gudrun Ensslin sentenced to life imprisonment for murdering four American soldiers in 1972.
May	1	Leftist extremists fire into a crowd of one hundred thousand in Istanbul. Thirty killed, two hundred wounded.
	23	Two groups of South Moluccan terrorists seize 165 hostages in a school near Groningen and board a hijacked train. Terrorists demand release of twenty-one South Moluccans imprisoned by the Netherlands.
June	11	Royal Dutch Marines assault terrorists. Six terrorists and two hostages killed in the attack on the train. One hundred children held by terrorists at the school had been released on 27 May.
July	23	Three Hanafi Muslims convicted of kidnapping, conspiracy, and second-degree murder for crimes committed on 9–11 March. Nine codefendants convicted of conspiracy and kidnapping.
September	5	Hanns-Martin Schleyer, President of the West German federation of industry, kidnapped by terrorists in Cologne.
	6	Muslims, convicted on 23 July, sentenced to life imprisonment.
	28	Japan Air Lines jetliner hijacked by Red Army terrorists in India. Japanese government pays $6 million ransom and releases six terrorists from jail. Terrorists flown to asylum in Dacca. One hundred fifteen of 151 hostages released in Bangladesh, ten in Damascus, seven in Kuwait, nineteen in Algiers.
October	10	Moros kill a Philippine army general and thirty-three others on Jolo Island.
	11	Colonel Ibrahim al-Hamdi, President of Yemen, and his brother, Abdullah Mohammed al-Hamdi, assassinated in San'a'.

October	18	Eighty-six hostages, held on a Lufthansa jetliner hijacked in Majorca, freed by a West German commando unit in Mogadishu, Somalia. Pilot killed in Yemen. Plane flown to Italy, Cyprus, Bahrain, Dubai, and Yemen before landing in Somalia. Three of four hijackers killed. Jan-Karl Raspe, Gudrun Ensslin, and Andreas Baader, principles in the Baader-Meinhof gang, commit suicide in Stammheim Prison near Stuttgart. Leftists claim they were murdered by prison officials.
	19	Hanns-Martin Schleyer found murdered in Eastern France.
November	17	France extradites Klaus Croissant, defense attorney of the Baader-Meinhof gang, suspected of establishing covert communications for the members in prison, to West Germany.

1978

January	10	Pedro Joaquin Chamarro Cardenal, editor of *La Prensa*, assassinated in Nicaragua. Thousands riot in protest against President Somoza's regime.
February	18	Palestinian terrorists assassinate Yusuf as-Sibai, editor of Cairo's daily *al-Ahram*, and seize thirty hostages at the Hilton Hotel in Nicosia. Cypriot officials allow the terrorists to fly off in a jet aircraft in exchange for nineteen hostages.
	19	Hijacked aircraft returns to Larnaca Airport after being refused landing rights in Kuwait, Somalia, Ethiopia, Greece, Yemen, Libya, and Algeria. Egyptian commandoes attack the terrorists and claim that the Cypriot National Guard and a PLO unit opened fire on them. Fifteen of seventy-four Egyptians killed. Hostages freed by the terrorists. Anwar Sadat severs diplomatic relations with Cyprus.
March	11	PLO guerrillas kill thirty Israeli civilians on a bus between Haifa and Tel Aviv.
	14	Israel conducts land, sea, and air attacks against PLO bases in Southern Lebanon in reprisal.
	16	Aldo Moro, former Italian premier, kidnapped in Rome by Red Brigade terrorists. Five bodyguards killed. Terrorists demand release of fifteen Red Brigade members on trial in Turin.
April	4	President Sardar Mohammed Daud Khan, Afghanistan, killed during military coup. Revolutionary council led by Nur Mohammed Taraki assumes control.

May	9	Aldo Moro murdered in Rome following Italian government's refusal to release fifteen Red Brigades from prison.
	11	Congo National Liberation Front (FNLC) guerrillas invade Shaba province, Zaire. President Mobutu Sese Seko accuses the USSR, Algeria, and Libya of backing the FNLC. Forty-four Europeans murdered in Kolwezi, an estimated one hundred fifty whites and three hundred blacks killed in the fighting.
	19	French and Belgian paratroops, airlifted in U.S. and British aircraft, rescue two thousand five hundred Europeans and Americans in Kolwezi.
June	23	Twenty-nine Red Brigade terrorists sentenced to prison in Turin. Renato Curcio and Pietro Bassi sentenced to fifteen years in prison for arson, kidnapping, and robbery. Sixteen acquitted.
	26	Radicals bomb the Palace of Versailles. French officials blame the Breton Liberation Front.
July	17	West Germany, Canada, France, Great Britain, Italy, Japan, and the U.S. agree to cancel flights to any country that refuses to extradite or prosecute air hijackers—and to deny landing rights to that country's aircraft.
	28	Iraqi officials attacked in London in reprisal for Iraq's refusal to negotiate peace with Israel.
	31	Iraqi terrorist seizes eight hostages at the Iraqi embassy in London.
August	2	Iraqi officials attacked in Pakistan and Lebanon.
	13	PLF headquarters in Beirut bombed. One hundred fifty members of various guerrilla factions killed.
	19	Four hundred thirty killed in a crowded theater in Abadan, Iran, burned by Muslim arsonists.
	22	Twenty-five Sandinist National Liberation Front guerrillas seize Nicaraguan National Palace in Managua. Six killed, twelve wounded, one thousand held captive.
	24	Sandinista guerrillas fly to Panama with fifty-nine released prisoners and $500 thousand ransom.
September	20	Corrado Alunni, Red Brigade leader, suspected in murder of Aldo Moro, sentenced to twelve years in prison for illegal possession of firearms.
November		Early in November the Spanish government approved stringent security measures in the Basque provinces. More than forty killings claimed by the ETA during the year.

1979

January	29	Emilio Alessandri, Public Prosecutor, assassinated by BR terrorists in Milan.
February	14	U.S. Ambassador to Afghanistan, Adolph Dubs, kidnapped, shot, and killed in Kabul by Muslim extremists.
	24	Italian court sentences right wing terrorists Franco Fredo, Giovanni Ventura, and Guido Gianettini to life imprisonment for bombing Milan bank in 1969.
March	1	Egyptian President Anwar Sadat warns Muslim Brotherhood that religion cannot be involved in Egyptian politics.
	22	Provisional IRA terrorists shoot Sir Richard Sykes, British Ambassador to the Netherlands.
	23	One hundred members of the Independent Fighting Brigades for Popular Autonomy riot during labor demonstrations in Paris.
	30	MP Airey Neave killed by IRA bomb in the House of Commons garage, London.
April	20	Palace of the Senators, Rome, bombed by members of the Armed Revolutionary Cells (or the Italian Popular Movement, both groups claimed responsibility).
May	1	Several night explosions occur in Paris and a number of terrorist organizations claim responsibility. Similar bombings occurred frequently throughout France during late April.
	3	Ten to fifteen Red Brigade terrorists bomb the Christian Democrat headquarters in Rome. One killed, two injured.
	6	Third anniversary of the Corsican National Liberation Front. Twenty-seven bombings occur in Corsica.
	8	BPR terrorists occupy the cathedral and seize the French and Costa Rican embassies in San Salvador. Both ambassadors taken hostage. Terrorists demand release of imprisoned BPR members. Twenty-three shot and killed by the police.
	11	BPR members take over the Venezuelan embassy. West German police shoot Elisabeth van Dyck, suspect in the kidnapping and murder of Hanns-Martin Schleyer.
	21	El Salvador officials cut off food, water, and electricity in the Venezuelan embassy held by BPR terrorists.
	22	Fourteen pro-BPR supporters killed by police while trying to supply the Venezuelan embassy in San Salvador. Guerrillas assassinate the minister of education in reprisal.
	25	BPR guerrillas peacefully vacate the Venezuelan embassy.

June	25	Red Brigades attempt, and fail, to murder General Alexander Haig, NATO commander, in Belgium.
	28	Syrian government executes fifteen members of the Muslim Brotherhood convicted of murder and subversion. Three sentenced to life imprisonment.
July	13	Colonel Antonio Varisco, Security Chief, Rome Central Courts, murdered by terrorists. Palestinian terrorists seize the staff of the Egyptian embassy in Ankara, Turkey. Two Turkish policemen and one Egyptian killed. PLO representatives mediate end to the siege.
August	27	IRA terrorists murder Lord Mountbatten in his fishing boat off the coast of Ireland. Two boys and Lady Brabourne also killed. IRA terrorists ambush and kill eighteen British soldiers and one civilian in northern Ireland.
	30	Irish police arrest two IRA members for the murder of Lord Mountbatten.
September	21	Carlo Ghiglieno, Fiat executive, murdered by the Red Brigades in Turin.
	26	Cesare Terranova, Sicilian judge, murdered by terrorists in Palermo.
October	10	Police arrest twenty-four students in Manila for opposing martial law in the Philippines.
November	4	Iranian militants seize the U.S. embassy in Tehran and take ninety hostages, including sixty Americans.
	11	Bassam Shaka, mayor of Nablus on the West Bank, Israel, arrested by Israeli military officials for allegedly supporting terrorists (Shaka freed on 5 December on the recommendation of the Israeli cabinet).
	20	Muslim extremists attack and invade the Grand Mosque in Mecca. Two weeks of bloody fighting follow before the extremists are driven out. One hundred fifty killed.
	23	Thomas McMahon convicted of Lord Mountbatten's murder in Dublin and sentenced to life imprisonment.
December	3	Puerto Rican terrorists kill two American sailors near San Juan. Ten others injured.
	4	UN Security Council unanimously passes resolution demanding release of U.S. hostages in Iran.
	11	Front Line (Red Brigade) terrorists "kneecap" ten students/faculty at the University of Turin.

Chronology

December	15	International Court of Justice rules 15–0 that Iran must release U.S. hostages in Iran.

1980

January	3	Leftist guerrillas, the Popular Liberation Forces, seized five radio stations in San Salvador.
	4	Popular Liberation Forces attacked the headquarters of the National Guard in San Salvador.
	9	Sixty three persons involved in the raid on the Grand Mosque in Mecca (November 1979) are publicly beheaded by Saudi Arabian authorities.
	31	Thirty nine Quiche Indians invaded the Spanish embassy in Guatemala City, took the Ambassador hostage, then died when the building was destroyed by fire.
February	4	Libyans burned the French embassy in Tripoli and wrecked the French consulate in Benghazi. France and Libya severed diplomatic relations.
	7	Iranians broke into the New Zealand embassy in Teheran and after closing the embassy New Zealand officials announced that Iran failed to provide guarantees of protection.
	17	Christian Falangists and Syrian troops aided by a rival Christian group battled in northern Lebanon.
	21	A general strike in Kabul resulted in the death of 300 Afghans and several Soviet soldiers. *Tass* announced that "foreign agents and mercenaries" were responsible for the violence.
	27	Members of the leftist M-19 movement seized control of the Dominican Republic embassy in Bogota, Colombia, took hostages, demanded release of accused terrorists, and ransom.
March	19	Cambodian factions of the National Liberation Movement engaged in a bloody battle inside a refugee camp near the border of Thailand—46 reported killed.
	24	Archbishop Oscar Arnulfo Romero y Galdamez murdered while conducting mass in San Salvador. Rival factions in Chad engaged in hostilities—more than 700 killed.
	30	Bombs and sniper fire resulted in the death of 30 mourners during the funeral of Archbishop Galdamez.
April	4	Police in Evanston, Illinois arrested 11 members of the FALN (Armed Forces of National Liberation) a terrorist

		group advocating independence for Puerto Rico. The group leader, Carlos Torres, was on the FBI "most wanted" list.
April	11	Two political opponents of Libyan leader Muammar al-Quaddafi assassinated in London, 2 students arrested.
	12	MSGT Samuel K. Doe seized the Liberian government. President William R. Tolbert, Jr. and 27 others are killed.
	25	President Carter aborted the rescue of American hostages in Teheran after three helicopters engaged in the effort experienced mechanical failure—8 crewmen killed when two rescue aircraft collide.
	27	Occupation of the Dominican Republic embassy by members of the M-19 movement ended after 61 days—16 terrorists and 12 hostages escaped to Havana aboard a Cuban airliner. Negotiations resulted in a guarantee of "safe passage" for the terrorists, and payment of $2.5 million.
	30	Iranian terrorists seized the Iranian embassy in London and threatened to blow up the building and the hostages unless 91 Arabs held in Khuzestan were released.
May	5	British commandoes stormed the Iranian embassy after the terrorists killed a hostage—3 terrorists killed, embassy destroyed by fire, 19 hostages rescued (2 dead).
	17	The acquittal of 4 policemen for the alleged murder of a Black insurance executive resulted in 3 days of riot in Miami, Florida—14 killed, 300 injured, 1,000 arrested, property damage estimated at $100 million.
	18	Antigovernment demonstrators in Seoul and 5 other cities in South Korea demanded constitutional reform and free elections—the government imposed martial law.
	21	Antigovernment dissidents took control of Kwangju, South Korea.
	27	Government troops retook Kwangju—170 dead (26 soldiers, 144 civilians).
June	1	Cuban refugees held in the Fort Chaffee relocation center in Arkansas rioted and tried to escape. Police and soldiers using tear gas and billy clubs contained the rioters—40 injured.
	2	Israeli extremists bombed the automobiles of two Arab mayors on the West Bank—several persons injured by hand grenades in other cities.
	8	Tribal factions in India's Tripura State massacred 378 immigrants from Bangladesh in the village of Mandai. The government in New Delhi dispatched paramilitary troops to quell the rioting.

July	8	The Christian militia of the Falangist Party defeated the militia of the rival National Liberal Party and captured NLP strongholds in Lebanon.
	10	A military coup in Iran allegedly led by ex-Prime Minister Bakhtiar is foiled by the government of Ayatollah Khomeini.
	17	Army General Tejada led a military coup to prevent the Bolivian congress from seating President Zuazo (elected in June). General Tejada disbanded the Congress and declared Bolivia to be a "military zone."
	18	Kingston, Jamaica placed under curfew to curb violence by armed gangs (70 people killed by gunmen during the first two weeks of July).
	27	Pro-Khomeini demonstrators clashed with fellow Iranians in Washington, D.C.—200 arrested.
	31	Eleven Iranian military conspirators executed by firing squad after being convicted of participating in the coup July 10.
August	2	Italian authorities blamed neofascist terrorists for bombing the central train station in Bologna—76 killed, 200 injured.
	6	French police in Nice arrested an Italian right-wing extremist suspected of complicity in the August 2 bombing.
	22	Police in Rome arrested 22 neofascists also alleged to be involved in the bombing.
September	12	Ayotallah Khomeini announced four conditions for the release of 52 American hostages—the U.S. would have to: (1) cancel all claims against Iran; (2) turn all property of the late Shah over to Iran; (3) promise not to interfere, militarily or politically, in Iran; and (4) release Iranian assets frozen in the U.S.
		General Kenan Evren led a bloodless coup and took control of the Turkish government; dissolved the Parliament, and suspended the constitution.
		A series of bombings in Manila killed 1, injured 60. Terrorists belonging to the April 6 Liberation Movement claimed responsibility.
	17	The President of Nicaragua, Anastasio Somoza Debayle, assassinated in Asuncion, Paraguay, along with his chauffeur and a financial advisor.
	18	Two Cubans hijacked a Delta Airlines jet in South Carolina and were arrested on landing in Havana.
	26	Gundolf Kohler, a member of the Defense Sports Group (an outlawed organization) killed when the bomb he is suspected of planting at the entrance to the Munich *Octoberfest* exploded prematurely.

September	26	Anonymous members of the National European Fascists claimed responsibility for a machine gun attack on a Jewish synagogue, school, and memorial site in Paris.
October	19	The April 6 Liberation Movement claimed responsibility for bombing a convention of the American Society of Travel Agents in Manila—20 injured.
	29	Nine people killed, 81 injured, by a bomb explosion set by an "unnamed person" inside the main railway terminal in Peking (Beijing).
November	2	The Iranian Parliament (Majlis) approved conditions for the release of American hostages.
	10	A team of American officials arrived in Algeria to negotiate the release of hostages held in Teheran.
	25	A coup led by Colonel Saye Zerbo replaced the government of President Sangoule Lamizana in Upper Volta.
	28	Police arrested 200 "communist inspired agitators" in Haiti for criticizing the government.
December	10	A federal grand jury in Chicago indicted 11 terrorists suspected of being members of the FALN on charges of complicity in several bombings beginning in 1975.
	12	Minister of Justice, Giovanni D'Urso, kidnapped by the Red Brigades, an Italian terrorist group.
	21	Iran demands $24 billion to release American hostages.
	26	The Algerian ambassador to Iran visited the American hostages and found their conditions "satisfactory."
	27	5,000 Afghans attacked the Soviet embassy in Teheran to protest the Soviet invasion of Afghanistan on December 27, 1979.

1981

January	15	Italian Minister D'Urso released by the Red Brigades after being forced to disclose government procedures for tracking terrorists.
	20	Iran released 52 American hostages after 444 days in captivity.
February	6	The ETA (Euzkadi ta Azkatasuna) a radical Basque separatist group murdered Jose Ryan, an engineer, to protest the construction of a nuclear plant near Bilbao.
	9	A general strike is called in Spain to protest Ryan's murder —crowds demonstrated in several cities against the ETA and its resort to violence.

February	11	The Corsican National Liberation Front allegedly conducted a series of 46 bombings on the French island of Corsica to protest the sentencing of 8 Corsican nationalists in Paris for kidnapping (in 1980) three people who opposed Corsican autonomy.
	16	The ETA organized a general strike in Spain to protest the death of Jose Izaguirre who was imprisoned for killing two civil guards. Demonstrators rioted in three cities. The PLO declared that "hundreds" of Palestinian military officers completed training at Soviet military academies.
	18	The Reagan administration announced that it would implement the agreements that resulted in the release of the Iranian hostages and that "future acts of state supported terrorism against the U.S. will meet with swift and sure punishment."
	19	Members of the ETA kidnapped the consuls of Uruguay, Austria, and El Salvador, attempted to kidnap the consuls of West Germany and San Sebastian, and demanded independence and the release of 300 Basque prisoners.
	23	Spanish civil guards attacked a session of the Parliament in Madrid with automatic weapons and took 350 legislators hostage. The leader, LCOL Antonio Tejero Molina, announced that he was taking over the government.
	24	Coup fails, government officials arrested Molina and the civil guards and released the hostages.
	25	President Mohammed Zia-ul-Haq of Pakistan ordered the arrest of several political figures who demanded an end to martial law. Political unrest was led by the People's Party supported by the Movement for the Restoration of Democracy.
	28	The three diplomats held by the ETA in Spain released unharmed.
March	2	Pakistani gunmen hijacked an airliner with 148 passengers and diverted it to Kabul, Afghanistan.
	4	The hijackers released 29 passengers unharmed.
	6	The hijackers killed one passenger who was employed by the Pakistani embassy in Iran.
	8	The hijackers released 4 more passengers.
	9	The hijackers obtained automatic weapons and ordered the pilot to fly to Damascus.
	12	The terrorists threatened to blow up the plane and kill the hostages aboard—the Pakistani government agreed to meet their demand, released 54 prisoners, and guaranteed the terrorists safe passage out of Pakistan.
	14	The three gunmen surrendered in Syria and freed the hostages.

March	16	An attempted coup was foiled by the government of Mauritania ending a conflict with Morocco over the Western Sahara (begun in 1975 when the Saharan area was abandoned by Spain).
	28	Five Indonesian terrorists hijacked a domestic airliner to Bangkok and demanded the release of 80 prisoners held in Indonesia, punishment for VP Adam Malik, and the expulsion of all Jewish officials and Israeli "militarists" in Indonesia.
	31	Thai authorities allowed Indonesian commandoes to storm the hijacked plane in Bangkok—4 of the 5 terrorists killed.
April	2	Fighting escalated in Beirut and Zahle, Lebanon—37 killed.
	4	Mario Moretti, a leader of the Red Brigades, and three companions alleged to have organized terrorist activities in Italy arrested in Milan.
	12	Riots in Brixton (Greater London) resulted in the injury of 150 police and 60 civilians—the riots apparently reflected public resentment of alleged police harassment.
	19	Filipino terrorists, members of the New People's Army, Philippine Communist Party, tossed hand grenades into the Catholic cathedral in Davao City, Philippines—13 killed, scores seriously injured.
	29	Muammar al-Qaddafi, Libyan Chief of State, visited Moscow and issued a joint statement intended to separate the "liberation struggle" of the people from "international terrorism."
May	9	Six members of El Salvador's military forces arrested as suspects in the murder of 3 U.S. nuns and a coworker.
	13	Pope John Paul II shot and seriously injured in St. Peter's Square, Vatican City, by Mehmet Ali Agca, a Turkish terrorist. Two women tourists from the U.S. injured by bullets.
	23	Gunmen seized control of the Central Bank in Barcelona, took 200 hostages, and demanded release of military officers arrested in the coup attempted February 23.
	24	Police attacked the bank and captured 9 terrorists alleged to be anarchists hired by right-wing extremists—some of the terrorists apparently escaped when the hostages were freed. Turkish hijackers commandeered an airliner enroute from Istanbul to Ankara.
	25	The hijackers, identified as members of a Marxist guerrilla organization, are overpowered by their hostages at an airport in Burgas, Bulgaria.

May	30	President Ziaur Rahman of Bangladesh and several aides and bodyguards killed during an attempted coup led by MGEN Mohammed Abdul Manzoor.
June	7	Israeli fighters and bombers attacked and destroyed a nuclear reactor near Baghdad, Iraq.
	19	President Anwar as-Sadat of Egypt accused the Communist and Socialist Labor parties of fostering violence between Coptic Christians and Muslims in Cairo—10 people killed.
	28	Antigovernment dissidents set off an explosion in Teheran—72 killed, including Chief Justice Ayatollah Mohammad Beheshti, 4 cabinet members, 8 deputy ministers, and 20 members of Parliament.
July	3	Race riots and violence erupted in Britain and continued for two weeks.
	30	Antigovernment dissidents bombed the office of President Ali Raja'i, he, Prime Minister Mohammad Javad Bahonar, and 3 members of the Iranian Supreme Defense Council killed.
September	12	Nine Italian terrorists suspected of bombing a Bologna train station and killing 80 people (August 1980) arrested in London.
	17	The Front for the Liberation of Lebanon from Aliens claimed responsibility for bombing the headquarters of the PLO in Sidon, Lebanon—20 killed, more than 200 injured.
October	6	Muslim fundamentalists assassinated President Anwar as-Sadat of Egypt during a military parade in Cairo.
	10	In Bonn, West Germany, 250,000 people marched to protest NATO's planned deployment of nuclear weapons in Western Europe.
November	14	The 4 assassins accused of murdering President Anwar as-Sadat and 20 accomplices indicted by the Egyptian government.
	29	Muslim Brotherhood terrorists accused by the ruling Ba'ath Socialist Party of blowing up a car loaded with explosives outside of a school in Damascus, Syria—90 killed, scores wounded.
December	8	Eleven Puerto Rican nationalists, Salvadoran leftists, and Venezuelans seeking the release of political prisoners hijacked 3 Venezuelan airliners and landed in Havana. Several

		hundred passengers freed and the gunmen arrested by Cuban police.
December	15	Iranian and Syrian terrorists destroyed the Iraqi embassy in Beirut—30 killed, 100 injured.
	17	BGEN James L. Dozier, U.S. Army, kidnapped by members of the Red Brigade in Verona, Italy.
	31	President Hilla Limann of Ghana deposed in a bloody coup led by Jerry J. Rawlings.

1982

January	27	Guerrillas attacked the Ilopango air base outside San Salvador and destroyed several aircraft.
	28	BGEN Dozier rescued by Italian antiterrorist forces in Padua, Italy.
February	2	The fundamentalist Muslim Brotherhood rebelled against the government in Hamah, Syria—numerous casualties on both sides and heavy damage in the city center.
	8	Tommy Manotoc, President Marco's son-in-law, reportedly kidnapped by leftist guerrillas.
	9	Manotoc rescued in a mountainous area east of Manila.
	13	Five former national guardsmen in custody for investigation of complicity in the murder of 3 Catholic nuns (December 1980) in El Salvador. A communist-led union federation allegedly attempted to overthrow the government in Portugal—several men arrested in a car loaded with guns, explosives, and recordings calling for a general uprising.
	23	Members of the Uganda Freedom Movement assaulted an army barracks in Kampala—69 killed.
March	17	Government troops killed 4 members of a Dutch TV crew while engaged in a firefight with leftist guerrillas in El Salvador.
	18	Right wing Muslims accused of rioting during an election rally organized by Golkar, a group whose members dominate Indonesia's House of People's Representatives. 60 injured, 240 arrested.
	23	Army officers deposed President Fernando Romeo Lucas Garcia and named a 3-man junta headed by GEN Efrain Rios Montt to lead the government of Guatemala.
	24	LTGEN Hossain Mohammed Ershad ousted President Abdus Sattar and imposed martial law in Bangladesh to "reestablish democracy."

March	25	The 17 Red Brigade terrorists who kidnapped BGEN James Dozier (December 1981) sentenced to prison.
April	7	Police in Uganda arrest 10,000 people suspected of supporting guerrillas in Kampala.
	15	The men (2 military, 3 civilian) convicted of assassinating Egyptian President Anwar as-Sadat (October 1981) executed.
	22	73 Shi'ah Muslims convicted of planning to sabotage the government in Bahrein.
June	3	The rebels accused of participating in an abortive coup (February 1981) are convicted by a military court in Spain.
July	12	Sendero Luminoso, a Maoist organization, attacked a police station in Peru's Trujillo Province. President Terry suspended constitutional rights in the area and ordered specially trained police to quell the violence.
	29	Mercenaries found guilty of air piracy in South Africa. (They hijacked an airliner in the Seychelles in November 1981 to escape following an unsuccessful coup).
August	1	The Kenyan Air Force attempted an antigovernment revolt in Nairobi—3,000 arrested, including all 2,100 Air Force personnel.
September	6	The Salvadoran Human Rights Commission accused government troops of killing 300 unarmed civilians in San Vicente Province.
	14	President-elect Bashir Gemayel assassinated by a bomb blast in East Beirut—8 others killed, 50 wounded.
	15	Sadeqh Ghotbzadeh executed by firing squad in Teheran after being convicted of plotting to assassinate Ayatollah Khomeini.
	16	Christian militiamen slaughtered more than 600 Palestinians in two Lebanese refugee camps.
	17	Terrorists took 107 hostages in the Chamber of Commerce building in San Pedro Sula, Honduras and demanded the release of political prisoners.
	25	Government officials allowed the Honduran terrorists to leave via plane to Panama—then to Cuba. Hostages released without injury.
	28	Prime Minister Menachim Begin ordered an inquiry of Israeli involvement in the Beirut massacre.
October	2	Explosion in the central square of Teheran, Iran killed 60, injured 700. Government spokesmen blamed "American mercenaries."

December	20	Defense Minister Lelio Lagorio told the Italian Chamber of Deputies that the attempted assassination of Pope John Paul II (May 1981) was an "act of war" perpetrated by Bulgaria.

1983

February	18	Hindus raid 17 settlements near Nellie, India—600 killed.
	24	Ethnic and political violence in Assam—1,300 killed. Prime Minister Indira Gandhi dispatched 90,000 troops in an unsuccessful attempt to control the situation.
March	21	President Efrain Rios Montt lifted the state of siege (begun in July 1982) in Guatemala but banned political activities, strikes, and news of guerrilla movements.
April	18	A car bomb virtually destroyed the U.S. embassy in Beirut, Lebanon—63 killed, including 17 Americans. The Islamic Jihad Organization claimed responsibility.
May	5	Chinese airliner hijacked while on a flight from Manchuria to Shanghai and diverted to Seoul, South Korea.
	7	Chinese airliner and passengers returned to China—6 hijackers remained in South Korea for trial.
	10	Thousands of Chileans demonstrated against the government in Santiago—police killed 2, arrested 1,000.
	20	Car bomb exploded by members of the African National Congress in Pretoria, South Africa—18 killed, 200 injured.
	24	Students marched in Paris to oppose reform of higher education in France—organized by left and right wing extremists.
	30	Numerous terrorist attacks in Peru killed and injured hundreds. Government declared state of emergency.
June	15	Cuba announced the sentences of several convicted hijackers after being queried by the U.S. State Department.
July	11	Terrorists, allegedly Sendero Luminoso (Shining Light) guerrillas, attacked the headquarters of the leading Popular Action Party in Peru—2 killed, 30 injured.
	14	Several Armenian terrorist groups claimed responsibility for murdering a Turkish diplomat in Brussels.
	15	The Armenian Secret Army for the Liberation of Armenia (ASALA) claimed responsibility for bombing the Turkish Airline counter in Paris—5 killed, 50 injured.

Chronology

July	21	David Dodge, ex-President of the American University in Beirut, released by Shi'ah Muslims after one year in captivity.
	26	12 Red Brigade terrorists convicted in Turin, Italy of committing 10 murders (1973–1980).
	27	Armenian terrorists attacked the residence of the Turkish ambassador to Portugal and blew themselves up—6 killed including 4 gunmen.
August	1	An additional 39 Red Brigade terrorists convicted of violence and murder in Sardinia.
	5	A car bomb exploded near the Bakkar Mosque in Tripoli, Lebanon. Sunni Muslims accused Christians of committing the atrocity.
	8	BGEN Oscar Victores led a coup and replaced GEN Efrain Rios Montt, President of Guatemala.
	18	6 Chinese hijackers convicted of hijacking a Chinese airliner (May 1983) in Seoul, South Korea.
	25	38 members of the Provisional Irish Republican Army escaped from the Maze prison in Belfast—1 killed.
	27	Argentina's military government passed a law to "protect democracy against terrorist activities."
October	9	North Korean commandoes confessed to the bombing of a wreath-laying ceremony at the Martyr's Mausoleum in Rangoon, Burma—4 South Korean cabinet members, 4 Burmese, 13 others killed.
	23	A terrorist drove a truckload of explosives into the USMC headquarters at the Beirut Airport, Lebanon—241 Marines killed, several others injured. The French barracks also destroyed in a similar attack—58 dead.
November	4	Car bomb exploded inside the Israeli military compound in Tyre—60 killed. Palestinian guerrillas questioned.
December	1	Sheikh Halim Takieden, president of the Supreme Druze Court in Lebanon murdered by an unidentified gunman.
	12	U.S. and French embassies and other sites in Kuwait bombed by Muslim extremists—6 killed, 63 injured.
	18	The Irish Republican Army (IRA) acknowledged bombing Harrod's Department store in London—5 killed, 91 injured.

1984

March	17	Irish police captured Dominic "Mad Dog" McGlinchey, leader of the Irish National Liberation Army and delivered

		him to British authorities to face charges of murder and terrorism.
April	3	Army forces seized control of the government in Guinea in a bloodless coup.
	7	President Paul Biya of Cameroon announced that an attempted coup led by COL Ibrahim Saleh of the Republican Guard failed—fighting continued for several days.
	17	Gunfire from inside the Libyan embassy in London kills a British policewoman during a demonstration by antigovernment demonstrators—10 Libyans wounded.
	20	Bomb exploded in Heathrow Airport, London by unknown terrorists—25 injured.
	28	Anti-Arab Jewish terrorists suspected of planning to blow up Arab owned buses arrested by Israeli police.
	30	Rodrigo Lara Bonilla, Minister of Justice in Colombia, assassinated in Bogota by illegal drug traffickers.
May	8	Canadian Army soldier shot and killed 3, wounded 13, in the National Assembly building, Quebec. Gunmen attacked a military barracks in Tripoli in an attempt to assassinate Libyan President COL Muammar al-Quaddafi—20 suspects reportedly slain.
	19	Four days of fighting between Hindus and Muslims in Bombay resulted in 107 deaths.
	24	5 former members of El Salvador's National Guard convicted of murdering 3 U.S. nuns (December 1980).
June	6	Indian troops attacked Sikh shrine in Amritsar to end violence between Sikhs and Hindus in Punjab—450 to 1,200 killed.
	30	Police and army officers kidnapped President Hernan Siles Zuazo of Bolivia in an unsuccessful attempt to overthrow the government—100 arrested (July 2).
July	5	9 Sikhs hijacked an Indian airlines plane enroute to New Delhi—255 passengers, 9 crew released unharmed in Lahore, Pakistan.
August	9	The Islamic Jihad ("Holy War") claimed responsibility for laying 190 mines in the Red Sea.
	20	Two weeks of violence involving the Tamil United Liberation Front and Sri Lanka government forces resulted in 95 deaths.
	23	The Maoist Popular Liberation Army and the Worker's Self Defense Force signed truces with the Colombian government.

Chronology 165

September	4	The Provisional Irish Republican Army (IRA) claimed credit for a car bomb explosion in Newry, Northern Ireland—71 injured.
	12	1,500 Muslims rioted in Jakarta, Indonesia to protest the arrest of 4 colleagues—unknown number killed.
	20	Car loaded with explosives blown up in front of the U.S. embassy in East Beirut. Islamic Jihad claimed responsibility—14 killed.
	29	Irish police seized a shipload of weapons intended for delivery to the IRA—5 arrested for trial in Dublin's antiterrorist criminal court.
October	12	IRA terrorists bombed the Grand Hotel, Brighton, England, in an attempt to assassinate Prime Minister Margaret Thatcher.
	26	3 Bulgarians and 4 Turks placed on trial in Italy for complicity in the attempted assassination of Pope John Paul II (May 1981).
	31	India's Prime Minister Indira Gandhi assassinated by 2 Sikh bodyguards in New Delhi.
December	4	4 Arabic speaking gunmen hijacked a Kuwaiti airliner. After leaving the United Arab Emirates the plane was diverted to Teheran—2 U.S. officials killed.
		Tamil guerrillas attacked an army convoy in Sri Lanka. Several days of violence between government forces and the guerrillas followed—395 killed.
	23	Terrorists bombed a train enroute from Florence to Bologna—29 killed, 200 injured.

1985

January	2	Ishmael Beet hijacked an American Airlines plane enroute from the Virgin Islands to New York. He was arrested in Havana.
	8	Gunmen kidnapped Catholic priest Lawrence Martin Jenco of Joliet, Illinois, in West Beirut.
	13	Libyan diplomat, Farag Omar Mahkyoun, assassinated by gunmen in Rome.
February	1	Red Army Faction terrorists murdered Ernst Zimmerman, an industrialist, in West Germany.
		Terrorists exploded a car bomb outside a mosque in Tripoli, Lebanon—12 killed, 58 injured.
	2	Bomb exploded in a bar in Athens, Greece—78 injured including 59 Americans.

February	14	Jeremy Levin, chief of the Cable News Network in Beirut, escaped from Islamic extremists after 11 months in capitivity.
	21	The leftist November 17th Group claimed responsibility for murdering publisher Nikos Momferatos in Athens.
	28	IRA guerrillas killed 8 British officers, 1 civilian, in Newrey, Northern Ireland—dozens injured.
March	6	Bomb destroyed building in Shi'ite Moslem area of Beirut—62 killed, 200 wounded.
	10	Car bomb killed 12 soldiers in Israeli convoy in Southern Lebanon—14 wounded in retaliation for March 6 bombing.
	12	Armenian terrorists attacked the Turkish embassy in Ottawa, 1 guard killed, 12 employees taken hostage and released 4 hours later.
	15	President Hojatolislam Ali Khanenei of Iran escaped an attempted assassination in Teheran—assassin and 5 others killed.
	21	Israeli soldiers swept Shi'ite villages in southern Lebanon to rid the area of "terrorists"—2 CBS cameramen killed, 1 wounded.
April	13	Islamic Jihad terrorists suspected of bombing a restaurant in Madrid near a U.S. air base—18 Spaniards killed, 82 injured (including 15 Americans).
May	10	Attacks and bombings by Sikh extremists in India killed 45, 150 wounded.
	13	FBI agents prevented Sikh terrorists from assassinating Prime Minister Rajiv Gandhi of India during a visit to the United States.
	20	Israel freed 150 Palestinian guerrillas in exchange for the release of 3 Israeli soldiers.
	22	Car bomb exploded during a battle between Palestinians and Shi'ite Muslims in Beirut—50 killed.
	25	Islamic Jihad claimed responsibility for bomb attack on motorcade of Kuwaiti ruler Sheik Jaber al Ahmad al Sabah—3 killed, Sabah injured.
June	9	Unidentified gunman kidnapped Professor Thomas M. Sutherland, American University, in Beirut.
	11	Shia Muslims hijacked a Jordanian airliner in Beirut, flew to Sicily and back to Beirut—hostages released.
	14–18	Shia Muslims hijacked TWA airliner enroute from Athens to Rome, ordered it to Beirut, demanded release of 1,195 Shia prisoners held by Israel. American sailor killed, hostages released after 17 days in captivity.

Chronology

June	19	Leftist terrorists shot and killed 13, including 4 U.S. Marines, and 2 American businessmen in San Salvador.
		Terrorist bomb exploded in Frankfurt airport—2 children, 1 adult killed, 42 injured.
		Car bomb exploded in Tripoli, Lebanon—75 killed.
	20	Car bomb exploded in North Lebanon—31 killed.
	23	Air India airliner exploded while enroute from Toronto to Bombay—329 killed. Sikh terrorists suspected.
		Canadian airliner blown up at Narita airport, Tokyo. Sikhs suspected—2 Japanese killed, 4 injured.
July	9	Car bomb exploded near Israeli checkpoints in Lebanon—12 killed, 6 injured.
	10	Israeli court convicted Jewish terrorists of murdering Arabs on the West Bank after a 13 month trial.
	11	French secret service agents bombed and sank the *Rainbow Warrior*, the Greenpeace flagship, in Auckland, New Zealand—1 killed.
	15	Car displaying the Red Cross flag exploded in the Israeli zone of Southern Lebanon—10 killed.
	22	Islamic Jihad claimed responsibility for bomb explosion in a Copenhagen synagogue—27 injured.
August	1	Shakib Hmeidan, ABC newsman, kidnapped by 4 gunmen in Beirut.
	8	Red Army faction terrorists suspected of exploding a car bomb outside U.S. Air Force headquarters in Rhein-Main, West Germany—2 killed, 20 wounded.
	17	Car bomb exploded near a crowded supermarket in East Beirut Christian suburb—50 killed; car bomb exploded in retaliation outside a mosque in the Moslem district—29 killed, 82 wounded.
	20	President of Akali Dal (Sikh political party) Harchhand Singh Longowal killed by Sikh terrorists in India.
		Gunmen in Cairo murdered an Israeli diplomat.
September	15	Terrorists attacked theater in Lala, Philippines with hand grenades—31 killed.
	16	Palestinian terrorist tossed a hand grenade into a sidewalk cafe in Rome—39 wounded including 9 Americans.
	18	Rev. Benjamin Weir, American hostage, freed in Lebanon after 16 months in captivity.
	25	Pro-Palestinian gunmen killed 3 Israelis on their yacht in Larnaca, Cyprus.
	30	Terrorists kidnapped 4 Soviet diplomats in Beirut—1 killed.

October	1	Israeli Air Force bombs PLO headquarters in Tunis in retaliation for murder of Israelis (September 25)—60 Palestinians, 12 Tunisians killed.
	7–9	PLO terrorists hijacked the Italian cruise ship Achille Lauro and demanded the release of 50 prisoners held by Israel; terrorists surrendered in exchange for guarantee of safe passage—1 American tourist killed.
	11	U.S. fighters intercepted an Egyptian airliner carrying the Achille Lauro hijackers to freedom and forced it to land in Sicily—4 terrorists arrested.
November	6	M-19 guerrillas stormed the Palace of Justice in Bogota, Colombia and take several hostages. Colombian troops attacked the guerrillas and ended the assault (November 7)—100 killed, including 11 Supreme Court justices.
	24	Palestinian hijackers forced an Egyptian airliner to land in Malta and murdered 2 women, 1 American and 1 Israeli. Egyptian commandoes attacked the aircraft (November 25)—58 passengers and 2 hijackers killed. Car bomb exploded at a U.S. Army shopping center in Frankfurt, West Germany—36 wounded, including 33 Americans.
December	27	Palestinian terrorists attacked El Al Israel Airline facilities in Rome and Vienna—19 killed, 100 wounded.
	31	Gunmen ambushed a motorcade with automatic weapons and grenades in an attempt to assassinate President Amin Gemayel in Beirut, Lebanon.

Ref HV.6431.T0